D1062211

CRITICAL ESSAYS

CRITICAL
ESSAYS

W. W. ROBSON

Routledge & Kegan Paul
LONDON

PR 99. R63

First published 1966
by Routledge & Kegan Paul Ltd
Broadway House, 68–74 Carter Lane
London, E.C.4

Printed in Great Britain by
Cox and Wyman Ltd
London, Fakenham and Reading

© *W. W. Robson 1966*

No part of this book may be reproduced
in any form without permission from
the publisher, except for the quotation
of brief passages in criticism

CONTENTS

830129

PREFACE

THIS book is a collection of essays, written during the last ten years or so, on a variety of specific occasions. It may, however, be found to display some sort of unity, in so far as all I have written is intended to promote (sometimes by appearing to take it for granted) a working measure of agreement about what, generally speaking, is good in literature; and to do this as part of the process of clarifying the doubtful, and hence controversial, element in particular literary issues.

Under modern conditions the public for serious writing on behalf of literature is largely confined to teachers and students. No one who attempts this form of writing can be unaware of that; but I believe that their interests, and those of literary culture generally, are best served by keeping in mind the possibility of a wider public of which they are a part. It is in this hope that I have written, not solely for specialist readers, but for men and women.

I should like to add a comment on one feature of this collection which might displease a reader otherwise in sympathy with my general aims: the absence from it of any discussion of the creative work of writers now active. I can assure such a reader that this omission is not due to lack of interest or concern, but to my conviction, which I trust will emerge from the essays themselves, that critical study of the authors of the past can be one way – and perhaps the most appropriate way for someone occupied academically with them – of searching for insight into the problems of writing now.

With the exception of the essay *Three Victorian Poets*, which has been substantially revised, these pieces are reprinted with only minor omissions or changes of wording.

W.W.R.

ACKNOWLEDGEMENTS

The Publishers and the Author are indebted, for permission to reprint, to the following Editors and Publishers: the Editor of the *Times Literary Supplement* and Messrs. Faber (*Purely Literary Values*); the Editor of the *Times Literary Supplement* (*The Romantic Poets, Wordsworth after 1803*, and the second part of *T. S. Eliot's Criticism: the Last Phase*); the Editor of *Mandrake* (*Henry James's The Tragic Muse*); the Editor of *The Review* (the first part of *T. S. Eliot's Criticism: the Last Phase*); the Editor of *Universities' Quarterly* (*Mr. Leavis on Literary Studies*); the Editors of the *Cambridge Quarterly* (*The Romanticism of C. S. Lewis*; the Editor of the *Oxford Review* (*Mr. Empson on Paradise Lost*); the Editor of the *Observer Mr. Auden on Poetry*, which appeared in the *Twentieth Century*); Messrs. Oliver and Boyd (*Kipling's Later Stories*); Boris Ford and Penguin Books (*Three Victorian Poets, D. H. Lawrence and Women in Love*); Routledge and Kegan Paul (*Paradise Regained: the Better Fortitude, Wordsworth's Resolution and Independence, The Dilemma of Tennyson*); Cambridge University Press (*English as a University Subject*); Oxford University Press and the British Academy (*Byron as Poet*).

ACKNOWLEDGMENTS

PART ONE

I

PURELY LITERARY VALUES

Two passages from T. S. Eliot's criticism have stuck in my mind for many years, and I will use them as a starting-point. In a lecture called *Religion and Literature*, published in 1936, Eliot writes, 'The "greatness" of literature cannot be determined solely by literary standards; though we must remember that whether it is literature or not can be determined only by literary standards'.

And in some lectures on 'Johnson as Critic and Poet', given in 1944, he observes that:

> In our own day the influence of psychology and sociology upon literary criticism has been very noticeable. On the one hand, these influences of social disciplines have enlarged the field of the critic, and have affirmed, in a world which otherwise is inclined to depreciate the importance of literature, the relations of literature to life. But from another point of view this enrichment has also been an impoverishment, for the purely literary values, the appreciation of good writing for its own sake, have become submerged when literature is judged in the light of other considerations.

These two passages are not, of course, making the same point; but they seem to carry the same implication: that there exist 'purely literary values', and 'literary standards', which are relevant to 'the appreciation of good writing for its own sake'. In one case it is said that these standards are not sufficient to decide whether or not a work can be called great; in the other, that they can be distinguished from the kinds of criteria applied by critics who bring to bear a psychological or sociological interest in literature. We are not told, in either context, what they positively *are*: Eliot

seems to assume that we already know, and merely need reminding. But in the context of the second quotation he does indicate
what in his view they are *not*, by referring to the connexion of
criticism, in the case of Coleridge, with 'philosophy and a theory
of aesthetics'; in the case of Arnold, with 'ethics and propae-
deutics'; and with an aberration unspecified in the case of Pater,
but which we might guess to be the use of ostensibly critical
writing for the purpose of quasi-creative 'self-expression'. Presumably, then, the implied contrast is with Dr. Johnson's approach to literature (Johnson being the subject of the lectures);
and this reminder is felt to be enough to give substance to the
phrases 'literary standards' and 'purely literary values'.

Eliot seems to be thinking of Johnson's practice, when discussing poetry, of detailed technical fault-finding. But is it not odd
to lay the stress on *this* as exceptionally characteristic and distinctive of Johnson's approach to literature; to insist that *this*
above all is the lesson we are to learn from it? Any really central
account would be bound to bring out how much Johnson was
concerned, precisely, with 'the relations of literature to life'; and
surely Johnson as little as any of the classical critics would have
been inclined to regard problems about the greatness of literature
as somehow extra-literary. Need one quote his remark about
Paradise Lost that 'the want of human interest is always felt', or
his famous paragraph on 'the praise of Shakespeare'?

But I have questioned the term 'purely literary values' not in
order to deny that there are such things but to urge that our conception of them should not be too exclusive. Clearly the domain
of the 'purely literary' *could* be very constricted. One might regard
it as limited, for example, to the preservation (at any rate in discursive prose) of conventional grammar and syntax – or spelling.
Or – advancing a little farther – one could refer it to the kind of
considerations dealt with in Fowler's *Modern English Usage*. Or
one might think of the corrective procedures used in Graves's and
Hodge's entertaining manual *The Reader over Your Shoulder*. But
even here larger questions are likely to intrude; for how can we
castigate, and try to rewrite, a supposedly faulty original without
risking possibly quite serious judgements on the author's quality
of mind, on his subject and his attitude towards it, on the purpose
of his writing and the extent to which it succeeds or fails? Stylis-
tics may be an acknowledged field of study; but as soon as considerations about *value* enter it – and questions of relative success

or failure cannot but involve them – its practitioner is committed to doing literary criticism in the usual sense, whether that is what he calls it or not. And we may note that Eliot speaks of literary *standards* as determining at least *some* questions of literary value.

To insist on the retention of 'literary standards' and 'purely literary values' ought merely to mean that criticism should be relevant. But this does not settle anything, for it leaves open the question, what are the canons of relevance. It seems plain that to frame these narrowly is undesirable. But more than that, it is quite unplausible. To take an analogy: there might well be a 'purely musical' analysis of Elgar's *Falstaff* which entirely ignored the fact that the music was intended, among other things, to recall the character and career of Falstaff. But it seems to me that there is simply *no equivalent* 'purely literary' analysis of Shakespeare's *Henry IV*. Twentieth-century critics of Shakespeare may be wary of talking about characters; Falstaff has even been called 'a walking symbol', or 'a triumphant particular crystallization' of some general element in the poetic drama. But the authors of these phrases would no doubt grant it to be of the first importance that whatever was symbolized or crystallized did not take the form of a *thin* man. In fact, of course, the whole of Shakespeare's Falstaff ought ideally to be present in the consciousness of the critic of Henry IV, as he need not be in the critic of Elgar's music.

'Purely literary values' may be found an objectionable expression by those who associate it with the discredited doctrine of aestheticism. What exactly this doctrine is (in relation to literature) I do not know. It does not seem to be stated clearly anywhere. To me, it suggests not a doctrine but a tendency or attitude, though one now perhaps existing chiefly in the imaginations of philosophers whose paradigm-situation for the experience of art seems to be a man gazing at a Chinese vase. How *his* postulated 'pure aesthetic experience' can intelligibly be compared with anything we are supposed to do with *Middlemarch* or the *Bacchae* or *The Death of Ivan Ilyich*, I do not know. Certainly I cannot believe that our ideal experience of these or any other great works of literature can be regarded as some sort of pure intuition of formal beauty unrelated to the human substance and significance of the works, irrelevant to our sense of human needs and purposes, or excluding (on the ground that a great work of art is unique and *sui generis*) our sense of comparative value in other literature and in life.

None the less, I think there is something to be learnt from the common tendency of aestheticians to assimilate literature to the 'purer' arts. And that is an emphasis on the *contemplative* element in our experience; or, to put it another way, on our sense that what we are experiencing is *art*, that of its nature it is not arbitrary or gratuitous, but made by a human being for certain purposes, in a certain mode, convention, or 'frame'. Our sense of what this 'frame' is may vary widely in different cases. Sometimes it is as if the writer actually asks us to include our awareness of the convention he is using as an important part of what he offers us; as perhaps in Marvell's Nymph complaining of the death of her fawn. At the other extreme, as in some of D. H. Lawrence's poetry, the writer seems to be doing all he can to make us forget the 'frame', and to participate directly not only in the experience offered by the completed poem but also in the experience that prompted it. And there are all sorts of other cases, more or less complex; Coleridge's famous 'suspension of disbelief', originally formulated with reference to dramatic illusion, is merely one refinement of the make-believe which comes naturally in the nursery, and which in the experience of art may take much more sophisticated forms. But all these modes of experience entail not necessarily a continuity of critical consciousness of what we are doing and of what is being done to us but at least the capacity to return at any moment to such consciousness. We may be imaginary participants in what is going on, but we can always resume the role of spectator. As a rule, perhaps, we seem to be both spectator and participant at once; and this is as near as I can get to suggesting the characteristic stance, or attitude, or frame of mind, in which we appreciate important art. Naturally the degree of involvement will depend not merely on the kind of work in question but on the recipient. I have the impression that in his experience of art the distinguished critic George Santayana was almost wholly a spectator, and that in his case we would not speak of a possible *reversion* to the contemplative mode, since he never left it. But this sort of detachment is rare. The essential experience of art is surely a more full-blooded and full-bodied response than the word 'contemplation' suggests. And yet I suggest that no art is worthy of the name if it cannot survive this kind of attention to how it does what it does.

But I do not wish to dwell on the subtler aspects of the literary experience, in case I should be thought to be implying that the qualities of a work which are relevant to criticism are in any way recondite. Indeed, the real difficulty is to know what to *exclude*; to commit oneself to saying what is not, or never, relevant. Certain considerations – say, biographical ones – can sometimes be ruled out as external, as not manifestly 'in the work'. But this familiar prescription can be harder to apply than it looks. Is Henry Fielding's personal character relevant to the appreciation of his writings? I should say, decidedly yes. True, we need not go outside *Tom Jones* to infer it. We can point to the warm, compassionate, masculine strength so evident in Fielding's best work. But it would be critical purism to maintain that our sense of this is not increased by our knowledge of the biographical facts; or that we ought, as critics, to try to keep this knowledge out of our minds. What we make of a work depends on what we bring to it; and justice and fairness in literary matters do not require that we approach literature with a blank mind, if indeed that is possible. Literature is a fully human product, and a sense of the author as a whole may be indispensable to our pleasure and our understanding. Certainly we need a sense of proportion, and some degree of critical – not to say ethical – conscience; but these need not be developed very far, in a reader whose interest is in poetry not gossip, before he can decide (for example) just how much of *Dylan Thomas in America* is relevant, or irrelevant, in making up his mind about Dylan Thomas's poems.

The objection to the hypothetical aesthete, or the critical purist, is the same essentially as the objection to those who censor literature in the interests of a conventional morality. In both cases too much that we know to be vitally important to literature, as literature, is being handed over to an external judgement. I certainly do not deny that literature reflects, or contains, or – perhaps it is best to say – embodies moral values. But it seems to me that these are merely certain of its characteristic values looked at in a certain way. Among all the curiously varied travesties that Dr. Leavis has been the victim of in his long career, the one that comes nearest to being recognizable is the label of 'rugged moralist'. This, of course, is applied sarcastically, with the implication that he tends to introduce non-literary factors into his criticism – the didactic, or the puritanical. But surely when we disagree with his more comprehensive judgements on literature, it is not because he has gratuitously introduced a 'moral' note at a point where it is unexpected, or inappropriate, but either because one does not agree with the moral views implicit in those judgements, or (as in my own case) because the work in question either does or does not seem to embody the moral values that he finds, or misses, there. To take a minor example that comes to mind: how much of Lawrence's customary respect for life can be found in his attitude towards Mr. Massy, the 'little abortion' in *The Daughters of the Vicar*? But even when such disagreements are more serious and far-reaching, does one really find that what Leavis's opponents are objecting to is some moralistic irrelevance? Or are they objecting to the introduction of moral questions at all? Surely the case is rather that the opponents have – or think they have – different moral views.

A point should be made here about terminology. It is an unfortunate by-product of the controversy about aestheticism (one going back to the last century) that the word 'moral' tends to be used to cover everything humanly important, meaningful and serious in the imaginative literature that we read with full attention. And the wide and vague application of the word deprives it of its value as a means of indicating a certain stress and focus in the preoccupation demanded of the reader. But despite all its possibly misleading suggestions, it can never be abandoned. It reminds us of a dimension of life from which we can never escape if we are to remain human. And the moral element in literature is unevadable on literary grounds, at any rate for the writer who is committed in any way ('realist', 'naturalist', or other) to fulfilling the standard of 'truth to life'. What truth to life can there be in his work, if it ignores the moral experience of mankind? It is simply a fact that human beings *are* moral, and attempts to evade this fact in the interests of 'realism' are as unrealistic as any romance. True, a writer may take up (or believe that he is taking up) a consistent attitude of moral detachment from the characters, *mores*, and conduct he is depicting. But once again literary considerations, considerations of art, make it difficult to suppose that a work composed in the spirit could be of any interest. It would require some pretence on the writer's part of being 'above' or 'below' the human level, which (again appealing to the realistic canon he has accepted) must inevitably falsify his rendering; we cannot see human life from the point of view of a fly, or of the deities of Lucretius. Of course, no successful or interesting work has ever been really composed in this spirit; if Flaubert thought he had done so, he was mistaken.

The question, then, whether moral judgements are relevant in literary criticism seems to me an unreal one, unless we are given a clear statement of the moralist's (or anti-moralist's) notion of the characteristically literary judgements with which the moral judgements are alleged to be contrasted. To take a familiar example: when we say, as most people do, that the business of Little Nell in *The Old Curiosity Shop* is mawkish, is that a 'moral judgement'? It certainly bears not only on the question of Dickens's application of his intelligence in this part of his work but also (if these can be separated) on the degree of his self-know-ledge and his respect for his art and for his readers. And yet this judgement is surely *typical* of the sort of thing we expect to be asserted or denied about a work like this; it seems no more extra-literary than the judgement 'People don't behave like that', which everyone would agree to be relevant to the appraisal of realistic fiction. To say that Little Nell is mawkish is simply to say that Little Nell is bad art.

Someone might say that this kind of concern is more likely to come up when novels and the like are before us. The scope and subject-matter of a *War and Peace* invite more portentous and far-reaching decisions than, for instance, a short lyric. But I do not think it is true that the essential criteria in the two cases are different in logical type. Obviously considerations of mode, weight, and substance must play their part in any intelligent dis-cussion; but we have only to reflect on the criteria according to which we might express a preference, say, for Wordsworth's 'A slumber did my spirit seal' over Housman's 'The night is freezing fast' to find that we are still appealing in the end to the same vital principles, at the same depth.

Anyone who has taken part in teaching literature to grown-up people, or in the public discussion of it, will have encountered the dogged and naïve questioner whose primary requirement of literature is the 'sincerity' of the author. This student is nowadays the object of sophisticated mockery from modern-minded acade-mics and literary reviewers. I believe that he is right; and my ob-ject in writing is to provide him with adequate intellectual defence against this derision. Clearly the term 'sincerity' is open to misuse. Being a psychological term, it can distract our attention from the only relevant object of literary criticism – the work itself – to dubi-ously pertinent and anyway difficult questions about the hypo-thetical state of mind of the author at the time of composition, or his motives for writing. And it has the further drawback that it seems only obviously applicable to those works (poems, say) in which the author speaks or appears to speak in his own person. And even 'personal' poems are not affidavits. Sincerity is easily confused with autobiography, and inquiries about where the author's materials came from. Nothing has done Sir Philip Sidney's reputation as a poet more unjust harm than the discovery that (having told us how on his Muse's instructions he looked in his heart and wrote) he looked into the work of Italian poets. Then, sincerity cannot be a *sufficient* condition of excellence, as many a hymn, epitaph, or undergraduate love poem will show. At most, it can only be a necessary condition; and as such may not be thought to tell us much.

For all these reasons I have sometimes thought that the word might be replaced by some such term as 'genuineness' or 'authenticity', which do at least point to the created object and not to the soul of its creator. But I have now come to believe that like the term 'moral', 'sincerity' cannot be abandoned. It implies, or should imply, a profound personal self-commitment of the writer. But this commitment is very different from that of 'committed' (or propaganda) literature, which cannot of its very nature reflect the inward and intimate movements of the human will. The relevant kind of sincerity is something that has to be *achieved* by an inner discipline. Our sense of it is a sense that the writer has himself lived through in imagination what his work affirms or rejects, expresses or fails to express, reveals or leaves in shadow; its doubts, its tensions, its final moral poise. I do not mean that a work need be, in our actual experience of it, *obviously* an imaginative living-through of the writer's own problems, in a way in which this quotation from *Jude the Obscure* may suggest: 'As you got older, and felt yourself to be at the centre of your time, and not at a point in its circumference, as you had felt when you were little, you were seized with a sort of shuddering. . . . All round you there seemed to be something glaring, garish, rattling, and the noises and glares hit upon the little cell called your life, and shook it, and warped it.'

Jude the Obscure itself looks in part like such a work, and one reason for its unsatisfactoriness is that we are not sure quite how far it *is* that, and how far it is an objective case-history with a sociological 'moral'; we have doubts as to whether Hardy altogether knows what he is doing. But that this process of imaginative living-through has *preceded* the work, and underlies what has become dramatic creation, we have a right to be assured; and our assurance comes not from external sources but from our own reading, when we do it with the full force of our minds. Our feeling about this profound and absolute sincerity of the author is an essential part of our recognition of his full humanity.

This full humanity in great writers can be the reverse of re-assuring. It can even be frightening. Let us professional teachers and aspirant critics of literature ask ourselves how much of our theroretical system-building, and conviction about our taste, springs from fear – fear of the greatness of literature, fear of our-selves or of our pupils, fear of sincerity whether in ourselves or in others. I do not wish to impute to anyone else; as George Herbert says, 'My God, I mean myself.' But I cannot help wondering if there is not something generally amiss about the frequent acade-mic insistence on the historical approach, or on the importance of genres. How pain-saving it can be to remind oneself and one's pupils that the humiliation of Malvolio was arranged for an Elizabethan audience which enjoyed bear-baiting; or that in order to get *The Merchant of Venice* right we should adopt in imagination what seems a very quaint and medieval attitude towards Jews (as I think we in fact have to do if we are fully to enjoy Chaucer's *Prioress's Tale*). How convenient it is to disallow any sympathy with the poor old carpenter of the Miller's Tale, on the ground that this after all is 'farce', without noting how the impulsion towards sympathy, inhibited in the tale itself by the farcical atmosphere, is given its rights in the reaction of the old Reeve who objects to it, with his monologue that is at once comic and pathetic and something else.

But these are not seriously testing cases. The most difficult test for me, as to whether I can accept the full humanity of great literature, is that dark note of misanthropy, which sometimes is to be heard there. One can perhaps 'place' the misanthropy of a Swift, as part of the case of a radically distorted genius. But what about the misanthropy to be found in Shakespeare, in Tolstoy, in D. H. Lawrence? All I can say is that we must be very sure of just what are our motives for rejecting it; if they arise purely from the instinctive movement of health; or if it is rather that we are not facing something in ourselves, something perhaps giving rise to, and concealed by, our desire to seem to ourselves and to others always 'nice', placatory, and well-adjusted social beings.

The real reading and teaching and discussion of literature are bound to be processes of self-testing and self-exposure; we have to find out, and be prepared to reveal, and to commit ourselves sturdily to, what we think funny, or cruel, or wise, or compassionate, or silly, or boring, or good. Perhaps what we shall eventually discover – the thing that matters most of all, finally, in our dealings with great literature – is what is our conception of *nobility*, of the noble life: or if we have one. We should not be afraid of this word because of its associations with outdated Victorian solemnity. I do not like – it seems to me revealing, in a tiny way, of something unwholesome in our society – the present fashion of casual sneering at one of the greatest Victorian writers, George Eliot. How much of English literature – how much of Russian – do the people who do this really have access to?

But I am not suggesting that we can take over (how could we?) any previous writer's conception of the noble. We have to work out our own; but since this is difficult to do, it is natural that we should turn more and more to the writers whom we recognize as classics. I have no wish to indulge in any topical jeremiads; but the obvious decline of, or – to put it less tendentiously – the obvious uncertainty about standards of honour, conduct and manners, to be seen in current fiction no less than in the newspapers and the life around us, makes it all the more important that we should get all the help we can from the past towards understanding ourselves and our problems. After reading Chapter LXXIV of *Middlemarch*, we might ask ourselves if there is alive and active in the literature of our own day the kind of compassionate intelligence that informs this treatment of human degradation and pain:

> It was eight o'clock in the evening before the door opened and his wife entered. He dared not look up at her. He sat with his eyes bent down, and as she went towards him she thought he looked smaller – he seemed so withered and shrunken. A movement of new compassion and old tenderness went through her like a great wave, and putting one hand on his which rested on the arm of the chair, and the other on his shoulder, she said, solemnly but kindly –
> 'Look up, Nicholas.'
> He raised his eyes with a little start and looked at her half amazed for a moment: her pale face, her changed, mourning

dress, the trembling about her mouth, all said 'I know'; and her hands and eyes rested gently upon him. He burst out crying and they cried together, she sitting at his side. They could not yet speak to each other of the shame which she was bearing with him, or of the acts which had brought it down on them. His confession was silent, and her promise of faithfulness was silent. Open-minded as she was, she nevertheless shrank from the word which would have expressed their mutual consciousness as she would have shrunk from flakes of fire. She could not say How much is only slander and false suspicion?' and he did not say 'I am innocent'.

1963

II

MR. LEAVIS ON LITERARY STUDIES

I am glad that Mr. F. R. Leavis has found in my essay[1] an opportunity for restating so trenchantly and stimulatingly his own view of literary studies at the University; and I must thank him for the courtesy with which he has treated my arguments, even while bringing to bear on them his characteristic force and incisiveness. I am very willing to grant that there are unfortunate phrases and turns of expression in that essay, and, what is worse still, that the main issue it purports to discuss is neither very specifically nor very clearly stated. I would like to mend matters. But first there are one or two points that Mr. Leavis has put to controversial use, in respect of which I must defend my intention.

Mr. Leavis represents me as proposing to substitute Locke, Bolingbroke, etc., as the central authors for study, in the place of what we usually and rightly regard as the classics of English literature: Shakespeare or Marvell or Pope, Johnson or Jane Austen. But my passing reference was not intended to suggest that Bolingbroke and the rest should be shifted from the margin of study to the centre, or that a literary student need give much, or indeed any, of his time to those authors – or to many others whom I could have mentioned; authors who, as Mr. Leavis would agree, are in various ways and in various degrees of *some* interest, and who can be made on occasion to serve the purposes of those whose primary concern, whether as teachers or as students or just as common readers, is with imaginative literature – with 'literature' as ordinarily understood. As to the names I actually mentioned, they were not chosen merely at random. Mr. Leavis in his

[1] The essay appeared in *Universities Quarterly* (August 1956) and Mr. Leavis's reply appeared in the November number.

own comments has very well suggested the kind of interest in Locke and Burke that I myself would think desirable for the literary student. I added Bolingbroke because Matthew Arnold recommended his historical writings; and because on taking this hint I found him to be the master of a strong direct, modern prose, evincing a remarkable grasp and force of mind. As for William Law, I am interested in him very largely as exemplifying a theme often explored by Mr. Leavis: the nature, significance, and influence of an age or a culture in relation to individuals who on the face of it do not conform to any received idea of what that was, and who yet can be seen in some curious respects to belong to it. Thus while Law by temperament, character and training is obviously utterly unlike Pope – his spiritual affinities being with the medieval anchorites – he still belongs plainly to 'the age of Pope' in social habit, style, and moral essence; illuminist as he is in tendency, and an earnestly practical moralist in his preoccupations, there is an odd note of the genial, the polite, the sociable, in his writings; and this seems to tell us something important, not only about Law, but about Pope: that is, about the religious and moral tradition which is at the basis of Pope's art. And I doubt whether that minor English classic the Serious Call is any more 'there' for the confident summarizer, the peruser of handbooks, than a great classic like *The Pilgrim's Progress*. I should add, however, that, in expressing regret that it should be neglected, I would not be taken to imply more than a dissent from the view that while Law's contemporary Steele is Literature, to be studied and lectured about and examined on, Law is not.

But my main object in referring to these neglected writers was to criticize the convention which fixes the line of literary studies so as to exclude, not only them, but the subject-matter, argument and substantial content of discursive prose in general. I mentioned here the 'terror of the cognitive' as responsible for this. And I can assure Mr. Leavis that I have good reason to think that the adoption of this convention *is* sometimes associated with the cultivation of 'style' and 'form' – with the cultivation of Sir Thomas Browne and his engaging quaintness. I had in mind, that is, the promoters of that variety of 'critical appreciation' which, in effect if not in theory, is a 'soft option': a means of relaxation from the rigours of Anglo-Saxon and the like. But I was far from wishing to attribute to Mr. Leavis, or to anyone who might reasonably be said to have learned from Mr. Leavis's work, any responsibility for this kind of thing.

Mr. Leavis censures my confident but ill-defined use of words like 'fact', 'intellectual', 'historical'. But I must be allowed to question his inference, from my incidental mention of a critic's mistake about *housel*, that my conception of 'fact' and 'history' is quite so simple as he says. In citing examples of this type of mistake, I was at pains to add that such linguistic changes did *not* constitute the most important kind of difficulty for the reader of old books. And I gave as an example a much more inward and subtle kind, typified by the 'frame of mind', the 'conception of purpose', of Christian devotional poetry. And surely this has its problems – problems of approach and criteria of relevance – for the mature critic as well as for the undergraduate, for the reader who shares the poet's religious beliefs and for the reader who does not. And don't we need, especially in these times, the limited and limiting suggestion of the adjective 'intellectual', to describe what must be at least one aspect of the comprehension that has to be achieved before we can talk intelligently about these works?

My unclear use of the adjective 'aesthetic' is similarly rebuked. And I agree that it is an unsatisfactory term, and one which promotes confusion, at any rate in literary discussion. But what other accepted term *is* there to describe those qualities, features, or characteristics of a poem, a play, or a novel, which they have in common (either directly or by analogy) with a work of musical or plastic art, as against what is not supposed to be or offered as 'art'? and which they have in common with each other as against (e.g.) an argument considered as an argument, or a sermon as a sermon? And surely no one will dispute that these characteristics have sometimes to be distinguished. Not that they are essential: so far from arguing, as I think Mr. Leavis takes me to do, that they are not the most important of the 'facts' about literature I insisted so much on, I took care to emphasize, in dissociating my position from that of the scholar who neglects the 'purely aesthetic' aspects of his subject, that these were usually just what made it what it essentially was; my quotation-marks were intended to be ironical.

Finally, apropos of my assertion that 'the standing of many great writers is simply a historical fact', Mr. Leavis (having asked who these are) goes on to relate the spirit of this remark to the emphasis on dry, dull, irrelevant, externals, rather than on the essential qualities of literature, which he diagnoses as characteristic of my approach. Well, it seems to me that some, perhaps many, of the great European classics are not very alive today; Dante, for instance: his *contemporary* standing is largely based on convention – and also, no doubt, on respect for Mr. Eliot's essay. I know that Mr. Leavis does not approve of his state of affairs; he thinks that the great poem of Dante should be more effectively honoured than it is. But how? We shall agree that there are many incidental pleasures, and even highly poetic pleasures, to be got by dipping into the *Inferno* and elsewhere; but I am sure that Mr. Leavis wants to recommend more than this; more, even, that the Dante who may be said to have influenced the revised *Hyperion* or *The Triumph of Life*. Now, it seems to me that if one is not seriously interested in the intellectualist vision which characterizes Dante's poem, one is losing something essential of Dante. I certainly do not believe that Dante is so inaccessible as some medievalists have made him out to be, but I don't agree either with someone who replied, when I argued in that strain, that a cradle-Catholic finds Dante easy because he imbibes a sort of instinctive Aristotelianism with his mother's milk. I don't believe that one can learn a way of thinking except by thinking. And mustn't one learn, at least to *some* degree, Dante's way of thinking, before the *Comedy* as a whole comes to life? This question is rhetorical; I don't wish for a moment to attribute absurd views to Mr. Leavis, but I do want to make it clear that my concern for 'history' was not a matter of insisting on externals. For the mind of Dante is not external to his poetry.

Now, suppose Dante did become, what he ought to be, one of the genuine centres of a truly vital humane school of study; and suppose one had a student who had a real interest in poetry, and was sensitive and intelligent, but who just *could* not get interested in Dante's remote and alien kind of intellectualism? A student who did appreciate the vivid dramatic quality of certain scenes and situations in the poem, and some local imaginative life here and there in the quality of the writing, but who found little else to engage his interest? (And I have a suspicion that many of those who read and enjoy Dante would have to admit, in a moment of candour, that they don't get much more than that out of him.) How could a teacher, knowing this very well, nevertheless justify the spending of any precious time on the medievalism of Dante? Surely his last line of defence (and that is what I was concerned with) would be that Dante's poem is a great historical fact; that it is more than a great medieval Italian poem, more even than a classic of European Christendom; and one might suggest to the sceptical pupil that if one *was* prepared to exercise one's historical imagination one might find some 'real' (in Arnold's sense) as well as 'historical' value, not only in the author of the *Comedy*, but even in the author of the *Convivio* – who was, after all, the same man. And I can't believe that Mr. Leavis would disapprove of the spirit of that approach. In practice, of course, one would no doubt expect, and seek, to foster a much more limited kind of interest in Dante, and I don't say that that would be wrong; but one would have to make it clear in doing so that the classical standing of Dante – the 'historical fact' – depends on much more than the things which may very well be all that even an intelligent and sympathetic modern reader can find to admire in him.

All these points regard what was my main theme, considered in its bearing on the question of literary studies: the relation between 'history' and criticism. It seems almost as if the interaction of these two were as complex as that of the Soul and Body explored in the great poem by Marvell which Mr. Leavis has so convincingly analysed. I am not quite clear whether Mr. Leavis rejects outright my opinion that history and criticism are separable, or whether he merely objects (fairly enough) to my somewhat obscure and elliptical way of stating it. That there *is* a distinction, I am still convinced; though I do not deny, and did not in my article, that the critic and the historian may be the same person.

I will not expatiate here on the relation between understanding and valuing, in reference to literary criticism, for I do not wish to incur again Mr. Leavis's charge of elaborating a 'dialectic' for its own sake. And anyway I find the whole subject very puzzling – as who does not, who is interested in the definition of criticism? On the one hand, valuing in the sense which matters to the literary critic, is not simply like awarding a certificate, or afixing a price-tag; it seems to refer to something which controls from the start the whole process of critical reading; on the other hand, I cannot believe that one recognizes the value of a work by a pre-reflective intuition: the very word 'judgement' that we tend to use ('value-judgement') carries the suggestion of a reflective act, a decision. (And we might say that a valuation based on a misunderstanding of a poem is not, in an important sense, a valuation of *that* poem.)

It seems, then, that understanding is, at least conceptually, distinct from valuing; that it is a prior requisite. But it does not follow from this (so to speak) logical priority, that as a temporal, psychological process 'understanding' precedes 'valuing'; and indeed I think few would accept that account, who recollect what the actual reading of a great poem is like: how it grows in the mind as the mind grows in comprehension of it, how it comes to be possessed by its reader and in turn possesses him. And so I have to grant that the distinction between understanding and valuing, as commonly stated or implied, strikes no real root in the experience of any lover of literature. There can be no doubt that Mr. Eliot, and Coleridge before him, speak for many when they declare that it is possible to admire and enjoy and be moved by poetry which in a strict sense one doesn't, and may not even want to, 'understand'. And in the same anti-academic spirit we may retort to our self-appointed enlighteners that many of the poems they affect to explicate or surround with 'facts about' them, we *already* understand, and that any 'help' they may offer will make no difference, since we will not *let* it make any. And I can sympathize all too easily with the mood in which one answers the question: 'What is the correct text of that poem? Which is the correct interpretation?' by saying, 'That which is most beautiful; that which gives me the most pleasure.' But I also have my share of that impulse which I will not dignify by calling it anything other than *curiosity*, to find out what the poet actually wrote, and what he probably meant it to mean – if I may perpetrate this 'intentionalism' without qualification or discussion. And I can only say that I think the teaching of poetry at the University should minister at one time or another to both kinds of reader; or rather, to the same reader according to his different states of mind, and his different purposes. And the ideal historian of literature would be that reader *in excelsis*. He would be a critic; reading his authors, he would know what the actual historian may not know: how to tell the quick from the dead. But the poet, and the critic, must have wherewithal to discriminate. And they may want other information too; wisdom is a higher and a better thing than information, but it is not the same thing; and the wise man may show his wisdom in consenting to inform himself.

I am sure that Mr. Leavis would not deny this. He is a literary historian himself; *Revaluation* is certainly literary history – its character as an experiment in historical method has been overlooked

by many of its critics. But if I may make a direct application
to him of a point I glanced at in my article: Mr. Leavis knows
what to remember in reading the literature of the past; he also
knows (which may be even more important) what to forget.
But one cannot either remember or forget what one has never
known. And I do find, and do hear about, historical ignorance,
not only in young students' work, but in nature writers. May I
however assure Mr. Leavis that I was not so impertinent, in both
the common and the strict senses of that word, as to imply that *his*
work does not make or propose a due use of history and 'scholarship'? True, I *was* concerned about the neglect and ignorance of
lower-order 'facts', a neglect not palliated by the reproduction
of the language of criticism. But I never meant to be
interpreted as advancing academic counter-proposals in a spirit
hostile or indifferent to *Education and the University*. I had in mind,
indeed, the conditions in which work in a spirit akin to that might
be made possible. But I was also aware of the local situation on
which Mr. Leavis had his eyes when he wrote his book, a situation
somewhat different from that which faces a teacher in the English
School to which I belong. And so I was thinking primarily in
terms of how to make the best of what is worth preserving in the
tradition of that School, with its primarily 'scholarly', linguistic,
and medievalist emphasis. I believe that life could be fostered there
too, for I can see no contradiction between the *ideal* purposes of
the scholar and those of the critic. And there was in my mind the
idea of an academic régime which would provide the same pre-
liminary training for the future creative writers, professional
critics, scholars, and above all the common readers – the literary
laymen – without whom literature cannot live. I specify the
'scholars' because Mr. Leavis acknowledges that scholars are
necessary. We agree that, to be useful, scholarship must be in-
formed by criticism. It must answer genuine critical questions.
But if this statement is not to be a mere pleonasm, we have to
assume that scholarship is not identical with criticism. And after
all, it will be generally granted that there is such a thing as special
scholarly training; and if scholars are to be trained, where else
than at a University? I cordially agree with Mr. Leavis that a man
isn't in a respectable sense 'trained' even for a special literary study
if he has not a trained intelligence about literature in general. And
the intended point of my article was that the ideal first-degree
course should provide at least some part of that general training.

I hope that Mr. Leavis will not think that I am exalting scholarship. I know that it is too often the case that, while a critic makes a little go a long way, a scholar makes a lot go nowhere. And few of us go to the leading academic 'authority' on a great poet for *critical* illumination about him; we go to one or other of the very few original critics present and past. But we need also what we *do* go to the authority for, a good text, together with the notes and commentaries that Mr. Leavis allows to be necessary – would that we always got them!

It is only too clear that there have been eminent scholars who have done useful services to literature without having much critical ability; I need not specify instances; there is, alas, an *embarras de choix*. But there have also been good critics who have been deficient in a historical sense. That 'history' is not enough, that uninformed by criticism it is not true history, is the moral I draw from the regretted A. J. A. Waldock's superiority to the academic champions of Milton that he strove with. But that there is none the less something distinct from the purely critical capacity, namely, a historical awareness that is needed to bring a literature, a tradition, a series of conventions, into full focus, is the further moral that I draw from the same author's very interesting but not quite satisfactory book on a Greek dramatist. This book has the critical virtues: but I must add that, while I can believe in Waldock's Milton, frankly, I cannot believe in his Sophocles.

1957

III

ENGLISH AS A UNIVERSITY SUBJECT

One lesson we may learn from the work of the great teacher and critic whom the foundation of this lecture commemorates, is that an effective concern for literature and education shows itself not in the uttering of grand generalities, but in the specific, the concrete, and the immediate. And so in speaking about this subject I should naturally like to be as precise and as down-to-earth as possible. But such an endeavour at once involves me in this difficulty: that the kind of detailed illustration and argument which I should have to provide in order to say anything of substance is both unsuited to exposition by lecture, and presupposes a patience and an intensity of practical interest in this large and complex problem which I have no right to assume from everyone present. I must then ask the indulgence of those who are thus intensely concerned if I over-simplify, dwell only on the broad lines of the problem as I see it, and throw out many bald assertions without argument. I can only plead that I have thought about the problem for many years, as one whose concern with it is practical as well as ideal, and that I hope I have good reasons for my positions which I should have elaborated if I had had the time and space to do so. And I should say at the outset that I shall confine myself for the most part, in what follows, to undergraduate studies; though to have a point of view about them of course requires having a point of view about graduate studies also, and in due course I shall have to say something about those.

To propose the topic of 'English as a university subject' suggests the question, What is a university subject? or (to make it clear that we are now passing from the real to the rational) What characterizes a subject as suitable for study at a university? or – to raise the question in a somewhat different and perhaps more challenging form – What distinguishes the *university* way of dealing with a subject? It is mainly in this form that our general question is examined in the opening pages of a recent report on higher education. This report does not, it is true, give much space to the explicit statement of the philosophy of education which underlies its proposals for indefinite university expansion. Indeed, one of the notable things about it is the very high level of abstraction of what it does say; this abstraction striking us as in marked contrast with the impressive and frightening particularity of the blueprints of complex institutional machinery which follows. It may be said that these opening pages are merely typical of official reports, high-sounding verbiage which it is a convention to utter before getting down to business. But to me those opening pages of the Robbins Report turn out to have a more important function; their argument, moving smoothly on its high plane of abstraction, contrives to beg or bury vital questions, while at the same time seeming to justify the subsequent disappearance of those questions – as if they had, somehow, been satisfactorily settled – in the mass of factual matter which follows. An example of the tone and bias which the report imparts from the beginning is what is here said about the *differentia* of university study:

> And it is the distinguishing characteristic of a healthy higher education that, even where it is concerned with practical techniques, it imparts them on a plane of generality that makes possible their application to many problems – to find the one in the many, the general characteristic in the collection of particulars. It is this that the world of affairs demands of the world of learning. And it is this, and not conformity with traditional categories, that furnishes the criterion of what institutions of higher education may properly teach.[1]

One consequence of the report's brevity about fundamental questions is that we are inclined to scrutinize its phraseology, when it does touch on them, rather suspiciously. Thus, a casual reader of this passage might find in it only an expression of the not very recondite idea that, while a course of dentistry is supposed to teach you nothing but dentistry, and a course of carpentry nothing but carpentry, 'the Greats man can turn his hand to anything'.

[1] *Robbins Report on Higher Education*, H.M.S.O., London, 1963.

But the proviso about 'practical techniques', as well as the context, makes it clear that the writers do not have in mind anything resembling the tradition I have symbolized by Classical Greats; and when we associate that proviso with the disquieting stress laid on what 'the world of affairs demands of the world of learning', in what is offered as a *criterion* for what institutions of higher education may properly teach, we are already wondering whether, at this level of generality, an unargued social pragmatism is not being introduced, or assumed; so that when we finally turn over in our minds the dismissing phrase 'conformity with traditional categories', we begin to suspect that along with these 'traditional categories' the whole case for liberal education, the whole history of the educational tradition from Aristotle to *Scrutiny*, is being tacitly dismissed. It is in these and the like unobtrusive phrases that our leaders of educational thought accomplish the shift from what used to be the English to what is now the American conception of university education – without ever having to make explicit what they are doing. The right reader will hardly notice that the older conception of a university is being replaced by the new conception of it as a finishing-school for democracy.

It may be said that the Robbins Report is not now topically agitating; it is certainly being said that the report is going to be left on the shelf. But the trend which it represents in modern thought – the thought, I must remind you, of the influential and powerful people in this country – is still going to be with us; and the questions I have raised with my undefined and undefended use of the old term 'liberal education' are going to be with us also. It is with this general preoccupation very much in mind that I have offered to tackle today only one, but, most people would agree, a very important aspect of the work of the university.

The passage I quoted from the report does in one or two ways, I think, at least turn our minds in the right direction. First, it is clear that, while too much may be quietly smuggled out of sight in the dismissal of 'traditional categories', few of those concerned with Arts courses and Arts subjects as we know them are going to feel happy about being forced tactically into the position of defending them. 'Tradition', we all know, is a dangerous word. Too many crimes have been committed in its name; and it is ambiguous in ways which make it easy for those who concur in the philosophy of the Robbins Report to discredit their opponents as reactionaries. Not that I am recommending that we should give up the use of the word 'tradition'. In so far as it suggests that there are good things which an educated and thoughtful person should be concerned to maintain and preserve, its suggestion is valuable. There are many occasions on which the force of the expression 'defence of tradition' is obvious. Thus when a gentleman wrote recently in the *Oxford Magazine*, apropos of the Oxford roads controversy, 'I couldn't care less about the Meadow Road. Society must progress and things must be changed', we may see in this and similar situations the positive content, and the strength, of the concept of 'defence of tradition'; for the defender of tradition against the gentleman who wrote in the *Oxford Magazine* can point to something real and definite and valuable which we have already got, to justify him and provide a reason for what he is saying; whereas the opponents have no reason to offer for what they are saying, but merely a habit of thought – or non-thought. Too many of the underlying assumptions about education in our time, even if less artlessly expressed, seem to me along the lines of 'society must progress and things must be changed'.

The obvious, and valid, objection to talking about the 'defence of tradition', in the context of discussions of liberal education, is that it is too purely conservative in suggestion; it implies more confidence than we have the right to feel, that out existing institutions, our faculties and Arts departments, do embody *as they stand* something real and definite and valuable which it is our duty to preserve. And this leads to a corollary: that what we are defending is nothing so palpably and unequivocally a value as the physical beauty of Oxford, the things which make Arnold's *Scholar Gipsy* nowadays so poignant a poem. Though the issue is fundamentally the same – the issue of civility against barbarism – the things which we have in mind, belonging as they do to the life of thought, and appertaining to the choices of men, are not just 'there', and then suddenly 'not there', like Hopkins's Binsey poplars:

> Ten or twelve, only ten or twelve
> Strokes of havoc unselve
>   The sweet especial scene,
> Rural scene, a rural scene,
> Sweet especial rural scene.

The traditions and the values we are concerned with do not live by nature; they can neither be destroyed, nor preserved, like the things of nature; they live – and it is a truism we shall do well to recall – only as a result of the countless conscious decisions, determinations and acts of will of individual men. To a larger extent than we always remember, the civilized man must constantly create, and re-create, the things he contemplates. That is why Dr. Leavis's term 'continuity' seems to me more satisfactory than 'tradition'; to my mind it brings out, as 'tradition' of itself does not, that we are to be concerned with ensuring a life, which being life implies growth; we must try to imagine our subject-matter, English literature, as an ideal totality; to see the present in the past, no less than to see the past in the present.

But we have still to ask, what does a care for literature and education, in the university environment, amount to? what is the cash-value of the language that speaks of 'continuity', 'life', 'growth', 'the present in the past' and 'the past in the present', in terms of the actual concrete situation of an English university of our time? What does it mean in terms of such prosaic realities as the standard of undergraduate admissions, the standard for graduates and their function in the academic community, the content of syllabuses, the role of lectures as compared with seminars, the advantages and disadvantages of the tutorial or supervisory system, the value or otherwise of conventional methods of examining – and all the numerous other practical problems which beset us all the time, if we are involved with university education in any way? And this is where the passage from the Robbins Report does seem to me, this time, to contain an element of helpful suggestion, to point to the place where serious positive discussion should start. What I am thinking of is the reference to some measure of *generalizability*, of applicability outside a particular field of study, as being a criterion, or, to use Newman's word, a 'note', of a genuine university subject – or of the characteristically university way of dealing with a subject. I do not particularly like the actual terms the report uses, when it speaks of finding 'the one in the many, the general characteristic in the world of particulars'. In subjects like ours, at any rate, the temptation to premature generalization is already great, and it is one that the student has to learn to resist. And for another thing, this and the other notes of university work that the report lists, seem, as I have said, remote from actuality in more than one sense – or at more than one level. It is an unsound philosophy of higher education which leaves us with no adequate theoretical means for distinguishing among technical and vocational training, general education, and learning; which leaves us in a cultural void, without any sense of a particular place and particular time – of England as a nation with its own history.

But there is certainly a serious difficulty about characterizing, in an industrial society such worlds away from Aristotle's, the distinctive note of the education of free men. And I am not prepared to propose a more satisfactory alternative to what the report says; that is, to try to lay down necessary and sufficient conditions for the definition of liberal education; only to remark that in its reference to potential generalizability we have at any rate the suggestion of something that distinguishes the method, the approach, the discipline, that are relevant here; the suggestion of the student's taking away from his studies not merely a skill, but a habit of mind.

Then, before descending from this plane of generality to what used to be called 'humane' education and to English in particular. I would urge the importance, as a criterion of university studies, of some reference to a *genuine body of knowledge*. This demand, I believe, is not tautological. For it is all too easy to recall that many places bearing the name of university have given hospitality, not only to what many of us would consider unsuitable subjects, but to what many of us would consider pseudo-subjects. In using the latter term I am thinking of the danger to which 'composite courses' are exposed. I am certainly not wanting to suggest that there is anything sacrosanct about the traditional organization of university subjects and faculties. No one interested in English literature as an academic subject can fail to see how it impinges on and interlocks with other studies which have not until recent times been regarded as falling within the scope of 'English' departments. And I welcome the experiments which are being made, in breaking down conventional barriers, at the new universities. But I have reservations; to be specific, I should not be happy if Oxford and Cambridge were to be in too great haste to increase the superficial attractions of 'English', to demonstrate its 'contemporaneity' and 'relevance', by turning it into one of these composite schools. One reason for these reservations is that some of these composites seem to me too much defined by their syllabus, and by the *ethos* and conscious intentions of the committees who put them together, rather than by the contours of reality. It is surely desirable that a university course, in however limited and sketchy a way, should bring the student up against a recalcitrance in his subject-matter, by making him find out for himself the way in which the things which are studied live together in the real world. And to say this is only to draw out the implication of the phrase I used, 'a genuine body of knowledge'. To put it in immediately relevant terms, English literature exists; its contents, its patterns, its relationships with the whole field of history and present experience are what they are; and they cannot be finally bent to the practical purposes of the present day, the purposes of syllabusmakers or of systematizing literary historians. To study literature without being compelled all the time to allow for the obstinate, individual, unmappable quality of what we are dealing with, is not education. Another danger of basing a course on selected highlights – American and European, no doubt, as well as English – as of introducing the student to a plurality of specialisms in related fields, is that he may become too dependent on his teachers and lecturers; finding in his subject-matter no self-evident principles of order, he is debarred by the vastness of his inevitable ignorance from working out one of his own. His chance of acquiring some independence of judgement is much less if there is no area of his work in which he can be at least temporarily on an equality with his teacher.

But I have already revived a hard question by talking of 'contours of reality'. No one is more conscious than I that when we are dealing with literature we are dealing all the time with mental things, intangible products of the interplay of individual minds. The pattern of order that matters cannot be chalked up on a blackboard, or schematized in a textbook; it must be felt and grasped by the individual himself, however imperfectly, and with however great a measure of what Dr. Leavis has well called 'the courage of enormous incompleteness'. It is one of the best-known and memorable achievements of T. S. Eliot's early criticism that he made influential the notion that the perspective of the past changes as really new works are added to literature. Eliot's argument, in this part of *Tradition and the Individual Talent*, is not altogether free from obscurity. It seems unnecessarily mystifying to say, as he does, that the ideal order of existing works of art is altered by the *creation* of the radically new work of art. Surely it was the publication and influence of Hopkins's poems (for example), rather than the writing of them, that altered the 'ideal order' of Victorian poetry; at the time he wrote them they could not do that, since they were not known. And Eliot seems to speak as if, not only the ideal order, but the individual works themselves, are altered. Surely the more common-sense view is correct, that what is altered is rather our interpretation, evaluation, and placing of them relative to each other and to ourselves. But one need not accept the mystical-metaphysical element in Eliot's argument to recognize in it a large measure of validity, and to admit that it has important consequences for the historical study of literature. I sometimes wonder whether those of us who are teachers of English literature realize what these are, realize just what we are committed to, in regard to our historical and critical principles, by the nature of our subject. We may pay lip-service to the proposition that 'English literature still goes on', but do we always realize its implications? One obvious, yet sometimes overlooked implication is that no one can know the whole of English literature, not only as a matter of fact (because there is so much of it) but as a matter of logic (because some of it does not yet exist). A trite reflexion! but does it not follow – and is it always felt to follow – that the history and criticism of English literature must be totally different from what is assumed by the traditional methods of education in the Classics? For us there can be no fixed canon of literature, no series of certified valuations. We may pride ourselves on being nowadays free from the academic prejudice illustrated by the old-fashioned French examination, which required of the candidate that, faced by a question about a particular author, he should do no more and no less than write out what is said about that author in Lanson's history of French literature. We may have gone beyond simply asking for the equivalent of Lanson: but exactly where? I wish I could feel that my colleagues and I could give a confident reply to that question.

But what I would emphasize at the moment is that, granted that the perspective of English literature is bound to alter from age to age, and granted that to achieve a particular contemporary perspective is only made possible by an exercise of individual judgement, however fragmentary and imperfect this must be – granted that, it is important to remember that the relationship between us at the present day, and a work of the past, is of the nature of a dialogue. If we simply impose our own interpretations and valuations, without listening to what they say, we shall not be learning from them, but teaching them. That is why I object to Eliot's saying that works of the past are *altered* by the arrival of new works. The justification for the academic study of literature must at least in part lie in a scrupulous attention to the other voice in our dialogue with the minds of the past. Professor Kott's *Shakespeare our Contemporary* is merely the most spectacular of recent examples of a tendency to silence that voice. We may contrast with that tendency what is said of Donne in *Revaluation*, that we read him as we read the living, without ceasing to be conscious of him as fully a man of his own time. This last illustration may perhaps make it clear that I am not here at all supporting the view that the historical approach to literature can be properly set over in some way against the approach of literary criticism. The most relevant evidence for the historian, as for the critic – and in the normal case these will be the same person – is the text itself; and many of the misreadings and aberrations by interpreters who emphasize their historical-mindedness may be traced precisely to an anterior conviction about the 'context' of the work which distorts or deflects their vision of its text. The individual work has its own meaning, is itself a fact of language and history; and to suppose that we have at least some access to that meaning, that we are not merely fabricating illusions about it, seems to be entailed by any coherent account of continuity, tradition, or cultural memory, of all, in fact, that we are committed to, whether wittingly or no, when we say our subject is English literature.

But to speak of English literature as a genuine body of knowledge at once stirs up the kind of controversy into which discussion of the nature of English studies has in the past so frequently turned. (Consider, for example, the publications provoked by the official report of the 1920's on the 'teaching of English in England'.) It would seem that for many people the only important points in dispute are things like: should Anglo-Saxon be compulsory? or, should the student whose interests are primarily literary be obliged to obtain a grounding in philology and linguistics? I have chosen not to begin with these questions – I am not, of course, saying that they are not important – because it seems to me that to *begin* with a question like 'Anglo-Saxon or not?' tends to eliminate questions which are more fundamental, by determining in advance the scope of the argument. I have been trying to define the concept of an English school with regard to its centre, not to its periphery; for surely not even the most enthusiastic supporter of Anglo-Saxon will claim that it is part of what has customarily been meant by English literature outside academic circles. The question about Anglo-Saxon and other 'fringe' subjects is to my mind subordinate to the questions, What is an English school for? and, What should be the sovereign discipline of an English school? But since that specific issue is so often brought up in practical discussion, I will say two things about it in passing. First, I would like to make it clear that to my mind there is no question but that a great international English university like Oxford or Cambridge should offer the fullest opportunities for the historical study of the English language, and for the pursuit of those Northern studies with which the Anglo-Saxon phase of our civilization is naturally linked. I hope I am justified in assuming that *this* is not in dispute at all. What is in dispute is whether the students whose interests are primarily literary – and these, in the normal state of affairs, are likely to be the great majority – should be compelled to spend any part of their admittedly very restricted time in acquiring what may be no more than a smattering of those disciplines. Secondly, I must point out that the Anglo-Saxon question is a separate one from the philology question. It is possible to support the inclusion of Anglo-Saxon in the syllabus, on the ground that Anglo-Saxon literature is part of English literature, while opposing the retention of compulsory philology; this was in fact C. S. Lewis's position. It is also possible – and this is a view sometimes expressed in Oxford today – to urge that the literary student should be introduced to the disciplines of linguistics and semantics, to acquire some sense of the historical developments of meaning, without requiring him to study Anglo-Saxon. The two questions are not the same; but in casual everyday controversies they are frequently confused.

I must apologize to those of you, here in Cambridge, who feel that these are questions which, so far as you are concerned, have been satisfactorily settled. I can only remind you that these are still open questions at my own university, Oxford, and, so far as many of our young men and women are concerned, questions that still burn. I would not like to predict the future of the Oxford English School in this regard, nor that of other university English schools which are similar to it in structure. All I can say is that the 'language-and-literature' formula is receiving more critical consideration today than it has had for many years. A point that might strike the unprejudiced observer is that the Oxford *Examination Statutes* reveal an anomaly in the curricular application of this formula; it is possible for the student whose interests are exclusively linguistic and medieval to choose a course which does not require him to deal with any author later than Chaucer; whereas the literary course, which the great majority of our students take, does require linguistic knowledge, and knowledge of authors earlier than Chaucer. If, then, the language-and-literature formula is already being ignored in the interest of the linguists, I do not see the rational grounds for opposing the setting up of a purely modern course (i.e. a course from the fourteenth century onwards).

But the strictly parochial aspects of the question of English syllabuses are not my concern today. If to many of you they seem strangely remote from the preoccupations of the teacher of English literature in the cultural crisis of the present day, this is itself an index of the degree to which university English schools have developed and travelled away from the shadow of the old classical-philological framework in which they began. (The *Oxford University Handbook*, not a noticeably revolutionary document, observes that 'English language and literature was slow in establishing its claims to professional scholarly standing because of the dominance of classical studies, and the theory, of very doubtful validity, that a good education in the classics sufficed to equip a man for the study of his own language and literature'.) The cutting away of English studies from the classical tradition, for which Mrs. Leavis called in 1943, has now been accomplished. Faculties of English are not now staffed from classical departments. Even at Oxford, where the Classics still retain a powerful social and intellectual prestige, the 'English' don feels himself less on the defensive. True, there are still traces of the old snobberies; intellectual and social snobbery, as is often the English way, are curiously intermingled. Of the English school a classical don remarked to me recently that an intelligent man could read it in his bath. It is noteworthy that All Souls offers no fellowships in English or Modern Languages; and one can still hear the view expressed, or implied, that a gentleman doesn't need to study English literature – or, for that matter, French: English, like Modern Languages, is a somewhat plebeian subject, read mainly by grammar-school boys. And of course many of those who read English are women. . . . But all this now wears a quaintly 'period' air. University English teachers now have the right to feel that the trend of the age is with them; Classics, the supreme academic literary subject of an aristocratic society, is being replaced, in the democratic society, by English. And in so far as certain snobberies and vested interests are being defeated, there have been great gains.

Yes, there have been great gains, negatively speaking – but can we be so confident in our affirmations? Can we say that English literature has yet found its characteristic discipline, in the sense in which the history of the English language, or traditional Classical studies, have their characteristic disciplines? To raise that question in your minds is my main aim today.

I take it, to begin with, that no one will deny that a university subject should have at least one characteristic discipline. And one of the marks of a genuine body of knowledge, as I see it, is that of itself it strongly suggests the nature of the particular approach which is most likely to make it accessible. I do not say that it is *defined* by this approach; for I have already expressed the opinion that a subject which is defined by the approach to it tends to be a pseudo-subject. But it seems clear that to admit, as we must, such multifarious content into a school of English literature makes it all the more incumbent upon us to offer some paramount co-ordinating approach, some sovereign discipline, which will give the subject, or rather the congeries of subjects, called 'English' a centre. And, like many others, I am convinced that the right view about what such a discipline should be is that which, as a matter of history, has been given by Dr. Leavis. It is he above all who has maintained that the typical, the central, the identifying discipline of an English school should be literary criticism. I propose to spend the remainder of my time in considering just what this means, and to what, in my view, it commits those who assent to it.

The propositions that English literature is a genuine body of knowledge, and that the appropriate discipline for its study is literary criticism, seem to me to be coupled and to move together. But this does not mean what some have taken it to mean, that criticism dictates to literature what it should be. On the contrary, it is the nature of literature which determines what criticism should be. Take, for instance, a well-known fact I have already referred to, that it is difficult, indeed impossible, to draw a hard-and-fast line round the domain of literature. One has only to take some great names at random – say, George Herbert, Hume, Gibbon, Blake, Dickens – to remember how many and how various are the interests into which the literary student, in pursuing the relevant

study of any of these authors, is likely to be led. But those who remind us of this – whether they know it or not – are in
fact strengthening the case for an overriding discipline. And it
must be a discipline which is flexible enough, and of general
enough application, and sensitive enough in its touch, to be able to
take into account, and set in some sort of order, everything that
may turn out to be relevant to the study of such authors. Now,
where else than in literary criticism can we find an approach that is
at the same time general enough, and flexible enough, and sensitive enough, to take such heterogeneous matters into account,
and provide principles of order which are spacious enough to
accommodate them all?

But, it might be said, there may well be *no* single discipline
which is, even theoretically, capable of organizing this vast
plurality of concerns and specialisms. And is literary criticism a
distinct discipline, in the sense in which, say, linguistics is a
discipline? Many would say that it is not, and never can be; others
say that it is, or could be, but *they* are not agreed among themselves
about what sort of discipline it would be. There are obviously
many problems here; and, to add to the difficulty, they are inter-
locking problems, so that to dwell on one or two of them, to the
exlusion of others, is artificial, and distorts them. But at this
point I am reminded of certain misconceptions which are so pre-
valent, and so dangerous, that at whatever cost of over-simplifica-
tion I cannot forbear to say something about them.

One of these misconceptions is derived from the attempt to present literary criticism on the analogy of work in the physical
sciences; when this attempt fails – as it is bound to do – the conclusion is drawn that literary criticism can be no more than a
world of undisciplined and subjective whims and fancies, where
every man does that which is right in his own eyes, and where
order is imposed, if it is at all, not by the strongest arguments but
by the loudest voice. This *either/or* ultimatum – either a science or
a mass of fancies – is the result of a misunderstanding that has
done a great deal of harm. The history of criticism is not like the
history of a science. There is no body of established results which
the next critic can build on. We cannot say about criticism, as it
seems reasonable to do in the case of at least some sciences, that
we are the heirs of the achievement of the past. We must rather
recall Freud's retort to Stekel, who had cited the saying that a
dwarf on a giant's shoulders can see farther than the giant, that a

louse on the head of the astronomer cannot. Consider the great names among the English-speaking critics of the past, such as Johnson, Coleridge, Arnold, Henry James, Eliot, D. H. Lawrence. The modes of thought of the great critics have to be studied in relation to their historical context; the problems of criticism are always the specific problems of a given time and place. We have, in the spirit of Collingwood, to try and find out what were the questions they were asking; we cannot see them as adding to a growing accumulation of knowledge, to be passed on intact to their successors; or even as engaged in a continuous debate – the true history of criticism, like the true history of philosophy, is not like this. Even if we were provisionally to define literary criticism as the sum of those inquiries that can profitably be pursued by the methods of Arnold (and the others), that will not get us very far. We may find in the great critics more than general inspiration; we may find hints and pointers to the accomplishment of specific tasks. But we shall certainly not find in them, nor in the work of any good critic, living or dead, a fool-proof technique which can be handed over, in the sense in which the calculus, the work of Newton's genius, can be taught to schoolboys.

It seems not superfluous to say this. For some *have* apparently held that we are in a happier position than the great critics of the past. They may have been men of genius, but they were wayward and undisciplined; we, who lack their genuis, can nevertheless manipulate techniques, and solve problems, which baffled them. I have heard this view expressed in England as well as in America. I think the common-sense view of the matter is here truer to the facts. Common sense takes it for granted that criticism must be personal. But this is because common sense takes it for granted that criticism must be evaluative, and those who see in criticism a domain for the working out of transmissible techniques find evaluation an extremely troublesome consideration. For it is plain that, whatever else can be handed over from a critic to his public, or from a master to his pupil, an evaluation cannot. (This comes out clearly if instead of 'evaluation' we say 'choice'.) Perhaps only a highly original critic can be the first to make a particular evaluation; but one has to be, at least in some measure, a critic one-self to be able either to endorse or to question it. I am surprised at the easy-going way in which people can say that they agree or disagree with this or that judgement of Leavis, or James, or Lawrence. To have come to the point at which agreement or disagreement becomes possible is already to have reached a depth at which agreement and disagreement cease to be appropriate terms; one's sensibility towards the object in question has been modified.

But could there be criticism without evaluation? About this difficult subject I must be content to sound brief and dogmatic. I hold, as many others do, that it is possible, ideally, to separate the critic's tasks of description and interpretation from his task of evaluation; that is, I believe that the descriptive judgement typified by 'There is a character in *Hamlet* called Osric,' the interpretative judgement typified by '*Hamlet* is the tragedy of a man who could not make up his mind', and the evaluative judgement typified by '*Hamlet* is most certainly an artistic failure', are logically different. Two points occur to me here. One is that the capacity to give correct descriptions of a work is important: descriptive judgements are not always trivial. A good example is given by Professor Morris Weitz:

> recollect Wilson Knight's reading of Claudius in the prayer scene. Who is closer to heaven in that scene, Claudius or Hamlet? But Bradley's report is a reminder that Claudius's prayer for pardon for his first murder, sincere or not, follows immediately upon his final arrangement for the second murder, that of Hamlet; hence, his report is sufficient to blow Knight's question and implied answer to the moon.[1]

Secondly, I would like to counter an objection that might be made to separating interpretation from evaluation in such cases as my example, '*Hamlet* is the tragedy of a man who could not make up his mind'. Someone might say that if the tragedy *were* that, it would be a lesser thing than some other interpretations would make it; so to endorse that judgement would be to make an evaluation, and a limiting one at that. But I would answer that the famous actor whose interpretation I have quoted was not – there is every reason to think – implying, by his interpretation, a 'limiting judgement'. His *Hamlet* was not a lesser thing – for him; though it might be for us.

So I do think that it is possible to concur in the description and interpretation of a work without concurring in its evaluation; and I think I have common sense on my side at this point. Indeed, if

[1] Morris Weitz, *Hamlet and the Philosophy of Literary Criticism*, Faber, London, 1964.

descriptions and interpretations could entail evaluations, I find it difficult to see how there could be room for the exercise of independent judgement – or for legitimate disagreement at all. It is true that I. A. Richards at one time seems to have thought that once the communication problem settles itself – once we have got, perfectly, the 'mental condition' relevant to the poem – the valuation problem is settled by our own nature and the nature of the world. But practical experience seems to be against him here.

Furthermore, at least one of the arguments used by those who maintain that the critic's activities throughout, and necessarily, involve evaluation seems to me unsound. Thus, it is sometimes urged that the mere choice of a work to discuss is itself an evaluation, if a tacit one; we choose to discuss *Paradise Lost*, rather than Blackmore's *Creation*. This seems to me to extend the meaning of the term 'evaluation' so far as to make it almost useless. And anyway, one might choose bad work to criticize, for a particular purpose.

A more plausible objection, and one that has been used with some effect against the practice of Professor Northrop Frye, who wishes to eliminate evaluation from criticism, is that the language that Frye and all other critics have to use, in order to talk intelligibly about literature at all, is itself already full of evaluative implications. This suggests that the idiom of criticism, without which any continuous literary discussion is impossible, and the continuity of a literature, in any important sense, is dubious – this shared idiom is, so to say, naturally inclined towards evaluation; because if men had not cared about the value of what they were talking about, and moreover cared to make their attitude towards that value manifest, it is probable that there would not have been any critical vocabulary at all. The things we are dealing with are, in some intimate way, of their very nature value-containing, or value-transmitting, or value-demanding objects – whichever is the appropriate term: to ignore this seems in some important sense to ignore *them*. And this argument seems to me a stronger one.

But the most cogent objection to a programme of non-evaluative criticism is practical: where it is to be found? Certainly not in the work of those who have traditionally ranked among the great critics. And consider any closely-wrought critical argument: say, Eliot's essay on Marvell. Surely it is plain that whatever felicities of description, or interpretation, Eliot's essay on Marvell may contain, these would not have been there without the pressure, by its nature committing the argument to evaluation, of Eliot's effort to define and fix his sense of Marvell's poetry. And that Eliot is precisely *not* the critic whom one would normally point to, in order to exemplify the statement that the great critics are all concerned with evaluation, makes the citing of him all the more appropriate; Eliot's criticism, it is commonly said, is at its best when it is related to his preoccupations as a poet; but even – and especially – when it is so related, it cannot help but be fundamentally evaluative.

But now we are faced with what may be called the paradox of evaluation. Let us suppose (what is by no means the case, since I am well aware that the questions I have raised are still quite open questions) – but suppose it is granted that criticism, to be effective in its descriptive-explanatory functions, must be evaluative, and therefore personal. How then can it be institutionalized? how can it be regarded as an academic discipline, which must *ipso facto* be an *impersonal* discipline, not merely a set of self-denying ordinances adopted by an individual critic at his own will and pleasure? This is where we come back from the general problem of literary criticism, which is what I have been discussing in the last few minutes, to the particular problem of critical training at the university. The problems here are of course both practical and theoretical; the theoretical problems underlie the practical ones, and are fundamentally more difficult; but with your permission I will take the practical ones first, because they are easier to formulate. They relate chiefly to student capacity, to teaching, and to examining.

It must be obvious from what I have been saying – and it is sufficiently obvious anyway to those who know anything about the problem – that the qualities required for successful initiation into critical practice are not likely to be common. In other words, the number of students who are naturally well qualified for higher literary education along these lines is not likely to be large. Literary criticism is difficult, and no good will be done by pretending that it is not. It is not difficult because it is highly technical, or a grind; A. C. Bradley's dictum 'Research, though laborious, is easy; imaginative appreciation, though delightful, is difficult' will suggest its true character. True, we can dismiss with contempt the sneers of those who say that we are expecting our undergraduates to be little Matthew Arnolds. Philosophy is none the less an acceptable undergraduate subject because few under-graduates are of the intellectual calibre of Descartes or Kant or Wittgenstein. But it is true that an English school whose centre is in criticism is not likely to resemble the broad general kind of school that, for historical reasons, university English in the twentieth century has tended to become.

I have no comprehensive solution to offer to this problem; it is a matter of taking opportunities wherever possible, doing what can be done in particular places and particular conditions. But, if I may limit my remarks henceforward to the situation at Oxford and Cambridge – and there is some reason to think that it is of some importance what happens there, in the matter of keeping up standards and maintaining continuity – if I may so limit my re-marks, I trust that we shall not be unduly troubled with the prob-lem of the *weak* student. It is the *middling* man (or woman) who troubles me; someone who may have a real liking for a literary subject, who one feels justifies their place at a university, and yet finds the proposed approach difficult or uncongenial. I have heard it suggested that people like this should be enabled to choose a different course, one with selected highlights, and not based particularly on the traditional monuments of English literature; this would not only be more closely related to their real needs and wishes, as present-day citizens or citizens-to-be, but would be easier. On this view, the traditional structure of English studies would be kept for the few who were able and willing to try it; its basis could lie in literary criticism, or textual criticism, or literary scholarship, or some conjunction of these and other disciplines; but the place of the traditional Eng-lish school, as the converging-point of the undergraduates with active modern literary interests, would be taken by the new com-posite course. I hope that Oxford and Cambridge, at any rate, will not adopt this solution of their difficulties. Let me not apply harshly the saying that 'wide is the gate, and broad is the way, that leadeth to destruction, and many there be which go in thereat: Because strait is the gate, and narrow is the way, which leadeth unto life'. (Though can any university teacher, if he is honest with himself, fail to recognize the special force of those words in application to his own task?) Let me, rather, appeal for sympathy with the middling man. Do we really want second-class citizens at our great universities? for that is what they would be, educa-tionally speaking, however grand the name that was given to

D

their studies. And would the middling people really like being segregated, in a vital part of their university lives, from the good people? Every college teacher knows that the presence of good men in a particular undergraduate generation has a wonderfully bracing effect on the middling men. And I do not think that we ought to underrate the middling or even the weak brother's capacity to perceive that he is not being asked to tackle a genuine body of knowledge – and to resent it. For myself, I think that syllabuses, and curricula, and examinations, and faculty boards, and college teachers for that matter, are at best necessary evils; 'the men teach one another', it is always being said at Oxford, and surely this is so.

But I have already reached my second practical consideration: the problem of criticism as it applies in *teaching*. And this seems the moment to reiterate the stress on the advantages of a collegiate university; I hope that these advantages, where they exist, will not be thrown away, but used more fully than they are; and I view with mistrust anything, on the teaching side, that strengthens the faculty at the expense of the college. From the point of view of this lecture, the college is the microcosm of that intellectual and social community which must be assumed to exist, or persuaded into existence, in the larger world, if there is to be any real continuity in criticism, or literature, or any higher collaborative mental activity whatsoever. It is in these small communities, and communities like them, that the student learns, if he ever learns at all, the feel of live, disinterested, eager discussion; it is there that the tutor (in the Oxford sense) is constantly stimulated by the need to justify his existence, and the relevance of what he is saying, by the presence of young people whose questions are none the less effective and forthright for being sometimes ingenuous. It is here that the graduate student performs an indispensable function, of providing the link, the liaison, between the undergraduate and the teaching generations. The Oxford or Cambridge college, in my view, is the true intellectual focus of the university considered as an ideal community; and on the character of that community I cannot do better than to quote the uninhibited pronouncement of a great Victorian:

I protest to you, gentlemen, that if I had to choose between a so-called university which dispensed with residence and tutorial superintendence, and gave its degrees to any person who passed an examination in a wide range of subjects, and a university which had no professors or examinations at all, but merely brought a number of young men together for three or four years, as the university of Oxford is said to have done some sixty years since, if I were asked which of these two methods was the better discipline of the intellect – mind, I do not say which is *morally* the better, for it is plain that compulsory study must be a good and idleness an intolerable mischief – but if I must determine which of the two courses was the more successful in training, moulding, enlarging the mind, which sent out men the more fitted for their secular duties, which produced better public men, men of the world, men whose names would descend to posterity, I have no hesitation in giving the preference to that university which did nothing, over that which exacted of its members an acquaintance with every science under the sun.[1]

These are the words of Newman in 1852; and they still are of interest, in a time when we have heard of 'universities of the air' and the like.

However, the realities of the situation are that we have to have syllabuses, curricula, faculty boards, and examining; and it is this last obligatory circumstance which suggests our third practical problem. That the traditional methods of examining, at any rate in English, are not satisfactory is becoming more and more widely known. An account of what is wrong with these examinations, together with practical proposals for reforming them, may be found in Dr. Leavis's *Education and the University*, or in Mr. F. W. Bateson's *English Poetry: a Critical Introduction*. It is sad that little seems to have been done to follow up these criticisms, or make these reforms effective; it seems particularly disappointing that the new universities, so far as I can see, with all their experimenting, do not seem to have made an attack on this notorious problem. But here I will mention that I was interested to learn from the report of the Hale Committee on University Teaching Methods that the University of East Anglia proposes that one third to one half of the marks in the degree examination in certain subjects should be awarded for the student's performance in a series of twelve seminars spread over seven terms. Perhaps

[1] J. H. Newman, *On the Scope and Nature of University Education*, Dent, Everyman edition, 1916.

this may encourage other experiments especially since I have gathered from the Hale Report that disquiet about examinations, among university teachers of English, is growing. Thus, in answer to the question 'whether the existing system of written examinations is the best practicable method of assessing undergraduate quality', 30 per cent of university English teachers said they were *not* satisfied. It should be borne in mind, moreover, that among those asked were teachers who had examined or were examining; as it is well known that people actually administering a system are apt to think better of it than those who are not, this figure is striking. The Hale Committee also report that, in the answers to the question 'whether the examinations taken by their students had an influence on the teaching of their subject which was good, neutral, or bad', among subjects the highest proportions of dissatisfaction were in Mathematics (22 per cent) and English (20 per cent).

All I will now say, with reference to the examination problem, is that exercises of the 'practical criticism' type, such as Cambridge has made us familiar with – the discussion of short passages of prose and verse – do not seem to be exposed to the same objections as the more conventional kind of examination-papers; and they bear an obvious relationship to what I hope will one day be accepted as the central discipline of the school. It is not, of course, that I take this atomistic inspection of exerpts to be the be-all and end-all of a literary education, or the paradigm of critical activity – though the view that it *is* thought to be that is surprisingly common. I assume that such exercises are merely aids to the assessment of the candidate; a means not an end. And the same could be said for the short dissertation, not done under examination conditions, which might also alleviate the existing system.

But in speaking of assessment of the candidate I have brought up the theoretical questions which cannot be avoided. Does literary criticism have determinate enough standards and criteria, are they intelligible enough, and widely enough accepted, to form the basis of a university discipline? Here, instead of giving a direct answer, I would answer, Scotch fashion, with a question, addressed to my colleagues in university English teaching: do you realize what, *in any case*, you are committed to when you set up as teachers of English literature? There is, I know, a tendency, particularly evident among those who are frightened of the term 'literary criticism', or who identify it with kinds of criticism, or

individual judgements, which they dislike – there is, I say, a
tendency among such people to insist that the basis of the course
is literary *history*, not literary criticism; they think that only if it is
accepted that what they call straightforward literary history is all
that an English School can properly offer, will it win to real
intellectual respectability among Schools in which the standards
and criteria of judgement are more fully agreed on and the subject-
matter they are applied to more objectively defined. I think this is
an illusion. At the undergraduate level, at any rate, the attempt to
distinguish between literary criticism and literary history seems to
me to make little sense. A candidate writes an essay in answer to a
typical examination question such as 'What do you understand by
Augustanism in English literature?'; if his essay has merit, it will
be as much a showing of critical perception, as a demonstration of
knowledge of literary history; who can say which is which? It is
surely at the level of graduate research, and still more when we
are considering such topics as why the *Oxford History of English
Literature* has been a failure, that the question of literary history
as a distinct concept arises. What Professor Yvor Winters said in
reviewing Professor C. S. Lewis's volume of that History raises
this question incisively:

> There are many men who have read more in this field than I
> have, and Lewis is certainly one of them. Some of them will
> find errors in Lewis which I have overlooked. I have found
> more errors in my own few publications than I have found in
> Lewis. It is not the errors in scholarship which trouble me
> primarily, however, for these are inevitable. It is the critical
> mind that bothers me. It is my own conviction that one cannot
> write the history of poetry unless one can find the best poems.
> The best poems are the essential facts from which the historian
> must proceed. The background of ideas is important; the char-
> acteristic eccentricities of schools and poets are part of the
> material; but without the best poems, the history is not a history
> but an impressionistic and perhaps (as in this case) a learned
> essay. Lewis cannot find the poems.[1]

It is easy to object that this raises more questions than it answers;
to ask, who is to say which are the best poems? or to raise a laugh
against Yvor Winters by asking whether, on the available

[1] Yvor Winters, *The Function of Criticism*, Routledge & Kegan Paul,
London, 1962.

evidence, *he* can find them. His words still utter a serious and perplexing challenge: 'The best poems are the essential facts from which the historian must proceed.' Unless the truth in this is grasped, there will never be a satisfactory literary history.

But this is the problem in its general form; what we have to consider is the specific problem of examiners' disagreement; and behind this, the delicate question, which we cannot finally avoid, *Quis custodiet ipsos custodes?* For it is no secret that some examiners are less intelligent than some examinees; this is one of the things people mean when they say 'English is different'. Of course, it may well be that we exaggerate the degree of unanimity and objectivity in subjects not our own; I have heard that historians and philosophers, and even mathematicians, have been known to differ about the merits of candidates; and even about the scope and nature of their subject. But 'English *is* different'; it is the nature of our subject, not only our shortcomings, which makes assessment difficult.

No simple answer can be given to this, any more than to any other of the problems I have raised; and anything I say at this point is bound to be rather lame. I can only offer a personal impression; that there is really less disagreement about general principles of evaluation than there sometimes seems to be (it is often more verbal than real), and it is in their application to particular instances that the disagreements begin; and that when they do begin, the influence of the best critical practice, and the best critical thought, has already has some effect in clarifying such difficulties, and may have more; and, finally, that the acceptance of the truth about some literary matters is sometimes more a moral problem than an intellectual one.

And so, thinking of the intellectual and moral demands of criticism, I come back to the name of Dr. Leavis; for as so often, so invariably, when criticism is seriously discussed in this country, it is his name we think of. It is he who has made such a difference to critical thought and practice that many university teachers, here and all over the world, feel they owe to his influence and example their conviction that the work they are engaged in is worth doing. Surely not the most hostile of his critics can deny him a high, perhaps a unique place in the history of 'English in the university'; at any rate, it is hard to imagine that this topic will ever be discussed in the future without a central place being given to his work. And just as his achievement in literary critics in general will always be associated with the name of *Scrutiny*, so his work in the academic field will always be associated with the name of Downing College. His career has been a signal instance of the capture of a particular historical opportunity – the history of the Cambridge English Tripos, together with the chance to make the English school at Downing a working model of that intellectual and social community in which living thought about literature can be encouraged to grow. In his honour, and that of Mrs. Leavis and all who have been associated with him in this work, I venture to apply, with a change of pronouns, those words of Arnold's which are a permanent source of inspiration.

They have not won their political battles; they have not carried their main points, they have not stopped their adversaries' advance, they have not marched victoriously with the modern world; but they have told silently upon the mind of the country, they have prepared currents of feeling which sap their adversaries' position when it seems gained, they have kept up their communication with the future.

1965

IV

T. S. ELIOT'S CRITICISM:
THE LAST PHASE

[i]

On Poetry and Poets, T. S. Eliot's volume of critical essays, has been greeted on the whole with respectful disappointment, more than one reviewer contrasting its elderly conventionalities with the iconoclastic liveliness of *The Sacred Wood*. But as a matter of fact these essays, like those in *The Sacred Wood*, are a mixed lot. On the one hand, they are entirely free from the tiresomeness characteristic of *The Sacred Wood*. 'How astonishing it would be, if a man like Arnold . . . had shown his contemporaries exactly why the author of *Amos Barton* is a more *serious* writer than Dickens, and why the author of *La Chartreuse de Parme* is more serious than either.' (The context offers no clue to what 'serious' means here, nor to this mysterious exaltation of *Amos Barton*.) On the other hand, the following is representative of a good deal in the later volume:

> Just as in a well-arranged dinner, what one enjoys is not a number of dishes by themselves but the combination of good things, so there are pleasures of poetry to be taken in the same way; and several very different poems, by authors of different temperaments, and different ages, when read together, may each bring out the peculiar savour of each other, each having something that the others lack.

But it would be easy to show that *On Poetry and Poets* contains passages which, besides showing greater critical maturity than

even the best pages of *The Sacred Wood*, are actually more *exciting*;
compare, for example, this paragraph from *The Three Voices of
Poetry* with the celebrated 'shred of platinum' passage in *Tradition
and the Individual Talent*; surely the poet is here giving us a much
more intimately felt and deeply considered account of the process
of composing poetry:

> In a poem which is neither didactic nor narrative, and not
> animated by any other social purpose, the poet may be con-
> cerned solely with expressing in verse – using all his recources
> of words, with their history, their connotations, their music –
> this obscure impulse. He does not know what he has to say
> until he has said it; and in the effort to say it he is not concerned
> with making other people understand anything. He is not con-
> cerned, at this stage, with other people at all: only with finding
> the right words or, anyhow, the least wrong words. He is not
> concerned whether anybody else will ever listen to them or not,
> or whether anybody else will ever understand them if he does.
> He is oppressed by a burden which he must bring to birth in
> order to obtain relief. Or, to change the figure of speech, he is
> haunted by a demon, a demon against which he feels powerless,
> because in its first manifestation it has no face, no name, noth-
> ing; and the words, the poem he makes, are a kind of form of
> exorcism of this demon. In other words again, he is going to all
> that trouble, not in order to communicate with anyone, but to
> gain relief from acute discomfort; and when the words are
> finally arranged in the right way – or in what he comes to accept
> as the best arrangement he can find – he may experience a
> moment of exhaustion, of appeasement, of absolution, and of
> something very near annihilation, which is in itself indescrib-
> able. And then he can say to the poem: 'Go away! Find a place
> for yourself in a book – and don't expect *me* to take any further
> interest in you.'

Thus there are pages of *On Poetry on Poets* which ought to become classical. Indeed, the essay printed first in the book, *The
Social Function of Poetry*, is as convincing and impressive a treatment of this vital subject as could be imagined; and if one finds
oneself wishing that its generalities had been supplemented by
rather more particular illustration, it is only fair to recall that it was
delivered to a foreign audience, so that this generalization seems
deliberate: Eliot is insisting on the universal responsibility of the

poet to the language in which he works, as not merely the record of civilized feelings, but as the necessary condition of their survival. It is a noble theme, and the manner in which Eliot deals with it is suitably authoritative without being in the least pompous. If the collection as a whole were like that we might be able to salute it as simply a dignified withdrawal by Eliot the critic into elder-statesmanship. But the book is both more and less than this. It is sometimes less than this, because Eliot can sink to a level which is unworthy of him:

> No poetic reputation ever remains exactly in the same place; it is a stock market in constant fluctuation. There are the very great names which only fluctuate, so to speak, within a narrow range of points: whether Milton is up to 104 today, and down to 97¼ tomorrow, does not matter. There are other reputations like that of Donne, or Tennyson, which vary much more widely, so that one has to judge their value by an average taken over a long time; there are others again which are very steady a long way below par, and remain good investments at that price. . . .

To reflect on the impossibility of finding anything like this in the writings of a Leavis or an Yvor Winters is to realize why Eliot's criticism does not nowadays command the interest of the young. But the curious anti-critical tendency which already reveals itself in this misguided little *jeu d'esprit* can take more interesting forms, and suggests further study of its relationship – its peculiar and ambiguous relationship – with the main theme of the whole volume: the scope of the poet.

Commentators have already remarked on the paradoxical way in which Eliot, his tone of voice mingling jocularity and exasperation, seems to repudiate (in the essay called *The Frontiers of Criticism*) the whole 'modern' critical movement which is usually said to descend from him. But it is important to realize that a fundamental scepticism, or even nihilism, in Eliot's thinking about the general discussion of literature is not a *new* tendency in his criticism. We can see it as early as *The Sacred Wood*, so often hailed as the chief manifesto of modern criticism, where the natural inference from a largely derogatory series of comments on Swinburne's verse is explicitly *not* drawn: 'The world of Swinburne does not depend upon some other world which it stimulates; it has the necessary completeness and self-sufficiency for justification and permanence.' True, at the end of the essay it is said that other uses of language than Swinburne's are 'more important to us'; but this is as far, in the direction of what would usually be called a critical conclusion, as Eliot will go. And this abstention (involving, surely, some internal contradiction within the argument) is very much to the fore in Eliot's middle period as a critic, a time when his theological moral and political 'commitment' was more apparent than it is now; his criticism in this period was very largely a repudiation, implicit and explicit, of the possibility of a 'common pursuit of true judgement'. Now the latest phase of Eliot's criticism has abandoned the inquisitorial manner of this period for a poised and quizzical urbanity, so that the scepticism is often barely distinguishable from a pervasive weary tolerance, or indifference. But it is still present even where Eliot is clearly intent on what he is saying, so that we cannot help relating it to the lack of interest in *communication* which is notable in the passage (quoted above) about poetic composition. It is hard not to suspect that Eliot's essential interest in Tennyson, for example, or in Kipling – I refer here to essays of his which have been condemned for their deference to 'conventionality' – is, though real enough, something so peculiar, private and limited that he despairs of communicating it; therefore, in order to substantiate his claims for these authors and fill up the framework of the essays, he resorts to the judgements already in currency – though, of course, restating these in his own distinctive style.

Eliot himself says in *The Frontiers of Criticism* that his best criticism is 'a by-product of my private poetry-workshop; or a prolongation of the thinking that went into the formation of my own verse'. This has been and will be much quoted; so it is desirable to see exactly where it applies. It should *not* be taken to mean that he is pre-eminently a critic who speaks with expert authority about the actual technique of poetry, who shows us how poems are put together, or how they 'work'. Indeed, this kind of analysis is surprisingly rare in Eliot, and to judge from some of his recent utterances he would not consider such a procedure useful or even possible. (The other critics he praises are either impressionistic, or prophetic, or fact-finding and 'scholarly'.) The way in which Eliot's criticism *can* be seen as the extension of his thinking about composition is illustrated by such remarks as these, from his interesting early (1926) essay on Sir John Davies: 'Thought is not exploited for the sake of feeling, it is pursued for its own sake; and the feeling is a kind of by-product, though a by-product worth far more than the thought. The effect of the sequence of the poem is not to diversify or embellish the feeling: it is wholly to intensify. The variation is in the metrics.' This is a useful reminder, in an uneven collection, that Eliot is not only the author of *Four Quartets* (to which the remark on Davies can be interestingly applied) but, after all, the most distinguished of living literary critics, almost the inaugurator of the 'idea' of criticism in our time. But this workshop-criticism does not predominate in *On Poetry and Poets*. Too often the critic clearly feels that his personal insights are too meagre, or too difficult to communicate, for purposes of reasoned argument; so that they are eked out by that kind of 'impartial' or 'detached' criticism which Eliot commends, in a singularly uninterested tone of voice, in that unsatisfactory essay *The Music of Poetry*, and which, as practised by him, turns out to be disappointingly conventional.

It is easy to see why so much discussion of Eliot's later criticism has centred on its tone and manner and intention, rather than on matters of substance; such characteristic specimens of it as *What is Minor Poetry?* do not seem to offer anything pointed or forceful enough for discussion, and even the more impressive performances like *What is a Classic?* plainly do not encourage it. Indeed, the general objection to these essays is that they inhibit any real debate; they *start* nothing; each is complete in itself, beautifully rounded, but calculated to promote respect rather than argument. Thus the celebration of Virgil, to which an essay is devoted, and which is also the culmination of the tortuous argument of *What is a Classic?*, hardly sounds like the celebration of a *poet*, of *poetry*. Once again, Eliot is clearly moved by something intimate and meaningful to him in the figure of Aeneas ('his reward was hardly more than a narrow beach-head and a political marriage in a weary, middle age; his youth interred, its shadow moving with the shades the other side of Cumae'). But the general effect of his account of Virgil is to endorse, in a distinguished and stately prose-style, the academic standing of the *Aeneid*; so that, just as Aeneas is a 'symbol' for Virgil, Virgil himself becomes a 'symbol' for T. S. Eliot. We are not in the end sent back to Virgil's *poetry*; and Eliot's tribute, though clearly much more meaningful for him than his apology to the shade of Goethe, comes to seem like it, an excursion into literary diplomacy.

No doubt the most frequented essays in the book will be those which revert to Eliot's old preoccupation with poetic drama: *Poetry and Drama*, which contains interesting comments, from the technical point of view, on his own plays, and *The Three Voices of Poetry*. The analysis of the first scene of *Hamlet*, in the former essay, shows what illuminating criticism of other people's poetry can arise from a poet's own technical preoccupations. But what is dissatisfying in these essays is that the discussion of problems of technique does not lead on to anything, does not seem to engage with questions which lie beyond what is suggested by the word 'technique'. It was the peculiar distinction of Eliot's early criticism to demonstrate, in practice, just how the expression, the definition, of technical aspects of verse could bring with it, if only by implication, *everything* relevant to the criticism of poetry. But in these essays the technical aspect is wholly isolated; so that the tension and urgency of the poet's struggle for expression is hardly conveyed, since we are not given a sense of what he wanted to express. Certainly it would be unreasonable to expect Eliot to write explanatory 'criticism' of his own plays; he was undoubtedly justified in discouraging inquirers after the 'meaning' of *The Cocktail Party* ('It means what it says'). But we cannot help relating what appears in these essays as the narrowly technical preoccupation of the dramatist to the plays themselves, at least since *The Family Reunion*. In these plays (though *The Elder Statesman* may be a partial exception) it is the technique by itself that seems to invite discussion: the dramatic material, the human substance, seems in comparison elusive or ambiguous.

In the two essays on Milton (which taken together could be used as sufficient texts for the study of Eliot's later criticism) this emphasis on technique is felt to preclude or prevent discussion of larger questions. The first essay has been much criticized for its frank warning-off of any but 'the ablest poetical practitioners of my own time'; it is also noteworthy that the second essay, apparently so much more modest and concessive, contrives to impede adequate discussion all the more effectively by this very show of reasonableness. This time a new figure, the 'scholar', is allowed on to the scene; but his interest is defined as an interest in the 'permanent', the historical background of the poet, and so on; what is 'immediate' in the art of Milton is still regarded as the province of the practitioner. The final effect of this mode of criticism is not arrogance but evasiveness; by insisting all the time on the strictly limited scope of his remarks, Eliot offers the appearance of a 'recantation' while at the same time not disguising that (as he admits in an introduction written later to Pound's critical essays) he 'still agrees' with Pound 'against the academic admirers of Milton'. Typical of this somewhat two-edged performance is the praise of Milton's 'inerrancy, conscious or unconscious, in writing so as to make the best display of his talents, and *the best concealment of his weaknesses* (italics mine). One sympathizes with the American scholar who remarked of the essay: 'Eliot still hates Milton's guts'. There is something about the manner, as well as the content, of Eliot's treatment of the Milton question that prompts that antithetical manner in response.

But it would be unfair to end on this note; the lecture on Milton is the extreme example in this book of 'dining with the opposition', and Eliot can be read with more pleasure and profit where, as in the lectures on *Johnson as Critic and Poet*, he is dealing with an author with whom he is really in sympathy. The treatment of Johnson is balanced and sound, and there are many interesting observations on Johnson's critical standards and the relation between his creative work and his criticism. There is, too, as always in Eliot's best essays, a contemporary 'moral': Eliot's discussion of the value of a technically disciplined versification, with its accompanying stress on good sense and the role of *judgement* in the composition of poetry, is clearly aimed at the then contemporary cult of Dylan Thomas (the lectures were given in 1944). Eliot's manner in this essay is that of the courteous judge 'guiding the jury'; his tone suggests various inflexions of the familiar judicial 'You may think'. (This tone may be contrasted with the embarrassed advocate's manner in the Kipling essay, in which Eliot seems unsure of precisely what he is trying to do.) The Johnson essay is indeed not faultless. There are some factual errors, and the treatment of Johnson's poetry is strangely disappointing – especially when it is compared with the earlier essay on Johnson's *London*. The negative note predominates; we do not feel, as we do in the earlier essay, that Eliot has really been stirred by re-reading Johnson's poetry. Here the judicial manner has an effect of chilliness. But when we are moved to criticize this or that point in Eliot's treatment of Johnson, we have to remember that it was Eliot himself who has largely re-created Johnson for us a a poet. And in their contrasting ways the astringent essay on Byron, which belongs to the thirties, and the moving personal tribute to Yeats, a lecture delivered in 1940, are reminders that Eliot's critical achievement, even in its later phase, does not lend itself to any simple summary. On putting down this volume we may feel that there are various ways in which it does not represent for us, completely and satisfyingly, the 'idea' of criticism; but we should not forget that it is very much owing to Eliot himself that we are able to form this 'idea' at all.

1962

[ii]

It is tempting but imprecise, to call this volume (*To Criticize the Critic*) a disappointment, for few readers in the past twenty years can have opened a prose book by T. S. Eliot with very high expectations. All the same, it is still mildly depressing to record the last example, *d'outre-tombe*, of this famous critic's sustained endeavour to undermine his own reputation and undo his influence. Thus the title-essay might be described as a deliberate attempt, by a genial and witty old gentleman, to nullify everything that a presumptuous young critic once wrote in an essay called 'Imperfect Critics', later reprinted in a book called *The Sacred Wood*. In the later pronouncement those famous phrases, those provocative assertions, those impressive and often illuminating turns into generalization, are written off, explicitly or implicitly, as youthful prejudices or foibles. We are not then surprised, in such a context, to find 'the lack of a sense of humour' – 'humour' being undefined – solemnly pronounced to be an important limitation in an author. But it is still saddening to find a writer of such gifts doing his bland best to perpetuate the kind of cultural climate in which poems with the originality of 'Prufrock' or 'Ash Wednesday' would be met – as *they* were met – with incomprehension and derision.

A proper diagnosis of this critical nullity to which Eliot committed himself in his later years must await – what cannot be long delayed – the radical appraisal of his whole achievement, not only as a critic but as a creative artist. In the meantime, a partial explanation may be hazarded. Eliot did not distinguish deeply enough between taste and fashion. He makes a show of doing so in the title-essay, but the distinction, at this stage of his career, had clearly ceased to be important to him. Bored with the fashions which sprang up as a result of unthinking deference to his prestige, irritated by the academic ossification of his living insights, he seems to have lost interest in criticism, and allowed it to become merely an exercise in diplomacy.

One odd effect of this relaxation – an effect very noticeable in several of the things here reprinted – is an inconsistency of tone in his writing. The urbane and ingratiating quality of his general manner is sometimes interrupted by sharp remarks which, because they have little or no context of critical argument, sound *merely* personal, and therefore rude. Thus in the very conventional and unprovocative speech on 'American Literature and the American Language' he suddenly says: '. . . I do not know whether Auden is to be considered as an English or an American poet; his career has been useful to me in providing me with an answer to the same question when asked about myself, for I can say: "whichever Auden is, I suppose I must be the other"'. Perhaps he did not mean to be rude here: but it is characteristic of this manner that we do not quite know.

The sense of inconsequence, which many of these essays produce, is increased by there being (so to speak) nothing *between* the vast generalizations ('It is observable of mankind that . . .') and the incidental specific remarks about books and authors, which at times seem no more than autobiographical chit-chat, depending for what dignity they have on the eminence of the author. Such anecdotal jocularities, while they make the book a necessary acquisition for those with a personal interest in Eliot, do little to relieve – indeed they accentuate – the pervasive bleakness.

Not all the pieces collected in this volume are so perfunctory as the title-essay, but there is nothing that shows the same degree of application to the subject as, for example, the lectures on 'Johnson as Poet and Critic' in the earlier collection, *On Poetry and Poets*. Thus 'From Poe to Valéry' (1948) takes up the interesting question (which must have puzzled many readers whose native language is English) why so inferior a poet as Poe meant so much to distinguished French poets like Baudelaire, Mallarmé, and Valéry. But the discussion peters out short of the conclusion – which is none the less hinted at – that the last two, at any rate, of those poets are of very limited achievement. And it is characteristic that Eliot never explains why, if Valéry's poetry is as uninteresting as he seems to imply, we should be so very interested in Valéry's account of the experience of composing it.

The lectures on 'The Aims of Education' (1950) relate to the same area of Eliot's interests as 'Notes Towards the Definition of Culture', but are much less good than the best parts of that book. Eliot's lofty style, his cheerfully conceded remoteness from anything practical, and his constant drawing of careful distinctions which never seem to advance the argument, impose a strain on the reader's attention out of proportion to his final reward.

The last items in the book are piquantly varied. The utterance on 'The Classics and the Man of Letters' (1942) might – apart from the excellence of its prose style – have been composed by a headmaster. Its measured formulations do not suggest that Eliot cared about 'the Classics' in anything like the immediate way he cared about Dante, as we can see by comparing them with the short piece, also reprinted here, on 'What Dante means to me' (1950). And they obviously lack the enthusiasm of the last two manifestos, on Ezra Pound and on free verse, with which the book closes. Period piece as the 1917 essay on Pound is, critically crude, badly organized, and unconvincing in its quotations, it unmistakably comes from the poet-critic who matters, even if he is not here at his best. And its place in the collection cannot but remind us of the span of Eliot's remarkable career; so that if we are tempted, as we put aside this volume, to recall the opening lines of Browning's 'Lost Leader', we should also remember the lines with which it ends.

1966

V

THE ROMANTICISM OF C. S. LEWIS

The writings with which Lewis reached perhaps his largest adult public may be called homiletic. Dr. Farrer writes of them, in the memorial volume – *Light on C. S. Lewis*, edited by Jocelyn Gibb, (1965) – from the theological point of view. He indicates (though this does not take the main stress in his chapter) some ways in which they are bad theologically. What he does not say is that they are bad in other ways as well. The farthest he goes in adverse criticism is to say this: 'Lewis wrote fairy tales but surely he did not believe them! It adds to our stupefaction, rather than detracting from it, when he solemnly submits such fantasies to the censure of the Church'. Giving a wider extension than Dr. Farrer does to 'fantasies', we could isolate an important and very disagreeable element in this part of Lewis's work. (And I note that Dr. Farrer, perhaps significantly, abstains from any comment on *The Screwtape Letters*, a book which Lewis himself came to dislike, and to have insight into some of the reasons for disliking.) But something more needs to be said. What we would very earnestly like to ask Dr. Farrer – or Dr. Mascall, or Dr. Vidler, who have also praised Lewis's religious writings – is whether they think *any* way of writing which aims at promoting Christianity is good. If *not*, do they not think some of Lewis's writing might have a bad effect? It is not only that he uses bad arguments, or that he frequently lapses in taste and touch and tone – though such failings must be significant. Many people remember, and dislike, that trick in *The Screwtape Letters* whereby things the author is prejudiced against, such as modern poetry, or congregational (as opposed to parochial) organization in churches, are discredited – that is the intention – receiving approval from the devil. But this is a minor lapse in comparison with the general moral pettiness of the book, and this is a fault, I am afraid, which is common in Lewis's homiletic writings. 'Take care of the pence and the pounds will take care of themselves' may be a sound maxim in economics, but is it so in morals? At any rate, no argument on the lines of 'Ah, but one thing leads to another . . .' will convince me that the old lady in *The Screwtape Letters*, who tells an overworked waitress 'That's *much* too much! take it away and bring me about a quarter of it' has any business in such a context. In the age which has produced Auschwitz, it is distasteful to have such slight topics associated with human damnation.

The ground for disliking Lewis's dealings with devils and hell, whether in the mode of *The Screwtape Letters* or *The Problem of Pain* or *The Great Divorce*, is not quite that he holds the 'robust faith' which a scholarly priest recently saluted in Dante. Leaving the question of literary merit apart, I do not know anything in his writing so morally confused as the *Inferno*. Nor is there anything like the unwholesome and spiritually snobbish element in Eliot's way of talking about Baudelaire and Original Sin. It is rather that Lewis's mode of interest in this subject reveals, as does that of Charles Williams, a mixture of horrified fascination combined with superstitious fright. An observation which must be made here goes beyond the realm of taste. 'His works,' says Mr. Chad Walsh in this volume, 'were particularly popular with clergy and were on the intellectual firing line – for example, college and university chaplains. It sometimes seemed that they bought his books by the gross in order to give them to eager young intellectuals who were disturbed by religious questions.' Mr. Walsh is speaking of Lewis's prestige in America, which he says remained high at least till the middle nineteen-fifties. And there is no doubt that in this country as well as in America Lewis's religious books have been read by a large number of young people. Is it right that young people, perhaps in the torments of puberty, should have books recommended to them which insistently relate a preoccupation with moral trivia to a frightened fascination with eternal flames? I think a person with genuine kindliness of nature, such as Lewis certainly had, should have been more alive to that consideration.

Even at their most amiable, Lewis's religious writings are apt to fall into a moral tone, and reflect a moral sensibility, which – to put it mildly – do not help us to overcome the modern sentimentalities he desired so vehemently to castigate. His later religious books are better than his earlier; they show less irritating overconfidence and insensitiveness; they are more humane, and sometimes touching. A good example is *Reflections on the Psalms*. But even in *Reflections on the Psalms* we come across a passage like this (Lewis is dealing with the question of how the 'cursing' Psalms can be used for devotional purposes):

> . . . I can even use the horrible passage in 137 about dashing the Babylonian babies against the stones. I know things in the inner world which are like babies; the infantile beginnings of small indulgences, small resentments, which may one day become dipsomania or settled hatred, but which woo and wheedle us with special pleadings and seem so tiny, so helpless that in resisting them we feel we are being cruel to animals. They begin whimpering to us 'I don't ask much, but' or 'I had at least hoped', or 'you owe yourself *some* consideration'. Against all such pretty infants (the dears have such winning ways) the advice of the Psalm is the best. Knock the little bastards' brains out.

Perhaps an exclamation-mark is the only comment necessary.

Mr. Owen Barfield, a close friend of Lewis, remarks acutely in the introduction to his volume that 'self-knowledge, for him, had come to mean recognition of his own weaknesses and shortcomings and nothing more'. This may be the reason for his frequent habit of dealing out to others, as moral advice, such very small change. It is a failing which injures his literary criticism, where from being a moralist (as any serious writer must be) he deteriorates into being a moralizer, and so takes some of the life out of the works he is seeking to interpret. The most striking example of this that I can recall is his chapter on the infernal debate in *Paradise Lost*, Book II, which he treats as if it were an episode in *The Screwtape Letters*. But there are other places in that lively, if often irrelevant, book, *Preface to Paradise Lost*, where Lewis seems to have forgotten that Milton is a very different author from Charlotte Yonge.

The general criticism to be levelled against Lewis's rligious-homiletic writings is not that they descend to the market-place, for everything that is of vital concern to men and women must in the end be debated there. Nor is it even that, like other writings of his, they are apt to substitute fireworks for brilliance, and sophistry for argument. It is that they propagate an unsatisfactory ideal of conversion. Where, as often, he is an apologist (he likes to begin chapters with 'When I was an atheist . . .') all the emphasis falls on conversion *to* something. There is much less awareness of it as conversion *from* something. What sort of conversion leaves so many prejudices intact? We cannot but relate this retention of prejudices to the lack of moral largeness. Lewis, in doubling the roles of father-confessor and nursery-governess, seems often to offer the latter as an unexpected substitute for the former. It is all in keeping that he can empty the theme of *Paradise Lost* of moral interest by representing it as 'You mustn't. You were told not to', so placing it, as he explicitly does, on a level with commands like 'Do not speak with your mouth full' and 'Bend over!'

Lewis, then, needs wary watching as a popular moralist. A man with that enviable gift of popularization, that facility of expression of which Professor Coghill speaks in this volume, he does not always show the sensitiveness and insight into moral experience with which he is credited, by many Christians. Where he has been perhaps under-valued is where he is writing at a more philosophical and abstract level. Here his qualities of lucidity, vigour, and uncommon common sense come into their own, and it may be for that very reason that he is wrongly regarded as superficial in comparison with more cloudy writers. Thus his book *Miracles* may well be open, as regards its fundamental argument (on which Lewis set much store – I am referring to the argument that naturalism is self-contradictory) to the objections which the philosopher Miss Anscombe made to it in *Socratic Digest*. But it does have the virtue, rare in this kind of writing, of setting out the issues clearly; and the common sense shown in the passage I now quote is refreshing to those who have ever wrestled with the kind of clerical 'higher criticism' about which Lewis here issues a warning:

When you turn from the New Testament to modern scholars, remember that you go among them as a sheep among wolves. Naturalistic assumptions . . . will meet you on every side – even from the pens of clergymen. This does not mean (as I was once tempted to suspect) that these clergymen are disguised apostates who deliberately exploit the position and livelihood given them by the Christian Church to undermine

Christianity. It comes partly from what we may call a 'hang-over'. We all have Naturalism in our bones and even conversion does not at once work the infection out of our system. Its assumptions rush back upon the mind the moment vigilance is relaxed. And in part the procedure of these scholars arises from the feeling which is greatly to their credit – which indeed is honourable to the point of being quixotic. They are anxious to allow to the enemy every advantage he can with any show of fairness claim. They thus make it part of their method to eliminate the supernatural wherever it is even remotely possible to do so, to strain natural explanation even to the breaking point before they admit the least suggestion of miracle. . . . In using the books of such people you must therefore be continually on guard. You must develop a nose like a bloodhound for those steps in the argument which depend not on historical and linguistic knowledge but on the concealed assumption that miracles are impossible.

Anyone who has read in this literature will know that Lewis was not here tilting at windmills.

The general formula, then, that suggests itself for Lewis's writings in this region, is that he is at his best when inwardness is not required, and at his most uneasy when it is. That this lack of inwardness is related to personal qualities which worried his close friends, is strongly suggested by Mr. Barfield's introductory essay, where he speaks of Lewis's

psychic or spiritual immaturity . . . which is detectable in some of his religious and theological writings; and occasionally elsewhere; for example, in the undergraduate humour of Weston and Devine's humiliation before Oyarsa in *Out of the Silent Planet*; and the opera-bouffe climax of *That Hideous Strength* – is this Kathleen Raine's 'a kind of boyish greatness'?

'Opera-bouffe', as those who have read the novel will know, is a very mild way of describing the climax of *That Hideous Strength*, with its gloating over the aphasia which spectacularly seizes the scientific villains, and the detailed description of their deaths, one after the other. The novel contains things which judicious admirers of Lewis will not wish to stress. It contains intelligent things too, of course; the common-room scenes in *That Hideous Strength* are much more amusing than C. P. Snow's. But its

mixture of fairy tale and thriller, science-fiction and theological
fable is unpleasant and unsatisfactory in the way that Charles
Williams's novels are. It seems to invite, in a half-defiant, half-
innocent way, the attentions of psycho-analysis, which a fantasy
that has been fully transformed into art never seems to do. And
even in those of his novels which are less unwholesome, if less
powerful, than *That Hideous Strength*, we cannot help following
a critical tip of Lewis's own and looking at the 'good' characters.
. . . Something has gone very wrong there.

In speaking of the novels, as of most of the verse, we are (I
think it is widely agreed) speaking of something that Lewis did
not do well. One striking feature is their extraordinary old-
fashionedness. Lewis's 'science-fiction' is Wellsian, not modern,
though inferior to Wells's. not only because of its admitted
derivativeness from him, but because it is less imaginative. Nor
has Lewis the myth-making quality Wells has in such stories as
The Door in the Wall, or the natural gift for allegory – for all
that Lewis talked about it – which Wells shows in *The Country
of the Blind*. But the Edwardian quality of Lewis's fiction is in
general not Wellsian, for as we should expect Wells's moral and
social outlook was abhorrent to him. The writer he obviously
resembles is Chesterton. Indeed, it is tempting to say that he was
the G. K. Chesterton of the academic world. So fragmented is our
literary culture today that this would be regarded as a compliment in some quarters and an insult in others. I mean it as neither,
but as an attempt at historical description. What a sad fate has
befallen Chesterton's writings! He can be so telling and unexpected here and there, amid all the paradox-mongering and
the papist axe-grinding and the verbal play that seems so often
only verbal. It is not for nothing that Empson has praised his flair
for the detailed analysis of poetry. And yet Chesterton is so clever-
silly, so garish and over-emphatic and 'personality'-conscious,
that (outside a limited circle of his fellow-Catholics) he has become
utterly unreadable. He is remembered only as having said a few
witty things.

Lewis admired Chesterton, and they have obvious resemblances.
They were both Christian apologists who reached large audiences,
and they shared a point of view, at the same time hierarchical and
democratic, which has now become rare, but which they expounded with gusto and conviction. As a critic, Chesterton was
more original than Lewis, but Lewis with his greater knowledge

and scholarship was much more responsible; Chesterton was a journalist, not a scholar. Their faults of style are not unlike: Chesterton is too highly coloured, Lewis too richly flavoured (he used too much quotation). Lewis was totally free from what is bad in Chesterton, that odious streak of old-fashioned anti-Semitism, and the fostering of sterile national hatreds. (Lewis might have said that Chesterton picked these up from Belloc, whom Lewis disliked.) On the other hand, Lewis did not have Chesterton's artistic gift; he never wrote a poem as good as *The Secret People*, and some of Chesterton's witty light verse has a way of running through one's head as Lewis's has not. But the main point of bringing Chesterton in is that he has 'dated' – whether this will prove a permanent characteristic need not now be discussed. We read him with the feeling that, for him, nothing has happened in literature since 1914 – at any rate, nothing good, nothing that has modified the critic's sensibility. We get this feeling too when reading Lewis's criticism. But it is more understandable in a man of Chesterton's generation, born in 1874. Lewis was born in 1898; his *floruit* (to use a word he liked) was not the Edwardian age. What need not have been a conscious rejection on Chesterton's part must, then, have been so in a man of Lewis's age and Lewis's intelligence.

The short way of dealing with this Edwardianism of Lewis is to say that it was just a pose, put on to annoy contemporaries and juniors whom he thought *should* be annoyed. Besides being dull, this account is unlikely to be true. Even in men whom it is natural to call *poseurs* (and Lewis was not one of these) the pose has its basis in something real. What is difficult to decide is why he chose in particular to be Chestertonian, and so to involve himself in the contradiction one detects in so many of Chesterton's writings. For in Chesterton we have a writer who flamboyantly proclaims himself to be a traditionalist, who is breezily and belligerently opposed to most of the characteristic trends of modern secular society, and who yet seems to *belong* to it in one of its least attractive aspects: he himself is part of the age of advertisement and propaganda which he attacks. How did it come about that Lewis was attracted by this confusion? Like Chesterton, and like Ronald Knox, he is tempted to the clever-silly; readers of his literary criticism are often exasperated by his habit of spoiling his best insights by some puerile deviation; two examples out of many might be his suggestion, in the essay on Donne in the Grierson *Festschrift*, that a criterion of love-poetry is whether you could read it to Britomart; or his demand in the essay 'High and Low Brows' that a literary theory of general application must cover *The Tale of Peter Rabbit*. Neither of these essays as a whole is foolish; they both raise serious critical points. But they are stultified by this Chestertonianism. What is the explanation?

The same problem arises when we consider the readability on which Lewis rightly prided himself. We must do justice to a point Lewis was fond of making, that a tortuous jejune style is no more a guarantee of profundity than a lively, flowing, figurative style is necessarily a mark of superficiality. But readability can be bought at too high a price: the leaving out of the qualifications and the modifications which a scrupulous writer leaves in, if he is more concerned with expressing the exact truth than with removing grittiness from his prose style. When Lewis is writing badly, his thought, if it enters the mind without resistance, does so because it is shallow, and ministers to complacency. But when he is writing well, as in the introductory chapter of his volume in the *Oxford History of English Literature,* his readability is identical with his mastery of exposition. No one can impart information so painlessly as Lewis, and here of course he is far superior to Chesterton, since he had so much more; he almost ranks with Macaulay. Yet like Macaulay, and like Shaw and Lytton Strachey and Aldous Huxley, he is likely to be an author to whom the young are ungrateful; having instructed and entertained them, he will be left behind, they will feel that they have outgrown him, that somehow he is empty.

Again it is that lack of inwardness that seems to offer the hint of an explanation of why Lewis, with all his gifts, is so disappointing. It comes out very clearly in his autobiography, *Surprised by Joy,* and this is all the more painful because Lewis commits himself there to achieving it as he does not in most of his other writings.[1] This book resembles Chesterton's autobiography in leaving us in doubt whether the author simply has not had the experiences that he claims to have been of transcendent significance in his life, or whether he has been unable to communicate them. Reticence, of course, is an old-fashioned quality which deserves respect. But

[1] *A Grief Observed* might be adduced in contrast as an exceptionally and effectively, 'personal' work; but I agree with John Wain (writing in *Encounter* 1964) about its failure to render key passages of reminiscence with essential human vividness.

if you want to be reticent, why write an autobiography? And, above all, why write it around what you claim to be the most important thing in your life – the discovery that Christianity is what gives it unity and meaning – and yet say so little about it? so little from the 'outside' even, let alone the 'inside'? Thus the book has a curiously self-conscious and patchy quality which resembles Ronald Knox's *Spiritual Aeneid* and distinguishes both these 'histories of religious opinions' from the great classic of the *genre*, Newman's *Apologia*. Not that Newman set out in the *Apologia* to *mettre son coeur à nu;* the *Apologia* originated in controversy, and is precisely what it sets out to be, a defence of Newman's consistency and intellectual honesty. But although Newman is not concerned with self-revelation, but with matters which to us are dry and churchy, he makes us interested in them because he convinces us that *he* was interested in them; and so we get a more vivid sense of his mind and character than Lewis or Knox give us of theirs, with their obvious concern about the picture, the impression, the emotional effect, they are conveying.

Was Lewis's Edwardianism a means of *guarding*, of *covering up* something? The contributors to this memorial volume sound oddly guarded themselves; Mr. Barfield hints at 'something *voulu*' about Lewis's literary personality, but he does not develop this theme. At any rate, Lewis had a formidable weapon for self-protection in his celebrated dialectic. He regarded this dialectic as a valuable educational discipline, and in his autobiography has given an amusing and vivid account of the man who taught it to him. Not that Lewis, of course, describes the dialectic as essentially self-protective. He saw it as intellectual armament in battles for impersonal causes. It is perhaps significant that it plays little part in Lewis's religious writings, contrary to what might be expected; perhaps Lewis did not feel the impulse to use it when he wanted to be serious down to the quick of life and death. But in literary matters the temptation to use it was strong, and Lewis often yielded to it. As a result, he won forensic victories which convinced nobody (did they even convince him?). I have some sympathy with his concern for the plain man who feels that modern literature and criticism are going wrong somewhere, but is too inarticulate to state his position cogently. But sometimes, it must be confessed, the plain man for whom Lewis is acting as advocate seems to be a very plain man indeed, and in the controversy with

Tillyard published as *The Personal Heresy* he allows himself to voice a hearty derision of the idea that a great writer's work *costs* him anything: 'what meditation on human fate could require more courage than the simple act of stepping into a cold bath?' Philistinism does not nullify a critic; we have a use for Walter Bagehot; and we can even find value in Macaulay's essay on Bacon as giving classic and amusing expression to the plain man's contempt for philosophy But Lewis had an intellectual agility superior to that of Macaulay or Bagehot, and the element of philistinism in his critical writings is therefore all the more regrettable.

It might be said, however, that what I have discerned as a note of philistinism may have been no more than an unfortunate manner of expression, into which Lewis was sometimes betrayed by his promptness to defend the common man and common things against the facile contempt of literary intellectuals. Certainly it would be paradoxical to describe as a philistine a man so steeped in poetry as Lewis, so much a philologist in the older and richer sense of the word. He was not in the least like the kind of professor he mentions in *An Experiment in Criticism*, whose subject has become a mere routine which one doesn't discuss 'after hours'. Small talk, politics, and gossip had no attraction for him; he was always eager to proffer and to hear about literary experiences, to engage in controversial debate, and, if this was desired, to speak of 'serious matters' (in Jane Austen's sense.) And his Chestertonian paradoxicality, tiresome as it could be, was often a way of stirring up stodgy minds; he liked a breeze to be blowing – and not usually a cold breeze, for the west wind nearly always prevailed over the east in Lewis's discussions. But his dialectic did not usually advance the cause of literary criticism – which I take to be the discovery of the truth about books. The most important questions could not be debated in Lewis's way; and indeed I suspect that one purpose of his mode of argumentation was precisely the exclusion of general issues. What is insidious is the suggestion conveyed in some of his writings that *his* way is the *only* way in which literature can be rationally discussed. This comes out in that disappointing book *An Experiment in Criticism*. I say 'disappointing' because this was a book (written late in his life) which Lewis wanted to be taken seriously, and which he regarded as a sort of critical testament. But the opponents he evokes in it are men of straw; the impression that Lewis is scoring bull after bull is not sustainable after inspection of his arguments, for everything has been so over-simplified that rational discussion – that is to say, discussion adequate to the complexity of the problems raised – has been ruled out In this respect Lewis, like Chesterton, seems in tune with an age of political propaganda. The reader after a while sees the unfairness, and resents it. Would Lewis have been so unfair when 'serious matters' were in question? Would he have assumed, for instance, that Roman Catholicism is disposed of by rebutting the (reported) assertions of a half-witted seminarist from Connemara? Yet this is the sort of 'evidence' – of the opinions of critics influenced by literature written since 1920 – which Lewis accepts in *An Experiment in Criticism* for his imaginary opponents' position; he takes on no foe more formidable than the Cambridge undergraduate who, he alleges, was deeply wounded because Lewis said that *The Miller's Tale* was written to make people laugh. How can literary questions be profitably or interestingly discussed at that level?

But here we have reached an area of Lewis's writings in which, except for his superior liveliness and energetic prose rhythm, he is indistinguishable from the voice of conventional academicism – though an academicism of an earlier vintage than that of today. In his attitude to the most influential critic of his time, T. S. Eliot, there is something sadly reminiscent of that academic campaign against original genius, which continued well into the nineteen-forties. An offence for which Eliot was long unforgiven was his essay on Gilbert Murray as a translator of Euripides. The reverberations of the official annoyance which this caused can be heard in Lewis's writings, and Eliot appears anonymously – and inaccurately, at that date – as 'a modern American critic' in *The Allegory of Love*, and is presumably glanced at as an importer of 'Franco-American' dandyism in the essay on Donne. What is depressing about all this is its conventionality, which appears even when Eliot was finally admitted into the fold of the respectable; Lewis, in making such *amende* as he ever did to Eliot, is quite frank about the part played by Eliot's religious orthodoxy in his own decision to accept him. But as a critic of modern literature, in so far as he was one. Lewis is not always so depressingly typical as this. For example, he had a respect for I. A. Richards as having set out the 'modern' theory of literature clearly, and frequently uses him as a starting-point for discussion. I think Richards's strong points and weaknesses were both of a kind which Lewis appreciated very well, and he was better in dealing with Richards, as a representative of the distrusted 'moderns', than when, later on, he attempted (in a regrettably oblique manner) to counter the influence of Leavis.

Once again, however, it is external, abstractable, theoretical issues that engage Lewis's mind; in the actual practice of criticism he is too often conventional. In urging, as he did, that matters of literary opinion should be forthrightly debated, and not confined to 'little senates', he laid too much stress (when he defined the requirements of a critic) on having the courage to say what one thinks, and not enough on having the intelligence to know what one feels. The first is vitiated without the second. Hence in his attacks on modern literature he is sometimes indistinguishable from a type Virginia Woolf was good at diagnosing, the clever detracting don who hates the creative literature of his time but has no secure basis of his own from which to judge it. Out of charity I abstain from examples, preferring to mention specimens of Lewis's criticism which seem to me good. His essay on Addison, in the Nichol Smith *Festschrift*, with its emphasis on Addison's 'good sense' and freedom from jargon, conveys at the same time that these were Lewis's own virtues as a critic. His remarks on Virgil in *Preface to Paradise Lost* make us feel that we ought to read Virgil, more than any of Eliot's pronouncements on that poet. And for all his twitting of Cambridge priggishness about Jane Austen (she writes *comedy*! he protests) his own essay on Jane Austen gives a more convincing, if not exceptionally penetrating, account of *Mansfield Park* than anything written by exponents of the cosy view. A certain community of outlook with the parson's daughter who wrote that novel steadies him and makes him serious in the right way.

For to Lewis 'seriousness' had to do with religion, the 'serious matters' of Jane Austen, the 'Serious Call' of William Law. Literature belonged to rhetoric, to the realm of means; and so he often, though unwittingly, conveys the suggestion that it does not really matter. In his essay 'Christianity and Literature' he explicitly states that literature which claims to be important as literature is merely solemn triviality, and in writing of Scott he asserts with apparent approval, that Scott would have acknowledged only the existence of 'conscience', not of 'artistic conscience' (for polemical purposes Lewis plays down the shame which Scott is constantly expressing in the *Journal* at having written so badly). His stress on literature as merely a *means* results in the loss of a vital note in his criticism, the

note that is heard in the impressive simplicity of Tolstoy's judgement that 'he alone can write a drama who has something to say
to men – something highly important for them – about man's
relation to God, to the universe, to all that is infinite and unending'.

On a less exalted plane of discourse, we may say that Lewis's
literary criticism suffers from his having no secure base either in
the modern world or out of it. His Edwardianism, as a country of
the mind, was not adequate, because Lewis, at his deepest level of
sincerity, could not identify himself whole-heartedly with it. And
his fairy-tale country, which *did* embody things that Lewis was profoundly sincere about, was not adequate because so much in literature is not amenable to translation into its language – though we
often feel that Lewis is doing his best, and with incongrous results,
to make it so.

But I have begged a question in talking of Lewis's 'literary
criticism'. We learn from his memorial volume that he associated
'literary criticism' with Cambridge, and insisted that what he himself was doing, in this region of his work, was literary history. It
has been a much discussed question whether good literary history
can be written without a critical purpose – that is, without a lively
interest in, and engagement with, the problems of writing *now*.
When speaking polemically on this subject Lewis was apt to give
the impression that he accepted the 'academic' view of literary
history, namely that it *can* be written without a critical purpose.
But in practice, I think, he had not quite made up his mind what
literary history was. In the book on the sixteenth century he argues
that the literary historian should give more space to 'difficult'
authors – that is, to authors who for one reason or another are uncongenial or inaccessible to modern taste – than he does to the 'important' ones, that is, to the authors who manifestly retain some
kind of life in the present. This represents the antithesis of the
position of the literary critic, and had Lewis carried out his programme consistently his Oxford History volume would have been
somewhat curious. As it is, however, his common sense saved him
from the grosser kinds of absurdity, and he does indeed set forth
in his volume a critical view of the sixteenth century – as, in his less
confused moments, he himself recognized that he was committed
to doing. (How acceptable his critical view of that century may be
found is another question altogether.) I venture to suggest an
analogy which Lewis himself does not use, to bring out what I
think he was doing as a literary historian, in so far as what he was

doing is consistent. (I believe the analogy is used by Lytton Strachey.) Some books of the past seem to be *dead*; no doubt in their day they served their turn, but they now belong only to the history of taste and fashion; Lyly's *Euphues* is a standard example. The literary historian's duty is not to administer the kiss of life to such works, and to pretend that he has revived them; but rather to make us understand (perhaps by citing modern equivalents) how they ever came to be thought genuine works of art, why they were widely read and influential. But other books can be said to be *sleeping*; Sidney's *Arcadia* would for Lewis have been an acceptable example. The historian's object here, as he cuts through the thorn-hedges of the past, is to awaken beauty. The trouble is that Lewis's practice not only does not convince us that he has actually found which works are 'dead' and which are 'sleeping', but even makes us doubt sometimes whether he knows the difference. As a result, much in his *Oxford History* is more satisfactory if we interpret it as recording the history of taste and fashion. Of course *some* critical powers are required to write even that kind of history; but I take it that not even Lewis's harshest detractor will deny that he had some critical powers. What is disappointing about his Oxford History volume is that its best parts are clearly much more than history of taste and fashion; but the necessity of conscientiously covering so much ground has frequently reduced Lewis to a liter-ary connoisseuring like Saintsbury's, and it is improbable that after drudging through vast masses of forgotten literature (say, after reading hundreds of Elizabethan sonnets) a historian is going to be in the mood in which critical discoveries are made. Neglected masterpieces have not usually been discovered in this way; they have been found when a reader was looking for something else, or was seeking to fulfil some other purpose (a creative one, per-haps) rather than making a chronicle.

The endeavour Lewis undertook for the Oxford History – and one cannot withhold respect from a man who took on and com-pleted so vast and unrewarding a task, while maintaining his deter-mination to read all the primary sources – this endeavour was bound to conflict, in practice, with the doctrine of historical imagination he preached with such eloquence. It is put simply, even badly, in his *Preface to Paradise Lost*:

> To enjoy our full humanity we ought, so far as possible, to
> contain within us potentially at all times, and on occasion to

actualize, all the modes of feeling and thinking through which man has passed. You must, so far as in you lies, become an Achaean chief while reading Homer, a medieval knight while reading Malory, and an Eighteenth-Century Londoner while reading Johnson. Only thus will you be able to judge the work 'in the same spirit that its author writ' and to avoid chimerical criticism.

Lewis here states with his usual clarity an assumption which lurks at the back of much academic work on creative literature. As always with Lewis, there is *some* element of good sense in what he says. Even to achieve a quite ordinary level of moral decency we have to have some capacity to 'see another person's point of view', 'put oneself in his place'; and something analogous must hold for the intelligent reading of literature. But the idea of *becoming* another person, entering the mind of someone in a remote age – does Lewis really recognize, even if we give full weight to his qualification 'so far as in you lies', the kind of task to which he is committing himself and his readers? Surely it is difficult enough, without any feats of impersonation, to find out and to articulate what *we ourselves* have felt; it may be nothing. I do not speak of the misleading suggestion that the audience of a writer was homogeneous at any time – though we are tempted to ask '*which* eighteenth-century Londoner should we become?' But the most suitable rebuttal is *ad hominem*: is there any reason to think that Lewis really entered into the point of view of a large number of his own contemporaries – let alone people in remote periods, of which we know so little? For example: did he really enter into the point of view of someone convinced, as he was not, that Pound and Joyce were not charlatans?

What is immediately relevant is that Lewis lends his prestige here to the notion that the 'mind' of another age – or even the mind of one individual in another age – is something we can go in and out of at will. This suggestion, so far from increasing the imaginative flexibility Lewis wishes to encourage, leads in practice to superficiality – at any rate in literary historians. Handling their huge mass of materials, they can only keep their sanity by putting most of their emphasis on what is picturesquely 'different' in the work of other men; to allow one's sense of a common human nature to be really involved in so miscellaneous and contradictory a mêlée of emotions as 'an age' – any age – is bound to be, imposes too much strain: who has the right to demand it from a historian, or from anyone?

I feel, then, that with all their attractive qualities books like the Oxford History volume and *The Allegory of Love* and *The Discarded Image* have more than a smack of antiquarianism about them. I do not think Lewis's doctrine of historical imagination functions actively in his own practice; rather, that it is the transposition into general terms of some personal desire for self-transcendence which he was not able to express in any of the modes of his own writing. This is suggested by the tone of the eloquent conclusion to *An Experiment in Criticism*:

> Literary experience heals the wound, without undermining the privilege, of individuality. There are mass emotions which heal the wound; but they destroy the privilege. In them our separate selves are pooled and we sink back into sub individuality. But in reading great literature I become a thousand men and yet remain myself. Like the night sky in the Greek poem, I see with a myraid eyes, but it is still I who see. Here, as in worship, in love, in moral action, and in knowing, I transcend myself; and am never more myself than when I do.

This gracious peroration was worthy of a better book. It certainly does not clinch the weak and superficial arguments of the *Experiment*. What it really does is to put us in touch with the frustrated minor poet in Lewis. I do not suggest that this was the 'real' C. S. Lewis; I doubt whether such a phrase has any meaning: a man is everything he is. But I do think this frustrated poetry is the key to both his strength and his weakness, as a man writing on behalf of creative work composed by other men.

The weakness can perhaps be localized by glancing at a writer of the past whom Lewis made four major attempts to 'put over' to a public he knew would not be initially sympathetic: I mean Edmund Spenser. Here, if anywhere, Lewis is fully involved in what he is doing; there is no mistaking the vibration of conviction in his writing. And yet I have never met anyone not professionally 'committed' to Spenser who could read Lewis's accounts of him, and his claims for the *Faerie Queene*, without astonishment. With Milton, or with Chaucer (to name two authors about whom Lewis still supplies critical currency) we feel that Lewis meets some resistance from the author he is 'rehabilitating'; with Spenser there

F

seems to be none. Rather, there are many signs of self-identification; see for example, in the sixteenth-century book, the account of the 'modern' Gabriel Harvey and Spenser's friendly ignoring of him. This consciously old-fashioned, serene, yet ambitious author Lewis presents may or may not be a true picture of Spenser. What Lewis does not make convincing is that 'his' Spenser is a great writer, one who deals centrally and vitally and effectively with things of deep and intimate concern to men and women. At times Lewis does not even seem to be trying to do this.

The point I am trying to make concerns Lewis, not Spenser. For all I know, the new 'arithmological' approach to writers of the Renaissance is going to supersede, in higher academic studies, the Lewises and the Hardin Craigs and the Theodore Spencers; their attempts to map the Renaissance mind for the twentieth century may already have become period pieces. I am not concerned with the question of just what was Lewis's contribution to cultural history. Though at this point I must remark that Professor Bennett, in what he says in this volume about Lewis the medieval scholar, has missed an opportunity; his _éloge_ does not make it clear how Lewis compares in eminence with Huizinga or Burckhardt; or whether he really demolished 'the Renaissance' or discredited the 'humanists' as he is supposed to have done; or whether in his most famous scholarly book, _The Allegory of Love_, while undoubtedly bringing out how much literature and literary convention influence 'real life', he was successful in establishing the decisive part played by poets in creating 'romantic' or 'courtly' love. These matters will have to await a fuller appraisal.

Lewis, so far as I know, has not convinced the common reader about Spenser; and this is not for technical reasons of Renaissance scholarship, but because for good or ill the common reader today rarely seems to share the boyish romanticism which I feel was Lewis's fundamental reason for liking Spenser – and many other authors. This boyish romanticism is responsible for some of Lewis's worst sillinesses; but it is also responsible for what was best and purest in his response to literature. Its perhaps least harmful feature was an insatiable appetite for youthful balderdash. The survival of that appetite in the high culture of the English-speaking world is a phenomenon which deserves investigation. Professor Coghill at the end of his tribute to Lewis suggests, though he does not press, a comparison between him and W. H. Auden; but it might well be pressed. There are a thousand differences between Lewis and Auden, but they both seem to share a wish to be reborn as Beatrix Potter in some other phase of the moon, and this hankering has a significant relationship with their work written for adults. Lewis, however, is a simpler writer than Auden, and there is no need to frown over his continued liking for the stories that charmed our childhood. It is where this natural nostalgia shades into something deeper – into Lewis's feeling for the 'joy' which he associated with his boyhood, and which he came to feel gave unity and significance to his life – that the critical problem becomes more problematic and more interesting.

I will put the problem in this way: what is *wrong* with having a boyish romantic taste? It would be a dull world of everyone had the same taste. Let a hundred flowers bloom! *That*, surely, is the position Lewis should have taken if he had been true to the principles of critical tolerance and eclecticism which he constantly preached. But why was he constantly impelled to *defend* a boyish romantic taste by so many ingenuities of sophistry? We sometimes feel that the whole dialectic Lewis was trained in, reinforced by an Oxford classical education, was elaborated just to do that. This might be said to be harmless enough. But there is always a danger that an academic figure so formidable and so justly respected may, with the best of motives, find himself institutionalizing his hobbies. We cannot help remembering the strong influence Lewis had on the English School at Oxford, which retains compulsory Anglo-Saxon and until recently ended the syllabus at 1830.

Lewis did not want to bully anyone, to force them to do what they did not want to do. His brief experience at a public school, which he describes in his autobiography, resembles that given by Louis MacNeice in his posthumous book *The Strings are False*, and (besides making us feel that those places should be instantly abolished) shows where Lewis acquired his lifelong hatred of bullying and forced conformity. Nor – though his controversial manner sometimes lends colour to this belief – was he a brow-beater. His fault as an examiner was quite contrary to what under-graduates feared; he was too kind, being apt extravagantly to over-mark the papers of a candidate whose views he disliked. Why did a man with so great a love of literature, and such gifts of ex-position, come to regard himself, as we are told in this book, as a failure? 'My medieval mission,' he remarked with typical candour, 'has been a flop *d'estime*.' Why did he fail to reach so many people whom he would have liked to help?

The opponents of Lewis sometimes represent him as serving up academic clubmen's prejudices in various colourful disguises. But I do not think he was essentially a clubman of any kind. He was very much an individual, and a strange one. (That is well brought out in this volume.) In the academic world he was capable of an independence and courage which a conventional member of it would not have shown. I will merely mention his forthright objections to what passes for 'research' in the humanities; the attitude epitomized in his remark that there were three categories, the literate, the illiterate, and the B.Litt.-erate, and that he preferred the first two, may well have cost him a professorship at Oxford.

As a representative figure, Lewis may well have been right in his genial (or rueful) recognition that he was a back number. The Oxford classical education has lost the unquestioning confidence it had in Lewis's younger days that it is *the* education for an intelectual *élite*. But was *his* classical education, acquired in the more confident days, the unqualified blessing he supposed it to be? How much of it was the 'trumpery' from which he prayed in a poem to be delivered before he died? Certainly it gave strength and solidity to his scholarship. But it also encouraged his propensity to dialectics; and in associating a taste for minor romantic poetry with a formidable ability to analyse and expound intellectual matters (this last being one of the strong points of the sixteenth-century book) it provided another illustration of the curious alliance, in English academic life, between the 'dry' and the 'watery'; an alliance of which the symbolic representative is the scholar-poet A. E. Housman. The exact value of Lewis's education is, then, another of the ambiguities which it is hard to resolve. Perhaps he was significant for us because – in the closing words of *The Allegory of Love*, he was 'a highly specialized historical phenomenon – the peculiar flower of a peculiar civilization, important whether for good or ill and well worth our understanding'. But it is as a person that he may prove most memorable.

Readers will have noticed with regret the touches of personal sorrow in Lewis's later books, often coming out in his choice, for illustrative purposes, of certain sad happenings in human life. Some of us are fortunate in remembering his cheerfulness; not the burly and breezy good nature of his popular *persona*, but something gentle and simple. It is not always clear whether the 'modern' world he supposed himself to be attacking was really the *adult* world; and I suspect that his dislike for the use of 'adult' or 'mature' as critical terms sprang from more than an understandable objection to cant. At any rate, his boyishness was always a very evident characteristic; here, to adapt a remark of Eliot's about Tennyson, his surface was intimate with his depths.

1966

VI

MR. AUDEN ON POETRY

Mr. Auden's inaugural lecture as Professor of Poetry[1] shows everywhere very evident signs of the kind of academic-social occasion for which it was composed; and one might be excused for assuming at first that a recognition of this fact was the only attention that the lecture required. The reader expects from such an occasion an agreeable piece of manners, and he is not disappointed. Mr. Auden offers an entertaining mixture of whimsical self-deprecation, interesting personal reminiscences, bright ideas, and jokes; whilst he nowhere supplements his often stimulating and provoking incidental comments with any very prolonged or serious tract of argument. Yet, difficult as it is to disengage ideas and propositions for discussion, from the disarming confessions of idiosyncrasy in which they are embedded, the attempt is worth making; for the ideas and propositions are there, and their content is likely to be not less but more powerful in persuasion, in proportion to the lecturer's disclaiming, on the ground of modesty, any appeal to the judgement of general experience and reason. A critical, or anti-critical, position, all too congenial to some of Mr. Auden's Oxford audience, is not the less effectively supported because Mr. Auden does not come forward as a critic. But there is also a pleasanter, because more positive, justification for a careful examination of what he says; there are things in this lecture that deserve to be disentangled and considered for their own sake, quite apart from the attention that may be given to their immediate context.

To dispose as quickly as possible with the distasteful task of

[1] W. H. Auden, *Making, Knowing and Judging*, Clarendon Press, Oxford, 1956; reprinted in *The Dyer's Hand*, W. H. Auden, Faber, London, 1963.

adverse comment, the first thing that it is necessary to say is that there is something not quite right about the *tone* of certain passages in the lecture. Putting it bluntly, why is Mr. Auden so deferential to the dons? It is one thing to be polite to one's audience; to apologize for one's Latinity or say nice words about one's tutors; it is quite another thing to give the impression that one is ranking deference to scholarship higher among the virtues than respect of poetry, for the poetic art. And that is the impression that Mr. Auden, I hope inadvertently, makes on at least one reader when he calls Yeats 'silly' for writing that poem *The Scholars*, of which the tenor is suggested in its closing lines:

> Lord, what would they say
> Did their Catullus walk that way?

Some years ago Mr. Auden, in a poem addressed to Yeats, said, 'You were silly like us'; but an intense devotion, followed by a phase of disillusion, and this in turn followed by a further phase at which devotion and disillusion are strangely co-present, seems to be a normal sequence in the reading of Yeats; and the passage in Mr. Auden's poem, which expresses that typical blend of admiration and exasperation, might be understood as recording it. But as to the remark in the lecture, I can only say that Yeats's poem loses none of its force when it is pointed out, as Mr. Auden duly points out, that texts have to be established and notes and commentaries provided; that exact scholarship is a good thing, and a thing we should be grateful for. The *point* of the poem comes out even more clearly in a version different from that quoted by Mr. Auden, which contains the line: 'If they have sinned, nobody knows.' Yeats is registering a characteristic poet's protest against the scholars' bleak inhumanity, their positive *dislike* of their subject. But it would be insulting to suppose that Mr. Auden doesn't see the point of the poem, and has never felt, as a poet, the kind of irritation that provoked it. The truth is that Mr. Auden has let his good manners, and a troubling conviction of his own deficiencies as an authority on literature, intervene between this poem and himself; and so has lapsed into a literal-mindedness hard to imagine in the Auden of the thirties.

The excuse for making this fuss about a small matter is that Mr. Auden was missing an opportunity, which was very much an opportunity for *him*, as a distinguished practising poet who commands a real, and really interested public in more than one generation of readers. Anyone who knows how desperately difficult it is to get a genuine, and not merely a conventional, assent to the proposition that to be interested in poetry is to prefer live poetry to dead, can only be disappointed that Mr. Auden spent so much time in urging scholars to take themselves seriously, and adjuring the rest of us to go and do likewise. The kind of public he was addressing needs no exhortation to comfort these people, to speak comfortably to them; the thing needful is a reminder of the *purpose* of the service which scholarship is supposed to perform.

The anti-critical element in Mr. Auden's inaugural is connected with this deference to 'scholarship', since he views the activities of the scholar as having a complementary relationship to the unhistorical and idiosyncratic explorations of the poet, his 'lazy habit of only reading what he likes'. It is hard to isolate this attitude as a subject for discussion, and still harder to discuss it seriously, since Mr. Auden excels in that celebrated Oxford talent for making *any* opposition sound like the protests of a solemn fool who doesn't know when his leg is being pulled. Certain types of critic are enumerated, the 'prig', the 'critic's critic', the 'romantic novelist' and the 'maniac', as exemplifying surrenders to temptation from which the 'poet turned critic' is immune; but they are mere men of straw, and all Mr. Auden need do to demolish them is to play for easily touched-off responses from his audience, which he does. Indeed, no figure is easier to guy than the critic who tries to communicate his sincere convictions about an art which he does not practise. Mr. Auden, of course, is not really being unkind or malicious when he is 'baiting the critic'; but some of his remarks sound suspiciously in harmony with conventional objections to criticism. For instance, his passing hit at Arnold, the greatest of his predecessors in the Chair of Poetry: 'Matthew Arnolds notion of Touchstones [*sic*] by which to measure all poems has already struck me as a doubtful one, likely to turn readers into snobs and to ruin talented poets by tempting them to imitate what is beyond their powers'. Arnold's recommendation is certainly open to some objections, one of which is that to follow it consistently might set up habits and anticipations in the reader which could interfere with the perception of a *new* kind of beauty; but to represent him as proposing the mechanical application to poetry of an external set of weights and measures is to miss the whole meaning of his proposal. He believed, as does Mr. Auden, that there is such a thing as great poetry, which is different from poetry that is merely good, and his suggestion, whatever one may think of it, was intended simply as a way of reminding ourselves *quickly* what that kind of poetry is. He used, and also misused, the method of 'touchstones' in his own criticism, but his intention was to keep the sensibility fluid, not to rigidify it. One of the many reasons for not accepting Mr. Eliot's judgement that Arnold is an 'academic critic', is the dislike and distrust of Arnold's criticism which seems to be so very common among academic critics; it is a pity to find Mr. Auden, even in such a casual reference, appearing to lend his support to this prejudice.

Associated with this quizzically-expressed scepticism about the standards of criticism, and about those who, like Arnold, try to base their judgements on them, there goes an appeal directed beyond the immediate audience, to the community of literate beings: 'Whatever his defects, a poet at least thinks a poem more important than anything which can be said about it.' This is the equivalent of certain remarks made much less temperately on the same subject by Wordsworth, and Wordsworth on this subject is in equally distinguished company; but it is legitimate to ask, as Arnold did, whether Wordsworth himself was not more usefully employed when writing his Preface to *Lyrical Ballads*, so full of criticism, and of criticism of the works of others, than when writing the *Ecclesiastical Sonnets*. Mr. Auden's proposition, that any given poem is more important than anything that can be said about that poem, at least sounds more reasonable than the more general proposition attributed to Wordsworth, that *any* poem is *ipso facto* more important than *any* piece of criticism; but it seems to entail the conclusion that a critique of an unimportant poem is necessarily even less important than the poem. I should have thought that, to take the first example that comes to mind, Middleton Murry's essay on Georgian poetry was much more worth reading (and so, in any reasonable sense of the word, more 'important') than most of the poetry Murry was discussing. But I have no doubt that Mr. Auden, in so far as he is not asking our indulgence for the poet's paternal pride in his compositions, is only claiming that a *good* poem is more important than anything that can be said about it; which may well be true, but which does not seem so effective in persuading us to rate the value of the critic (who may sometimes be of use in pointing out that it *is* a good poem) as low as Mr. Auden here appears to do.

Mr. Auden's conclusions about the advantages and limitations of the poet-critic are elicited from an account, based on experience, of the immaturities, mistakes and temporary 'transferences' upon his Masters which are a necessary part of the education and development of a young poet. 'His experience as a maker', says Mr. Auden, 'should have taught him to recognize quickly whether a critical question is important, unimportant but real, unreal because unanswerable or just absurd'. The very large implicit assumption here, that the experiences of all poets are similar, becomes explicit immediately when Mr. Auden goes on to dismiss Dr. Hotson's attempt to find internal evidence of its date in a sonnet of Shakespeare (CVII). Here Mr. Auden, just by consulting his own experience of writing poetry, is enabled to decide that the question whether Shakespeare's poem does or does not contain a specific historical reference is 'unanswerable'. One need not be a defender of Dr. Hotson's thesis to feel that Mr. Auden is claiming rather a lot for the experience of even a very gifted modern poet, as a basis for deciding such difficult questions. Coleridge, the type surely of 'the poet-critic', is as remarkable, in his Shakespearean criticism, for his sheer knowledge of Shakespeare, as for his ability to turn to critical use his reflections on his own experience of composition. But then it looks from Mr. Auden's next paragraph as if he were shying away from committing himself seriously to the position he has just outlined:

> A poet [he says], would generally be wise, when talking about poetry, to choose, either some general subject upon which, if his conclusions are true in a few cases, they must be true in most, or some detailed matter which only requires the intensive study of a few works. He may have something sensible to say about woods, even about leaves, but you should never trust him on trees.

Presently his claims to authority have dwindled even more: 'Speaking for myself, the questions which interest me most when reading a poem are two . . .' (a 'technical' and, 'in the broadest sense', a 'moral' one). And at last he is confessing that 'a poet' may well have 'nothing but platitudes to say' about poetry; 'firstly because he will always find it hard to believe that a poem needs expounding, and secondly because he doesn't consider poetry quite that important: any poet, I believe, will echo Miss Marianne Moore's words: "*I too, dislike it*".' This is sad. Even the academic, in the rare moments of candour when he admits to himself that he doesn't like his subject and doesn't believe in the value of what he is doing, at any rate feels guilty about feeling like this; it is no business of a poet to reassure him that he needn't.

There is surely no need for Mr. Auden to be so apologetic about the powers of a poet-critic (and, for all the apparent pretension of his claim for 'the maker's experience', the total effect *is* of an apology – and not in Sidney's or Shelley's sense). He gives evidence in this very lecture of what those powers could be, even though his manner is disjointed and epigrammatic, and he does not (and of course could not in the limited space at his disposal) work anything out or pursue the implications of what he has said. The good parts of the lecture are on a very different level from the anecdotes, unilluminating frivolities and 'social' values, of the parts I have been discussing; it is unfortunate, and I am afraid characteristic of Mr. Auden, that they should be so interlocked with those bad parts, the lecturer passing from one to the other without any obvious recognition that he is doing so. This exasperating discrepancy is itself a significant supplement to the auto-biographical comments on the genesis of his poetry which Mr. Auden has supplied as part of his subject-matter. One can easily sympathize with his difficulty in finding tone and level on such an occasion. There is nothing distasteful about the solution of it he chooses, which is to present himself *qua* poet, and by implication the poet in general, as a harmless eccentric; he is not himself smug; but I fear he might be the cause of smugness in others. A poet, he says apologetically, 'may even find himself lecturing';

> Nécessité fait gens mesprendre
> Et faim saillir le loup du bois.

But a poet lecturing not only supplements his income, but performs a social function; and the most useful function, on this occasion, might have been to be contumacious. To have been healthily so, he need only have given us less sociability and more in the spirit of his best insights.

Apart from the purely autobiographical passages, the most striking things in Mr. Auden's lecture seem to me to be his comments on the poetic use of language and his discussion of what he calls his 'private' theory of the imagination. Early in the lecture he refers to that mysterious sense of *fittingness* which appears to characterize the relation between poetic language and the experiences which it seems in an extraordinarily suitable way to describe or suggest. He quotes from Valéry: 'The power of verse is derived from an indefinable harmony between what it *says* and what it *is*. Indefinable is essential to the definition'. This 'harmony', about which Valéry, following Mallarmé, delighted to spin hermetic and elegant mystifications in his criticism, also preoccupies Mr. Auden, but he does try to resist the mystificatory impulses which such a subject so often arouses in poet-critics of the Symbolist tradition, and to bring it within the framework of the rationally discussible. Unfortunately he introduces a confusion with the term he chooses ('Proper Name') to describe the use of language which refers with this peculiar and untranslatable, yet 'publicly recognizable' aptness. His choice of the term is suggested by the 'uniqueness' of reference of Proper Names 'in the grammatical sense'. On the one hand, he says, 'To know whether *Old Foss* was an apt name for (Edward) Lear's cat, we should have to have known them both'; while on the other hand, 'a line of poetry like (Shakespeare's) *A drop of water in the breaking gulf* is a name for an experience we all know so that we can judge its aptness'. Yet, he maintains, 'Shakespeare and Lear are both using language in the same way'. Apart from the triviality of the parallel proposed, it is also irrelevant. Mr. Auden is here discussing the power of the poet – the poet who really *is* a poet – to bring home to us what we seem to have felt before, without our having the ability to communicate it: or indeed, the intelligence to *know* it (I leave to philosophers or psychologists the question whether these two latter capacities can be separated). Hence while in reality we are entering into someone else's experience – and so one that is *new* to us – we respond to it as if it were a memory of our own. 'I have never seen the notions in any other place; yet he that reads them here, persuades himself that he has always felt them.' (Johnson, *Life of Gray*.) What useful analogy can be drawn between exercising this power, and choosing a name for a cat?

In his discussion of the Imagination, Mr. Auden adopts Coleridge's terms Primary and Secondary, since he believes he is 'trying to describe the same phenomena' as Coleridge. He says:

The concern of the Primary Imagination, its only concern, is with sacred beings and sacred events. . . . A sacred being cannot be anticipated; it must be encountered. On encounter the imagination has no option but to respond. All imaginations do not recognize the same sacred beings, but every imagination responds to those it recognizes in the same way.

The Secondary Imagination is of another character and at another mental level. It is active not passive, and its categories are not the sacred and the profane, but the beautiful and the ugly.

The impulse to create a work of art is felt when, in certain persons, the passive awe provoked by sacred beings or events is transformed into a desire to express that awe in a rite of worship or homage, and to be fit homage the rite must be beautiful. . . . In poetry the rite is verbal; it pays homage by meaning.

Just as in the previous example Mr. Auden reduced the poet's creative power over language to a knack for nomenclature, so here he diminishes the significance of the word 'sacred'. For when he allows us a glimpse into his own 'private world of Sacred Objects', it turns out to be a very private world indeed, though one not unfamiliar to readers of his earlier poetry: Jules Verne and *Struwwelpeter* and Latin mnemonic rhymes, *Underground Life, Machinery for Metalliferous Mines, Lead and Zinc Ores of Northumberland and Alston Moor.* . . . If he is going to use words like 'worship' and 'homage', and speak so loftily and solemnly about the creation of art, he should not in consistency convey the impression (though this is the tenor of much else in the lecture) that a poet is merely a harmless eccentric. I cannot help connecting this with his admiration, which he mentions elsewhere, for Robert Frost's feeble line 'I had a lover's quarrel with the world', and with the semi-ironical self-deprecation which, like some of the younger English poets he has influenced, he has tried so incongruously to turn into a creative force. Of course it is impossible to withhold sympathy from the predicament of a verse-poet in a world where, like the priest, he is an anachronism testifying mainly to the inertia of cultural institutions. But I feel that Mr. Auden has not here been able to strike the right note. I wish I could say with confidence what the right note would be.

1957

PART TWO

VII

MR. EMPSON ON *PARADISE LOST*

Before succumbing to the natural temptation to fix on 'eccentric' as the proper term for this book,[1] there are one or two considerations which should make us pause for a moment. The book sets out to confute the account of *Paradise Lost* advocated by such writers as C. S. Lewis and Tillyard; are we then to regard *them* as representing the critical centre? Surely not: one of the things that emerges most clearly from Empson's book is that *they* are eccentric. In their zeal for their self-appointed task of making *Paradise Lost* make sense as a whole, they seem to lose touch with any of the normal standards and criteria which it is usual to apply to poetry traditionally considered great; and in their frenzy of special pleading they inadvertently reveal many grounds for thinking that Milton was decidedly *not* great. Here Empson restores the critical balance, by insisting that Milton was large-minded, generous, humane; and that his poetry is often delicate and sensitive.

Another reason for not calling *Milton's God* eccentric is one's sympathy for Empson's revulsion from that literary and Christless Christianity which derives from T. S. Eliot. His campaign against the critics for whom 'humanist' and 'liberal' are words of abuse, deserves full support. In so far as it is a contribution, and a weighty one, to this campaign, the book should be welcome. But it has some direct relevance too to literary criticism in a narrower sense; for Empson argues convincingly against two common and still influential ways of dealing with *Paradise Lost* – in some critics they are not clearly distinct – the 'neo-Christian' way,

[1] William Empson, *Milton's God* (Chatto and Windus) revised edition, London, 1965.

G

which finds the conventional account of the poem intellectually satisfying and morally sound–Milton *did* justify the ways of God to men; and the 'historical' way, which asks us, in the name of scholarly interpretation, to *pretend*, while reading the poem, that Milton justified the ways of God to men – and in doing so, to suspend our ordinary assumptions in respect of logic, good sense, and common humanity.

Finally, there is one other sense in which Empson's book helps Milton, and helps the common reader. Many modern books on Milton seem to be written by people who wouldn't touch politics and the world of great affairs with a barge-pole. This is not a help in dealing with *Paradise Lost*. There is no evidence that politics is a religious passion for Empson, or that his religious feelings run in that direction. But there is plenty of evidence that Milton's did, and Empson has enough moral and political concern himself, and enough capacity for imaginative sympathy, to get inside the skin of the harsh, bickering idealist whose God, in Book X, to the accompaniment of heavenly choirs, orders the angels to inflict deliberate damage on the universe (X, 648 ff.). It is a great advantage to Empson to have this positive feeling for Milton's cast of mind, its compound of revolutionary, apocalyptic fervour with harsh grimness, of single-minded idealism with the advocate's passion for 'stating a case'.

At this point, however, it is time to record regretfully that Empson's book is confused and inconsequent, in so far as it uses *Paradise Lost* as an opportunity for attacking Christianity. I am not here concerned with whether or not Milton was a Christian at all, in any useful sense of that word, or whether his Christianity was Christ-less; what I am saying is that, if we accept Empson's account of *Paradise Lost* as essentially a *private* work – in one place he even links it with the name of Kafka – it is thereby invalidated as the central statement of Christianity which his anti-Christian thesis requires it to be. Whether indeed *Paradise Lost is* best regarded as a 'private' poem hidden in a 'public' framework is another matter; personally, I should judge this to be a truer account of the *Aeneid*. But this is a side-issue. The point I want to make is (using Empson's own reference to Kafka) that Kafka's work may well *throw light on* Judaism; but it would be absurd to use it as a means whereby to *expose* Judaism as irrational and morally vicious. Perhaps Empson has not sufficiently made up his mind about what sort of author Milton is.

And perhaps because of this there is a general unclarity in the book. What exactly *is* Empson maintaining about Milton's God? Empson believes that the poet's intentions are relevant; now, while 'intentions' may cover a great deal, the term cannot be stretched so far as to affirm that Milton would have accepted, as a fair account of his intentions, that 'the poem is wonderful because it is an awful warning not against eating the apple but against worshipping that God' or that 'the reason why the poem is so good is that it makes God so bad'. One can, however, infer from the book a weaker form of the thesis; that the contradictions and inconsistencies to be found in the poem (and Empson finds even more than earlier critics have done) are due to Milton's artistic *naïveté* or clumsiness perhaps, but still more to misgivings unconscious, pre-conscious, or semi-conscious, about the validity of what he was doing. To take the book as asserting *this* thesis, and dwelling especially on the last-named group of reasons, makes it more plausible and more discussible, but is hardly consistent with many of Empson's explicit statements about his own intentions.

'Motives', possibly, is a more helpful word than 'intentions' here; and certainly an account of Empson's motives, in so far as they bear directly on *Paradise Lost*, increases one's sympathy and respect for his book. What Empson, like all Milton's good modern critics, feels about the poem is that there is a fundamental decency in Milton's treatment of Adam and Eve, and occasionally even of Satan. Thus what he wants to show is that the great romantic poets who wrote *Prometheus Unbound, Milton*, and *The Vision of Judgment* were not essentially wrong, were not grasping at a mirage, when they felt Milton to be one of them. This is an entirely praiseworthy aim; but Empson loses touch with common sense and critical justice in following it, for he tries to generalize this human fineness in Milton so that it applies to the whole poem; and, finding it where it is not, he unintentionally devalues it where it is (just as if we acclaim all Shakespeare's rhetorical bombast as great poetry, we tend to blunt our sense of the places where he is truly sublime). A more logical extension of the thesis that Milton had no total control over what he was doing would be to admit that 'Milton's God' is a will-o'-the-wisp; Milton had so little consciousness of his artistic problem, and so much confidence in his flood of honorific superlatives, that he never realized how incoherent a conception his God would seem to

a reader who had not already made up his mind what to find in
the poem.

But I have slipped into assuming that Empson's thesis is that
Milton was not in total control of what he was doing. Now it
must be said at once that parts of the book (for example those
parts where Empson is giving his own account of what he thinks
Milton meant to convey about God's total plan) might seem to be
directed *against* that view; but when Empson brings out the
dignity and pathos of Eve, or the impressive distinction and personal tragedy of Satan, we feel that he is admitting that, as he
himself wrote in the *Pastoral* book, Milton's feelings were crying
out against his appalling theology. The problem may be ap-
proached in this way. On p. 21 Empson quotes the following
from Shelley: 'This much is certain: that Milton gives the Devil
all imaginable advantage; and the arguments with which he exposes the injustice and impotent weakness of his adversary are
such as, had they been printed distinct from the shelter of any
dramatic order, would have been answered by the most conclusive
of syllogisms – persecution.' Empson comments; 'Shelley cannot
have meant that Milton's God was "impotent" to persecute Satan,
but I expect he would have denied meaning only that this god could
not have defended his conduct by rational argument.' I quote this,
not to catch out the most brilliant critic of our time (for surely
what Shelley means is that, if Milton had presented Satan's
arguments in his own person, *Milton* would have been persecuted)
but to raise the main difficulty about Empson's book: is he maintaining Shelley's thesis about *Paradise Lost*, or Blake's – that
Milton was 'a true Poet and of the Devil's party *without knowing it*'
(italics mine)? The first edition of the book seemed nearer to
Blake's position; the appendix to the second edition suggests that
Empson has gone over to Shelley's.

At any rate, Empson's book sets out the case for the prosecution of the Most High Eternal Father. Towards the end, by a surprising turn, it also sets out a new case for the defence, which the
orthodox apologists had not thought of. Much of what is new in
the case for the prosecution is, though ingenious, unconvincing:
it would not take a particularly clever counsel to pick holes in it;
indeed, the unanswerable objection is the pedestrian one: 'That is
not what the poem says.'

Let us look at some details. Empson's main case against God is
that he deliberately connived at the fall of Satan, Eve, and Adam.

I will briefly discuss a few points relating to the first two of these. According to Empson, Satan (cf. p. 95) really did doubt the credentials of God the Father. But God, instead of settling the question reasonably, behaved towards Satan with an abominable mixture of deceit and malignity. We naturally ask: *how* could God have settled the question reasonably? I do not know whether Milton can be supposed ever to have asked himself that question; but Empson suggests that one thing God might have done would have been to demonstrate, to the sceptical Satan, his creative power; instead of which, in his deceitful way, he waited until *after* Satan's revolt, to allow Satan to see the beauty of the newly created universe, and to hear from Uriel, who has no reason to lie, an account of how he saw God (the Son) creating it. Hence Satan's breakdown in the Mount Niphates speech, hence his later intellectual and moral corruption (admitted by Empson). These can be blamed on God, not merely in the general metaphysical sense in which he is ultimately responsible for everything whatever, but in the straightforward moral sense in which the concept of blame is applicable in the relations between man and man.

But Satan says nothing like this in the Niphates speech, which, being confessional, and being the speech in which he nerves himself for his final, awful decision ('Evil, be thou my Good') *must* be crucial for any account of his motives. Empson's argument is extremely weak here. He has to admit 'a logical gap' (p. 62) between this Satan and the Satan he wants us to believe Milton is presenting. But how can an argument based on a logical gap, i.e. something that is *missing* from Milton's poem, have force for those who feel the power of what there actually *is* in Milton's poem (IV, 32–113)?

Did Satan really doubt the claims of God at all? To show that he did, Empson has to clutch at straws. He finds things in the text that Milton did not put there. And he has to make what to any unprejudiced reader is at best a vague and shadowy background to Milton's story, seem important and vital. Thus he makes a great deal of a passage in Sin's narrative in Book II. This Spenser-like episode is not, Empson insists, to be regarded as a mere extravaganza, but as organically relevant to the main story. It has to be harmonized with Raphael's narrative in Book V. 'Milton regarded this previous conference of the rebel leaders as an actual event in the story he was imagining.' Previous conference? we inquire.

Yes, Sin's narrative implies that 'Satan called a council about the claims of God before he revolted.' 'This seems an important point,' says Empson, 'because it lets us recognise their [the rebel leaders'] theological opinions as rationally considered.' But Sin says *nothing* about the claims of God. She speaks only of 'a bold conspiracy against Heav'ns King' (751). And no unprejudiced reader, surely, could feel that this council was important. It is mentioned only as the *mise en scène* for the spectacular incident of Sin's birth.

Many readers must agree with Empson that God's behaviour towards Adam and Eve is even more dubious than his behaviour towards Satan. So conservative a critic as Douglas Bush compares God to an almighty cat watching a human mouse; John Peter calls his behaviour 'distinctly suspicious'; and Empson's favourite critic, Phelps Morand, analysed the incident of the scales (IV, 1010–15) as a contrivance by God to further Satan's purposes. Empson's God is subtly and ingeniously wicked. This wickedness comes out most in the analysis of the fall of Eve. According to Empson, God did not only *allow* Eve to be misled – that is the straightforward reading of the story – he deliberately misled her himself. A labyrinthine intrigue, enthrallingly related by Empson; note particularly the correlation he brings out between what Raphael tells the human pair about their future 'wings', and what the mysterious voice (Satan's) had whispered to Eve in her dream. God must have known what Satan whispered; why then did he permit his angel such dangerously misleading language?

The reason, to my mind, is simply Milton's inadvertence – though I would not disagree with the view that these inadvertences occur so often as to suggest uneasiness on Milton's part about his self-imposed task of reconciling providence and free will; there is even a suggestion of occasional demoralization ('God to render Man inexcusable . . .', he lapses into saying in the argument to Book V.) But all this is very different from the cunning, plotting Milton proposed by Empson.

Here, surely, we have an example of Empson *not* getting inside Milton's mind. Milton's mind was one of solemn simplicity – all the evidence points that way. His greatness is closely related to that simplicity. So is his decency (as for instance in the touchingly solemn way he insists on the sexual life of Adam and Eve before the Fall). Even his celebrated style, which is undoubtedly the product of great skill, is not *sophisticated*. He is no seventeenth-century *précieux*. I do not deny that Milton's mind was very independent; and, with Empson, I feel in *Paradise Lost* the continuing presence of the intrepid champion of the free mind of *Areopagitica*, the worried and worrying private speculator of *Christian Doctrine*. But the mind of the thinker of the prose is simple and single; and the thinker of the prose is the thinker of the verse, though in verse he speaks often with a sweeter, more poignant, suppler voice.

Empson is paying Milton the highest compliment he can, when he tries to make Milton seem as clever as himself. But Empson's own work, in verse and prose, is a more convincing demonstration that it is possible for a mind to be subtle and devious, yet kind and honest.

But these are unargued generalities. Does Empson's argument about the fall of Eve survive confrontation with the text? The upshot of God's intrigue, according to Empson, is that Eve at the moment of her fall thinks:

'The reason why all the males keep on saying I mustn't eat the apple, in this nerve-racking way, is obviously that they are longing for me to do it; this is the kind of thing they need a queen to have the nerve to do'; so she does it. It is a splendid invention by Milton; true to life, and the only way to make sense of her story; and he makes her later behaviour support it. In effect, she presumes that God will love her for eating the apple, at any rate later on, when she has realized that that was what he wanted her to do at bottom (p. 163).

Of Milton's own attitude to Eve's fall Empson says:

He thus believed when he wrote the poem that Eve would have been justified if she had eaten the apple with sufficient faith that God wanted her to do it, in spite of God's repeated instructions to the contrary. This would make Milton less likely to describe her as falling through triviality; and his account can only blame her, I think, for trusting Goodness rather than God, one side of the divine nature rather than the other. She does indeed take a rather petulant tone towards God, but only (so to speak) if he is not good. There is a lack of tact [!] in the presence of the All-Knowing, but Milton could not

seriously regard this as enough reason for the appalling consequences to all mankind (p. 180).

I can only observe that the relevant passages of *Paradise Lost*
(IX, 745–80, 795–833, 856–85, 961–90, 1144–61) simply do not
support Empson. Taking up the main point: let us grant that the
serpent's words entered Eve's heart (550), and that the serpent
does suggest (692 ff.) that God may praise Eve for her courage. But
Eve's speech (745–80), which shows the influence on her of the
serpent's arguments, does not repeat this part of them; and this
omission is impossible to explain, if the decisive factor in Eve's
decision were what Empson says it is.

The whole argument depends on Empson's extremely free
paraphrases of Milton's verse. We must all enjoy these; I particularly enjoyed the epitome of God's genial speech to Adam (VIII,
399–411): 'What d'you want a woman for, hey? *I* don't want a
woman.' But how can any *detailed* interpretation of Milton's meaning be founded on such rewritings? One's heart warms to
Empson's interpretation of Adam's famous speech about the
'fortunate fall' (XII, 469–84); what he [Adam] is really saying,
apart from the emotional condition he has been reduced to, is 'Oh,
so you did want us to eat the apple, after all? Well, I'm pleased to
hear that, because Eve rather thought you did, at the time.' But I
am afraid Adam says nothing like this. He does not mention Eve
at all. Empson is implying the presence of a bit of evidence that is
not there. Here as elsewhere we have Empson's kind heart
prompting his ingenious head to make *Paradise Lost* more emotionally and morally coherent than it is.

Empson's moral generosity finally leads him into making the
case for the defence of Milton's God. No orthodox Miltonist
could have thought of anything so ingenious. All the deviousness,
malignity and horror turn out to be the prelude to a consummation of the world in which God, like the Marxists' State, will
whither away. This bold stroke, whereby God becomes a stern
and masterful character struggling to renounce, is one of Empson's
most imaginative ideas. Abdication is the only ethically satisfying
resolution of the divine ruler's dilemma: 'Sith 'twas my fault to give
the people scope, /'Twould be my tyranny to strike and gall them/
For what I bid them do.'

But did Milton hint that God the Father was going to abdicate?
A hint is all it can be, for the only passage which supports

Empson is God's speech in Book III (274–343), with its culmination in 'God shall be all in all', taken from Paul in 1 Corinthians. It is difficult to know what Empson is now maintaining. In the first edition he boldly committed himself to the word 'abdication'; in the second edition (see his note on p. 280) he half-withdraws the word, admitting that Milton would not have accepted that term.

The question of what Milton meant here is obscure and difficult. I wish Empson had followed up his suggestion that Milton may have been influenced by the Cambridge Platonists towards a more humane – and more mystical – conception of the Deity. I only know these writers from Grierson's *Cross-Currents*, and can offer no first-hand opinion on this point. I note in Michael Fixler's recent book (*Milton and the Kingdoms of God*, p. 85) a parallel between the religious-political thought of Milton about the millennial Kingdom of God, and that of Ralph Cudworth, the Cambridge Platonist, preaching before the House of Commons in 1647. There may be a clue to be followed up here.

But if the meaning of *Paradise Lost* depends on something so abstruse and allusive, so vaguely hinted at, then it is a private work, and all that has been urged against (e.g.) Saurat's view of Milton, as an eccentric theologian composing *Paradise Lost* around his eccentricities, becomes once more *actuel* and relevant. I hope this is not so. At any rate, part of Empson's own book turns against him here; when he is defending Milton's style against adverse critics, he protests that Milton uses words with exactness; what then becomes of all the passages (cf. III, 373–4; X, 31–2 and *passim*) where God the Father is called 'Eternal' and 'Immutable'?

At times Empson speaks as if *Paradise Lost* had been written by T. F. Powys. ('Then in the name of Man,' said Mr. Hayhoe boldly, [to God, the 'only penitent'] 'I forgive your sin; I pardon and deliver you from all your evil; confirm and strengthen you in all goodness, and bring you to everlasting death.' For Empson, after all, has a soft spot for Milton's God; though losing no opportunity to convict the old monster of his ultimate responsibility for all evils, he argues with some force that this God is at any rate less distasteful than the God believed in by many Christians; at least he takes no pleasure in torture.

Empson's book, to my mind, does not remove the incoherences in *Paradise Lost*, but increases one's sense of them. That an argument so extraordinary as his can be made to sound so plausible, is itself a consideration to be very seriously pondered when we are trying to make up our own minds about Milton's poem. I do not think a defence of Milton against Empson's mistaken apologia can be undertaken along Lewis's or Tillyard's lines. We have to go back to older critics, to a critic with the rare honesty of Johnson, who will admit the mixture of admiration and boredom which the great work engenders in him. 'The want of human interest is always felt' – is it not for this reason, rather than those given by Leavis, that the common reader keeps away from *Paradise Lost*?

Empson does succeed in making Milton's theology sound more interesting than the common reader usually finds it (though this is more true of his quotations from the *Christian Doctrine* than from *Paradise Lost*). He makes us wonder whether it was not a disaster that Augustine, rather than the more humane Origen or Gregory of Nyssa, became the central influence upon Christian theology. But he does not succeed in showing that Milton in *Paradise Lost* was an especially original or first-rate theological mind – could a first-rate theologian be as contemptuous of metaphysics as Milton is? (cf. II, 557–61). Part of Milton's artistic problems, surely, arose from his lack of interest in metaphysics; it was rash for a writer so preoccupied with Free Will to ignore the metaphysical and logical trickiness of the problem – as Milton does.

Few will doubt – and Empson convincingly shows this, both by quotation and commentary – that Milton's God was the expression of some of the strongest impulse of Milton's nature. But few will be convinced – and Empson does not enforce the conviction – that it was these same impulses which made him humane, sensitive, and a great poet.

The second edition of Empson's book does not differ greatly from the first, as regards the main body of the text; but Empson had added some notes, in which he deals with objections raised by critics of the first edition. There is also a new appendix, a piece of scholarly detective-work done to show that Milton probably was responsible for the foisting of Pamela's prayer into the *Eikon Basilike*. It may seem strange that an admirer of Milton should devote so much effort to convict him of this dirty trick, whereby the new régime, having destroyed the person of Charles I, sought to blacken his memory. But this is all perfectly consonant with Empson's whole paradoxical thesis: if Milton did connive at the

foisting of the prayer, this would be for Empson a suggestive confirmation of the view that Milton's God himself is not above using
distinctly shady means to achieve a good end. Empson here and
elsewhere does not give due weight to the moral commonplace –
which, in regard to *Paradise Lost*, has its artistic corollary – that
the chosen means infects the end.

But this is a book of rare interest and distinction. What other
professor of English literature could have written it? (I intend no
ironic inflexion in this question.) Milton himself described *Paradise Lost* as an 'adventrous Song', and Empson's book, in its own
way, has a comparable quality. His interpretations and commentaries often bring out an extra sparkle and vivacity in the great
poem. There can be few critical books which are at once so amusing and so serious and passionate. Empson puts his cards on the
table, tells us what he has read, and invites us to broaden our own
minds and our own reading. We find here no conventional propaganda for The Epic, the kind of thing you have to be a head of a
college to appreciate; *Paradise Lost* is treated as a living work, not
'a monument to dead ideas'. And if the book contains nothing
quite so brilliant as the analysis of Herbert's *Sacrifice* with which
Ambiguity culminates – and I say this as one willing to concede
to Rosemond Tuve's objections everything that *should* be conceded – this seems only because the poetry Empson is dealing with
affords less opportunity for such a wonderful demonstration of
what 'close reading' can do. And that Empson's strictly critical
power has not deteriorated, is proved by a part of the book which
(because it has nothing much to do with the main thesis) has been
neglected by reviewers; I am thinking of the magnificent discussion of the Dalila scene in *Samson*. But indeed it can be generally
said that, where Milton's poetry itself is most impressive and convincing, Empson's critique is at its best. Though more provocative
and more brilliant, it is not so scrupulously careful, so critically
central, as John Peter's discussion of the poem in his *Critique*.
Peter's book can be recommended to the student with less reservations. But Empson, partly because of the (sometimes perverse)
novelty of his approach, the originality of his attack, can often
bring more of Milton's poetic genius through. (It may be significant that Peter's chapter on the style is so poor and perfunctory.)
Empson, with all his paradoxes, conveys to us the Milton who in
one's litany of praise is the fount of noble eloquence, the wel-
comer of every noble pleasure – the second phrase is Empson's.

He memorably suggests, especially in the earlier chapters, the epic thrust and buoyancy of *Paradise Lost* at its best – all the qualities that make Books I and II so much more exhilarating than *Hyperion*. Empson, then, has done good service to Milton and to poetry. Even his recurrent tone of exasperated sarcasm is excusable in one who has spent so much time with Milton's God the Father.

1966

VIII

PARADISE REGAINED:
THE BETTER FORTITUDE

Paradise Regained seems not to have received much critical attention. Perhaps this is because it is the least popular of Milton's
poems. Although the poet himself 'could not endure to hear
Paradise Lost preferred to it', no one from that day to this seems to
have agreed with him. It has never attracted the same sympathetic
interest as *Samson Agonistes*. And even the academic authorities
who thought themselves obliged to rank it above *Comus*, and even
above *Lycidas*, may well have felt that they preferred those poems.
Paradise Regained, then, is clearly not a *tempting* poem. The very
terms in which it is usually praised (as by Landor or De Quincey)
suggest that it has been deferred to more than genuinely admired,
and more admired than enjoyed. At the same time, *Paradise Regained* has not usually been judged to be a failure. The consensus
of opinion seems to be that it is a success, though a success of a
limited kind. If critics are unenthusiastic, it is not as a rule because
they find in the poem a discrepancy between intention and performance. It is rather that there is felt to be something unsympathetic, something even repellent, about the intention itself.

The problem with which the poem at once confronts the reader
of poetry can be suggested by quoting two passages, which when
taken together are fairly representative of a contrast of modes, or
qualities, pervasive in the poem:

> But to guide Nations in the way of truth
> By saving Doctrin, and from error lead
> To know, and knowing worship God aright,
> Is yet more Kingly; this attracts the Soul,
> Governs the inner man, the nobler part,

The other ore the body only reigns,
And oft by force, which to a generous mind
So reigning can be no sincere delight.
Besides to give a Kingdom hath been thought
Greater and nobler don, and to lay down
Far more magnanimous than to assume.
Riches are needless then, both for themselves,
And for thy reason why they should be sought,
To gain a Scepter, oftest better miss't.

(II, 473–86)

Have we not seen, or by relation heard,
In Courts and Regal Chambers how thou lurkst,
In Wood or Grove by mossie Fountain side,
In Valley or Green Meddow, to way-lay
Som beauty rare, *Calisto, Clymene,*
Daphne, or *Semele, Antiopa,*
Or *Amymone, Syrinx,* many more
Too long, then layst thy scapes on names ador'd,
Apollo, Neptune, Jupiter, or *Pan,*
Satyr or Fawn or Silvan? But these haunts
Delight not all; among the Sons of Men
How many have with a smile made small account
Of beauty and her lures, easily scornd
All her assaults, on worthier things intent!

(II, 182–95)

Neither of these passages will be judged to be among the best parts of *Paradise Regained*. But the second none the less is decidedly better than the first, and it is not difficult to establish the nature of its superiority. The first passage is strangely colourless and tone-less. We have the sense of a mind behind it, but we have little or no sense of a voice expressing the mind. What made it poetry for the poet? Clearly the metre – the even beat of the remarkably regular verse, with the typical monosyllabic thud at the end of so many of the lines, which, without interrupting the consecutive flow of the argument, reinforces the general effect of flat unin-cantatory assertion – the effect that makes it impossible to mistake the passage for even one of the more didactic parts of *Paradise Lost*. It is this metrical movement which underlines and empha-sizes the order of the poet's interests here, the stress tending to fall on demonstrative distinctions ('*this* attracts the Soul . . . *That other* ore the body only reigns') and grammatical particles (*'both* for themselves,/ *And* for thy reason why they should be sought'). This assertive bent, this habit of emphasis, results in a noticeable devaluing of the quality of the emotionally toned words. Consequently, although the passage is clearly the product of strong conviction, it is virtually impossible to convey this in any vocal effect. Indeed, it is best not to try, for the attempt could only draw attention to such unfortunate effects as the last line quoted, with its clutter of dentals and sibilants, suggesting a particular intensity of spat-out or hissed-out contempt.

In comparison the second passage appears tonally much more adequate. It conveys a peculiar mixture of knowing sneer and indulged aesthetic pleasure. The second line epitomizes this effect, the voice lingering a little over 'Courts and Regal Chambers' to come down with a grimly savoured dissonance on 'lurkst'. Satan is enjoying this speech: he is *with* Belial in the 'scapes' even while he is consciously dissociating himself from them; and the lift into superiority is appropriately accompanied by a lift in the verse itself, after the pause on the long sound of 'lures', to the expression of that easy scorn.

There is nothing remarkable about the writing in the second passage; by itself it would not prompt us to analysis; it is only the contrast with the first passage that brings out how well written it is. And it may be said that there is nothing remarkable either about this kind of contrast in Milton's poetry. It seems to be accepted as matter-of-course that Milton writes better poetry for 'bad' characters than for 'good'. I am always surprised at this casual assumption about so great a poet – and none of the sensible detractors of Milton denies that he is, after all, a great poet. Yet here we have a great poet writing on a theme with which he is beyond question seriously engaged, but producing work which considered by the standards of his own best writing is inert, jejune, and dull. The problem is surely a more interesting and difficult one than the common account of the matter suggests.

For it is not always true that Milton fails to make 'good' characters speak good poetry. Here are a few lines from the Lady in *Comus*:

> Yet should I try, the uncontrouled worth
> Of this pure cause would kindle my rapt spirits
> To such a flame of sacred vehemence,

> That dumb things would be mov'd to sympathize,
> And the brute Earth would lend her nerves and shake
> Till all thy magic structures rear'd so high
> Were shattered into heaps ore thy false head.
>
> (792–8)

The motive force here is obviously an impassioned moral fervour, but in contrast with the lines of Christ quoted from *Paradise Regained* the words, the phrasing, the run of the verse, all seem to 'sympathize' with it. We feel that invoked 'shaking' in the reading, and the 'structures' (finely placed word) already unsubstantial and tottering before the last line brings them down in ruins (the alliteration of 'shake' and 'shattered' contributes to this effect of a continuous process). It is true in suggestion to say that this kind of verse is more 'dramatic' than the passage from *Paradise Regained*. But this is not because the one creates the presence of a particular dramatized *person* and the other does not. Neither is dramatic in this sense, but the passage from *Comus* employs the method of poetry, in using language to carry the mind to what it says.

It may be objected that a local dryness or dullness is not an adequate ground for condemning a long poem. But the radical criticism is that this failure in the blank verse is merely the local manifestation of an essential failure of life in the poem, and that our perception of this affects our sense of the poet's whole grasp of his theme and casts doubt upon the whole form through which he has given it expression. It is important here to avoid an elementary misunderstanding. *Paradise Regained* is certainly, in a sense, 'about something'. It is an explicitly didactic work, whose burden could be paraphrased. And on the face of it the formal outline of the poem is correspondingly clear and unambiguous. But what criticism has to deal with here is not what would be conveyed by a prose abstract of the argument, nor by a general account of the Renaissance epic tradition in which Milton was perhaps writing. The question at issue is whether the chosen form of *Paradise Regained* corresponds in any intimate way to the chosen matter. I have here to disagree with some remarks of Mr. Northrop Frye. 'Most of us,' he says, 'tend to think of a poet's real achievement as distinct from, or even contrasted with, the achievement present in what he stole, and we are thus apt to concentrate on peripheral rather than central critical facts. For instance, the central greatness of *Paradise Regained* as a poem, is not the greatness of the rhetori-

cal decorations that Milton added to his source, but the greatness
of the theme itself, which Milton *passes on* to the reader from his
source.'[1] But surely the 'passing on' of 'the greatness of the theme'
is a more creative process, requires a more positive contribution
from the poet, than the phrase 'passing on' by itself suggests. The
great subject does not in itself make a great poem; and the only
way in which we can establish relevant distinctions between
Paradise Regained and (say) Blackmore's *Creation* is by examining
everything in the poem which may be said to represent the poet's
own unique sense of the theme he is handling.

The manifest undertaking to which Milton committed himself is clearly foreshadowed in the prelude to Book IX of *Paradise
Lost*, where the traditional subject-matter of classical epic and
chivalrous romance is rejected in favour of the epic of heroic
magnanimity ('the better fortitude / Of Patience and Heroic
Martyrdom'). This promise is scarcely fulfilled in *Paradise Lost* itself, and it may be conjectured that Milton's consciousness of this
played a part in his decision to write the shorter epic, in which the
epic 'machinery' which occupies so much of *Paradise Lost* is
drastically reduced, and the formal and the actual centring of the
poem on its Hero coincide. The denial of scope to the epic
'machinery' is accompanied by a denial of elaboration to the style.
This new style, at its most typical, takes its colour from the character of the Hero. He is laconic and terse. Even the actual Domini-
cal *logia* in his mouth ('Tempt not the Lord thy God . . .', etc.)
partake of this Senecan terseness. Milton's Christ (if this may be said
without offence) is rude – 'rude' here occupying an intermediate
position between Othello's 'Rude am I in my speech' and the
modern 'brusque, ill-mannered'. He characteristically speaks 'in
brief' (IV, 485, 'So talkd he, while the Son of God went on / And
stayd not.') His more extended speeches are in the 'majestic un-
affected stile' (IV, 359) which Milton attributes to the Hebrew
Prophets. Satan in contrast represents the polished orator. But
even he at times partakes in the new plain vocabulary and 'un-
poetical' manner:

> . . . harmless, if not wholsom, *as a sneeze*
> To mans less universe.

> (IV, 458–9)

Compare Christ's:

[1] *Anatomy of Criticism*, Princeton University Press, New Jersey, 1957.

H

> . . . collecting toys
> And trifles for choice matters, *worth a spunge*.
>
> (IV, 328–9)

This is an overflow from the manner of Milton's controversial prose. Yet the plain style, with all its laconism ('He added not . . .') can have a certain ideal dignity of its own:

> He added not; and Satan bowing low
> His gray dissimulation, disappear'd
> Into thin Air diffus'd: for now began
> Night with her sullen wing to double-shade
> The Desert, Fowls in thir clay nests were coucht;
> And now wild Beasts came forth the woods to roam.
>
> (I, 497–502)

Even after no more than forty lines of *Paradise Regained* it becomes plain that our habit of expectation, brought over from the earlier *Paradise Lost*, of a large amplitude of sonority and grandeur of *sostenuto* is not going to be gratified. The occasional expansions in the manner of *Paradise Lost* stand out sharply in contrast with the surrounding verse:

> . . . and led thir march
> From Hells deep-vaulted Den to dwell in light,
> Regents and Potentates, and Kings, yea gods
> Of many a pleasant Realm and Province wide.
>
> (I, 115–18)

Expansive 'allusions' are rare, and their orotund style seems to point to their ironic use:

> Such forces met not, nor so wide a camp
> When *Agrican* with all his Northern powers
> Besieg'd *Albracca*, as Romances tell . . . , etc.
>
> (III, 337–9)

But the prevailing gravity and formality of the poem's characteristic manner forbid us any sense of having passed to a 'lower' style or a less impressive subject-matter. On the contrary, Milton's way of contrasting the new poem with the old (*ille ego qui quondam*), in the first line of *Paradise Regained*, offers the promise of a *greater* sublimity: *Paradise Lost* becomes in retrospect a song about a 'happy Garden'; the poet is now to sing of deeds 'above Heroic'. Yet until Satan's first 'undisguis'd' speech to Christ, when some sort of life begins mysteriously to stir in the verse, little or nothing is done to capture the imagination. The general impression is of a pervasive dull distinction. The frequent paraphrase of the language of the New Testament has much the same effect in Milton's stately verse as in many a sermon; the suggestiveness of the original is diluted. The landscape evoked is of the vaguest: the 'pathless Desert' into which the Son of God is led has the thinness of allegory. The style is inelastic and mannered. Milton without magniloquence, we begin to feel, is hard to read. It is against this soporific background that we hear a new note, which, in D. H. Lawrence's phrase, makes us prick our innermost ear: 'Tis true, I am that Spirit unfortunate . . .' (I, 358). But here we are brought at once to the central peculiarity of the undertaking of *Paradise Regained*.

Milton, it has often been observed, is a striking example of that type of divided poetic personality in which the *prédilection d'artiste* for certain themes is accompanied by a moral antagonism towards them. Closely allied to this is the observation that there is apt to be a cleavage between Milton's expounded doctrines and his unconscious sympathies; and this in turn prompts the judgement that Milton's imaginative creations show a consequent tendency to 'get out of hand': Satan in *Paradise Lost*, and in a different but related way God the Father, Adam at the moment of the Fall, are said to illustrate this tendency; and the criticism has been so generally made that it might be called the characteristic adverse judgement on Milton's poetry. Now whatever general validity there may be in this criticism, it is not clear that it is at all precisely applicable to *Paradise Regained*. Whether the Satan of the later poem is or is not 'the same' character as the Satan of *Paradise Lost*, no one surely would judge that here at any rate he 'gets out of hand'. On the contrary, in the presentation of Satan as in everything esle in this poem, we have the impression of the poet's measured control of his artistic intention. For example, the residual pride and self-pity of Satan in the speech just quoted (I, 357–405), so finely evoked in the tone and movement of the lines, are clearly part of the intended effect. He is presenting himself, after all, as a 'sympathetic' character:

> Men generally think me much a foe
> To all mankind: why should I? they to mee
> Never did wrong or violence
>
>   (I, 387–8)

It is the detection of these arts that provokes the Saviour's 'stern' reply. But what is at issue for the reader of poetry is not the ethical content of Satan's speech or of Christ's reply, but the degree of 'presence' which the poet succeeds in bestowing on both of them. And it is impossible to judge that both are equally 'present'; this is why attempts such as that of Mr. Arnold Stein[1] to interpret the whole poem as a drama must fail. At the same time, it is equally impossible to believe that Milton was unaware of the nature of the contrast between the two speeches – of the nature of the contrast between the presentations of the two disputants generally. That contrast is too systematic, too consistent, too representative in the poem to have been unintentional. In investigating it we are led to the heart of the matter, the singularity of Milton's central purpose.

The difficulties inherent in that purpose – the presentation of Christ as the hero of an epic – can hardly be exaggerated. Certainly, 'epic' in *Paradise Regained* means something very peculiar, and it is significant that there is no real classical model for the poem – whatever ecouragement for his undertaking Milton may have derived from such dubious forerunners as Vida's *Christiad*.[2] Nor can neo-classical accounts of the form of certain books of the Bible have given adequate precedent. It seems to me that in its formal character *Paradise Regained* is essentially *sui generis*, and that this is consonant with Milton's sense of the unique and unrepeatable character of the Hero. (It is perhaps significant too that such typical features as the epic simile, so famously exemplified in Book I of *Paradise Lost*, do not occur in *Paradise Regained* until Book IV, and none of the similes when they do occur is at all remarkable.) But the *suggestion* of the qualities of ancient poetry is with equal certainty part of Milton's intention; in order to bring out the transcendent character of Christ's heroism, it is necessary to keep before the reader persistent reminders of the traditional heroism which Christ transcends. Now in inviting this comparison between Christ and the epic heroes Milton runs at once into a formal difficulty. In the background of comparable traditional epic is the theomachy; on the human plane the hero is the repre-

---

[1] *Heroic Knowledge*, University of Minnesota Press, Minneapolis, 1957.

[2] The nearest parallel is possibly the *Oedipus at Colonus,* and Sophocles's 'gnomic' manner may well have played a part in the formation of the style in *Paradise Regained*. But the formal relationship of the two works is far from close.

sentative of a god, or of the nation favoured by the god. But in Milton's poem the uniqueness of the relationship between the hero and the god forbids even the possibility of any tension between the hero's purposes and those of the god. The whole point of the story, the ethical significance of the paradigm, is the completeness of the subordination of the hero's human purpose to the divine purpose. But respect for the tradition of Christianity – a respect which, *pace* Saurat, Milton does nothing to disturb – rules out the imaginary evocation of an even conceivable temporary contrast between the two. The result is that Milton runs the risk of presenting Christ as a demigod, one in whom the divine and the human purposes are not so much *united* as *identical*; thereby not only falling into theological unorthodoxy, but emptying Christ's conduct of its exemplary character of *obedience*. It is a general point to be pondered here, whether any poet who presents the Incarnation as part of his subject does not run this risk.

But in any case this formal problem is a minor difficulty in comparison with the substantive problem Milton faced in portraying the *character* of his Hero. Now here we have at once to distinguish between superficial and essential criticisms. Those who complain that Milton's Christ is not like 'the Christ of the Gospels' must make it quite clear to themselves that they are not relying on sentimental half-memories of the Parables. They must recall the mysterious and baffling figure, so starkly presented in the Gospel of Mark and never altogether absent from the pages of the other Synoptics or of John. They must recall the 'hard saying'. They must recall the sacred character of Christ as it has come down from the New Testament and the central tradition of Christianity – a character and a tradition which (despite once popular accusations of 'Arianism' and 'Socinianism') Milton in *Paradise Regained* nowhere abjures. But once mere sentimentality is disposed of, legitimate occasions for criticism remain. Doctrinal objections, even if they were likely to worry most modern readers, do not in my opinion arise. (The view to be found in some authors that Milton is covertly substituting the Temptation in the Wilderness for the Passion as the central mystery of Christianity is directly refutable from the text, e.g. I, 115ff. or IV, 633–5.) The real objections are on grounds of taste and feeling, not doctrine.

It is commonly said that Milton, however doctrinally orthodox he may be shown to be in his poetry, is deeply un-Christian in feeling. Nor can this objection be brushed aside as irrelevant, since part of Milton's task as a poet is to convey the feelings appropriate to what he says. And the objections to the 'feeling' in *Paradise Regained* can be localized. The Christ who speaks of the people as 'a miscellaneous rabble' (III, 50) is not the Christ who had compassion for the multitude. It is not simply a question of Milton's representation being at variance with that of the gospels; for in order to assimilate Christ to his idea of the Magnanimous Man, the paragon of surly virtue, the poet has invented a detailed context for Christ's remarks, and it would be possible therefore to plead some dramatic justification for the variance. But whatever these excuses, the insensitiveness of the presentation remains. It is not possible, at these points, for Milton both to benefit from legitimate preconceptions about his Hero and to exhibit his Hero as speaking in a manner which affronts them. The error of feeling is closely related to the error of taste illustrated in Christ's discussion of the Roman worthies (III, 443 ff.) or of the Greek philosophers (IV, 291 ff.). Here again the objection is not to the historical impossibilities of these remarks – even assuming their historical impossibility. We must be prepared to grant the poet his conventions: such as making Christ speak in English blank verse. But the objection here is to imagine incongruity. And we must go further than this. Milton's presentation of Christ, as a whole, must stand convicted of either an error of feeling or an error of taste. If he imagined that the traits of his Hero are all to be found in the historical character of Christ, he was guilty of the former; if on the other hand he supposed himself to be legitimately adding traits to it, he was guilty of the latter. It may be objected that these criticisms are not strictly relevant to a literary appraisal of *Paradise Regained*, since they depend upon the accident that Milton's poem – unlike the *Iliad* or *Aeneid* – happens to draw upon a still living religion. But this, if urged as a defence of *Paradise Regained*, is a dangerous argument. For it seems clear that the success of the poem depends upon the reader's willingness to imagine himself in sympathy with certain religious and ethical doctrines. To a reader without this sympathy, or without the capacity for it, *Paradise Regained* will be indeed a frigid work. And the fair criticism of the poem here is that Milton, by his presentation of Christ, has done something to disturb that sympathy where it already exists, and to hinder its attainment where it does not.

The conclusion is inescapable: that Milton's portrayal of Christ does not succeed in uniting the sacred figure with the epic hero. And this judgement must be associated with the criticism already passed upon the desiccation and tonelessness of so much of the verse Christ is made to speak. Both strictures regard what may be called a *failure of incarnation*. The peculiarity of *Paradise Regained* among Milton's poems is that the division of the poetic personality which prompts these strictures seems to be perfectly conscious. Milton gives all the imaginative and emotional appeal – the characteristic appeal of poetry – to the temptations: Christ rejects them as the spokesman of pure reason. But this involves Milton in an artistic contradiction. In allowing Christ to speak poetry at all, he is obliged to supply *some* tone, *some* presence, to the voice of pure reason. The result is the acerbity in Christ's speeches which strikes the ear so disagreeably. This is the failure of incarnation in its most obvious form. Christ as the silent patient figure amid the storm conjured up by Satan is impressive. Christ's stately rudeness is less so. Imaginative temptations should be met imaginatively. The quality of feeling for a lesser good must be opposed by the quality of feeling for a higher good. To try to write poetry on another supposition is to go against the grain. It is, indeed, hard to feel that an element of penitential exercise, of deliberate self-mortification, did not enter into Milton's conception of his purpose in *Paradise Regained*. When we hear of '*Sion's* songs, to all true tastes excelling', we cannot but recall that Milton's one undoubted failure as a poet is his own translation of Psalms. And the note of the famous passage on Athens (IV, 237) is unmistakable. It is the note of love; not the intimate love for a particular actual place that sounds in the great choral ode of Sophocles, but the bookish man's love, no less real and longing, for an ideal country of the mind. The reply of Christ is not even intellectually satisfying. Who can listen without irritation to the scholar-poet evolving the ingenious paradox (IV, 321–5) whereby reading is discredited? But what is really objectionable is the note of feeling. The fine-writing of the passage of Athens, and the speech of Christ which rejects it, seem both self-indulgences – indulgences of different 'selves', different habits of feeling, in the poet.

The more successful parts of *Paradise Regained* depend on a more equivocal relation between Milton the artist and Milton the moralist. As a moralist, Milton deals in simple heroic opposites: good against evil; temptation and rejection; to stand or to fall. The climax of the poem, when Christ miraculously is sustained upon the pinnacle of the Temple, epitomizes this grand simplicity:

> To whom Thus *Jesus*: Also it is written,
> Tempt not the Lord thy God: he said, and stood.
> But *Satan* smitten with amazement fell.
>
> (IV, 560 ff.)

Good and evil are confronted: good stands and evil falls. Such is
the bare *schema* of the poem. But who can feel that the actual Satan
of the poem is 'evil'? However discredited and contemned, he is
'serviceable to Heaven's King' by Christ's own admission. He is
even a Son of God; the title, as he employs it polemically, has a
terrible irony; but at one moment (III, 203 ff.) the tragedy of the
rejected Son beside the 'Son beloved', allowing himself to dream
of Christ's intercession with their common Father, is fully
realized. This dramatizing of the figure of Satan raises the story
above the level of a mere debate. Satan is made 'serviceable' to the
poet: it is in Satan's language, rather than in anything Milton
directly tells us about Christ, that we feel the *attractiveness* of
heroic virtue. Yet Milton does not allow the dramatization of the
suffering Adversary to conflict with his function as the Tempter.
Rather, the personal appeal of Satan is made to reinforce the
temptations.

> If I then to the worst than can be haste
> Why move thy feet so slow to what is best . . .?
>
> (III, 224–5)

Satan is the servant of Milton's art. That is, I think, why his 'evil'
remains in the poem merely schematic, nominal. Milton required,
more than most poets, a positive feeling for what he was writing
about. A certain *uncritical* element in his genius is at once his
strength and his weakness. It is the weakness that we chiefly see in
Paradise Regained. Every reader notices the close relationship,
amounting virtually to identification, between Milton – or one
side of Milton – and his Hero. A rigid, uncompromising angularity
is set up as the standard of value. Surely – apart from the error of
taste involved in making Christ impersonate it – so *simpliste* a
procedure is open to criticism. The Hero at the worst moments of
the poem is made to sound like an irritable snob: but Milton,
owing to the uncritical simplicity of the moral position he had
adopted, has no means of avoiding this. It was a tactical mistake
to confine courtesy to the Devil. There is a certain guilelessness

here. Milton has no sense of the dangers inherent in so unqualified an identification between the Hero's righteousness and his
own. 'Si fort qu'on soit, on peut éprouver le besoin de s'incliner
devant quelqu'un ou quelque chose. S'incliner devant Dieu, c'est
toujours le moins humiliant.' I wish I could feel that the Milton of
Paradise Regained had been capable of sucn a reflection.

1960

PART THREE

IX

THE ROMANTIC POETS

Even after a century or so of being canonized, embalmed, and petrified in textbooks as 'the Romantic Movement', the great outburst of English poetry at the end of the eighteenth century has still not ceased to put out vibrations of its power. For the last time, perhaps, in the history of English literature our poetry felt itself moving *with* the forces that move the world; and the excitement of that far-off moment can still be felt in the rhythms, the imagery, the mythological creation of the great romantic poets. And when since the beginning of the seventeenth century have there been (by the most stringent critical estimate) five major English poets alive and writing? The triumphant phase was of course brief. Indeed, some of the most memorable romantic poetry records not triumph but defeat, despondency, disillusionment. But the force and moving quality of this disillusionment – whether felt in the broken rhapsody of Blake, the even-voiced, yet essentially lyrical, meditations of Wordsworth, or the impassioned, hectic tone of Shelley – themselves testify to the grandeur and strength of the illusions.

Of course the impact of romanticism, at any rate in English literature, was not so flamboyant as, in the nineteenth century, it was customarily thought to be. Housman was right to call Wordsworth 'the pivot of the epoch', but exaggerating when he called him 'the chief figure in English poetry after Chaucer, if redemption ranks next to creation'. In comparison with some other European countries – think for example, of French or Spanish poetry of the period – England had still kept up the standard of its poetry even in the unpoetic eighteenth century. Dr. Donald Davie is right to call Wordsworth as much the last poet of the eighteenth century as the first of the nineteenth. Wordsworth and Coleridge had forerunners, even if we neglect Blake as he was neglected: *Lyrical Ballads* is now often regarded by scholars, and with some justice, as the doing better of something that many others had tried to do, rather than as Housman's 'new thing upon the earth'. This is not to depreciate their originality: only to point out that originality, as is so often the case, need not be a matter of total novelty, but of the discovery of *unexpected* origins. It was a rather unpromising by-line of eighteenth-century English poetry which Wordsworth and Coleridge cultivated; but it was to lead to a radical transformation of English imagination and sensibility, while the lurid 'German romances', the products of the self-conscious 'romanticism' of the age, are forgotten.

This reminder of the many different things that 'romanticism' has meant, and means, compels us to recall the important truism that 'the romantic movement' is a dangerous thing to generalize about – especially the English romantic movement. It is not only that English poets and artists are notorious individualists; the whole nature of 'romanticism' itself was determined by a stress on the individuality, the uniqueness, of the individual poet himself. So it turns out to be safer, and more proper, to generalize about the romantic tradition as it appears in the poetry of the (on the whole) disappointing Victorian sequel, than in work composed during the romantic prime. (This suggests a curious contrast between the fortunes of English and French poetry in the nineteenth century; whereas the first period of French romanticism seems somehow not quite to 'come off', its successor, the phase of Baudelaire and the Symbolists, has remained intensely interesting and vital, and has dominated the whole movement of later European poetry; our Victorian romantic poetry on the other hand, would be generally agreed not to have fulfilled the promise of its great forerunners and inspirers'.)

A common romanticism – this phrase seems less and less applicable, and what it points to more and more elusive, as we study the work of the greatest romantic poets. Dr. Ian Jack, in the *Oxford History*, has recently reminded us that there is no equivalent, among them, of the Continental-style 'movement', school, group, or *cénacle*. But Dr. Jack perhaps goes too far in hushing up their sense of common purpose: however vaguely this may have to be defined. After all, *something* happened in English poetry at the end of the eighteenth century. To do without the word 'romantic', in describing the period, does not mean that we can do without the thing – whatever exactly it was – that this word points to (of course one should say things); and it must be significant that the *Oxford History* itself should feel obliged to devote a whole volume to seventeen years of English literature.

Perhaps a well-known passage from the preface to Shelley's *Revolt of Islam* does most to reconcile the apparent contradiction between our vivid sense of the individuality, and our equally strong sense of the *Zeitgeist*, in the work of the great romantics: 'There must be a resemblance, which does not depend upon their own will, between all the writers of any particular age. They cannot escape from subjection to a common influence which arises out of an infinite combination of circumstances belonging to the times in which they live; though each is in a degree the author of the very influence by which his being is thus pervaded.' This may suggest the spirit in which the literary historian of the romantic period should go to work; but it does not by itself furnish the particular terms in which this 'common influence' should be described. And it is possibly a limitation of Dr. Jack's volume, as of the previous volume on the age of Wordsworth by Professor Renwick, that they do not take us very far in this direction either. Naturally, if one is more interested in poets than in *Zeitgeister*, it is the individuality of a poet's work that will be in full focus; and most British readers of poetry nowadays will be too wearisomely familiar with critical insistence on 'the words on the page', the treatment of poetry as a particular unique expression of a particular unique sensibility, to need warning against the 'queer aquatic monsters in a tank', words ending in -ion and -ance and -ity and -ism fighting out their spectral battles, which Q long ago derided in George Brandes. Yet poetry has a history; and in poets so conscious of their time as the romantics were (as the quotation from Shelley implies) the unsatisfactoriness of dealing with poet after poet, poem after poem, without any coherent organizing principle of historical criticism, is obvious.

Chance brings together two books which in their different ways represent an attempt to attack this problem. Patricia Hodgart and Theodore Redpath have brought together in *Romantic*

Perspectives[1] various essays, reviews, and *dicta* about the work of Crabbe, Blake, Wordsworth and Coleridge; some of this material comes from friendly contemporaries, some from uncomprehending or hostile ones; and some from the poets themselves. We are thus given a broad view of the contemporary response to this new poetry, and it suggests some fresh thoughts. For instance, in the stock account of the matter Crabbe, of course, is not regarded as one of the new poets, but as a mere survival from the eighteenth century, and as such saluted and befriended by the traditional reviewers of the time, for example Jeffrey. That this account is misleading can be shown even from the extracts from Jeffrey given by Miss Hodgart and Mr. Redpath. (It is a pity, by the way, that so much of their book is devoted to 'extracts'; we could have done without some of the editorial matter, valuable as much of it is, if to enjoy in return the full sweep and scale of a Jeffrey review – despite their long quotations and repetitiousness, the 'great reviewers' of the early nineteenth century might impress the modern reader more if their painstakingness and their weightiness, at their best, were more fully suggested.)

A study of Jeffrey's prose, his sensibility and even his particular judgements brings out how much he – gibbeted in conventional literary history as the arch-anti-romantic, notorious for saying that *The Excursion* 'would never do' – was affected by the new currents that were moving in the poetry of the age; and so, as a consciously suspicious and sometimes adverse critic of those trends, all the more interesting a witness to the truth of Shelley's proposition about the 'common influence'. And what Jeffrey saluted in Crabbe was not merely the eighteenth-century of Augustan virtues he might have been expected to salute, as a means of rebuking what seemed to him *niaiserie* in a Wordsworth, but originality – 'the most original writer who has ever come before us'. Crabbe's very remarkable later work, appearing after his twenty years' silence, was not missed by the 'great reviewers', and they recognized the variety of the influences upon it. Modern criticism has perhaps still to catch up with their insights; the time is long overdue for a thorough reconsideration of Crabbe's position in English poetry. As Mr. Howard Mills recently remarked, the *Oxford History* depicts him on the whole as a Parson Adams left over from the eighteenth century; and the common

[1] Harrap, London, 1964.

reader's notion of Crabbe, if that indispensable fictitious character
can be said to have one at all, is too often in resonance with the
little anecdote in Sir Walter Scott's *Journal*, quoted in *Romantic
Perspectives*:

> Sir George Beaumont and Wordsworth were sitting together
> in Murray the bookseller's back room. Sir George after sealing
> a letter blew out the candle which had enabled him to do so,
> and exchanging a look with Wordsworth began to admire in
> silence the undulating thread of smoke which slowly arose
> from the expiring wick, when Crabbe put on the extinguisher.

Crabbe, then 'had no imagination' and so the stereotype has been
fixed. Even *Peter Grimes* and *Sir Eustace Grey* – to name two poems
of Crabbe that seem to be reasonably current – would have done
something, one would have thought, to modify it; but the reappraisal of *Tales of the Hall*, the sorting-out and weeding-out of
Crabbe's work that needs doing, might do much more.

It is useful, it gives a feeling of actuality, to the study of
romantic poetry to see it in the context of the best critical thought
of its age – and other thought which was not so good; and Miss
Hodgart's and Mr. Redpath's volume performs a useful service.
But of course a compilation of past criticism cannot be a substitute for critical thoughts of our own. And so we turn to *Romanticism Reconsidered*,[1] edited with a foreword by Professor
Northrop Frye, to see what is happening among the present-day
academic critics of the romantic period – in this case, American
academic criticism. The result, it must be said, is a certain disappointment. This collection of essays comes from distinguished
hands – Professor Frye himself, Professor Abrams (the author of
that valuable book *The Mirror and the Lamp*), Professor Lionel
Trilling, Professor René Wellek. And, naturally, it reaches a high
level of learning and lucid writing, and contains material for which
we are grateful (the quotations alone, from writers and thinkers of
the period, in Professor Abrams's essay form an inviting antho-
logy). What is wanting is that sense of actuality which, for all
their inevitable crudities and misjudgements, we can find in the
comments and reviews in the Hodgart and Redpath volume.
Take Professor Frye's own contribution, for example. This is an
erudite, witty, informative piece of writing, in the mode which
Professor Frye practises in his larger works with the energy and

[1] Columbia University Press, N.Y., 1963.

synoptic effort of a Spengler. Here, having shown himself in agreement with Professor Abrams's important judgement that the romantic poets were, centrally, social and political poets, inspired by the French Revolution and the ideological stir of the time, he sets out to show how they evolved an imagery and a mythological framework in which to express their insights.

Professor Frye is a highly sophisticated writer. Indeed, with him as with Professor Trilling, one feels a certain incongruity between the sophistication of the essayist and the unsophisticated minds of a Blake, a Keats, or a Wordsworth who are the subjects. But these were profound minds; and Professor Frye seems all the time to be moving only on the surface. He is well aware of the pitfalls of his approach; he sees, and recognizes, the fundamental and very important differences between the poets he is dealing with; and yet the total effect of his essay is to assimilate them into a skilfully drawn but highly artificial pattern. So smooth is the mode of his writing that it is only rarely that we can notice where recalcitrant details are being blurred over; as when Professor Frye, listing examples of romantic symbolism, cites 'the corn-goddess in Keats's *To Autumn*, the parallel figure identified with Ruth in the *Ode to a Nightingale* . . . [as] all emblems of a revealed Nature'. We all remember the reference to Ruth 'amid the alien corn' in the 'Nightingale' ode; but in what sense does this have an effect really comparable with the figure of Autumn in the other poem? and if Ruth is Nature, why is the corn alien?

This, it may be said, is a very small and debatable point. But what is more serious is that his whole procedure is a substitute for any strong engagement of the writer with his subject. Professor Frye's essay consequently suggests little of the power of romantic poetry (for all that he says, rightly, about the 'metrical excitement' in some of Wordsworth's best, if not best known poems, and the *élan* of the whole movement) because he has not conveyed that it operates powerfully on him. As a result, his romantics seem merely studious eccentrics. When, in contrast, Housman writes of Blake in *The Name and Nature of Poetry* – of Blake as 'the most poetical of poets' – we feel, whether we agree or disagree, that this is a real judgement: this is what Blake meant to him, and it has altered his life: and the note that is altogether missing from Professor Frye's writing can also be suggested by quoting Dr. Leavis on Wordsworth:

Behind, then, the impersonality of Wordsworth's wisdom there is an immediately personal urgency. Impelling him back to childhood and youth – to their recovery in a present of tranquil seclusion – there are the emotional storms and disasters of the intervening period, and these are implicitly remembered, if not 'recollected', in the tranquillity of his best poetry. In so far as his eyes may fairly be said to 'avert their ken from half of human fate', extremely painful awareness of this half is his excuse. . . . Probably not many readers will care to censure him for weakness or cowardice. His heart was far from 'unoccupied by sorrow of its own', and his sense of responsibility for human distress and his generously active sympathies had involved him in emotional disasters that threatened his hold on life. A disciplined limiting of contemplation to the endurable, and, consequently, a withdrawal to a reassuring environment, became terrible necessities for him.

We may contrast a passage from Professor Frye:

For Wordsworth, who still has a good deal of the pre-Romantic sense of nature as an objective order, nature is a landscape nature, and from it, as in Baudelaire's *Correspondances*, mysterious oracles seep into the mind through eye or ear, even a bird with so predictable a song as the cuckoo being an oracular wandering voice. This landscape is a veil dropped over the naked nature of screaming rabbits and gasping stags, the nature red in tooth and claw which haunted a later generation. Even the episode of the dog and the hedgehog in *The Prelude* is told from the point of view of the dog and not of the hedgehog. But the more pessimistic, and perhaps more realistic, conception of nature in which it can be a source of evil or suffering as well as good is the one that gains ascendancy in the later period of Romanticism, and its later period extends to our own day.

This quotation suggests the representative blandness, the detachedness, which seem to go with the excessive 'intellectuality' of Professor Frye's writing (an intellectuality which is still more marked in Professor Trilling). The 'personal urgency' is missing. But do we need that? Certainly Professor Frye's essay is orderly and informative, and serves some purposes very well. It is certainly arguable, and probably true, that the ultimate significance of romantic poetry lies in its effort to create, by means of imagination alone, something approximating to a religious myth which would be valid for a modern world in which would be valid for a modern world in which the old myths have lost their foothold. But we would feel happier about this exposition if we could feel that these men, and other men, and the expositor himself, had ever felt the passionate need for a religious myth. If this need is not conveyed, the intellectual constructions abstracted from the experience of the romantic movement will seem only like pretty and ingenious toys. This ingenuity seems sometimes a temptation to Professor Frye; in some of his other work, if not here, he is rather given to the working-out of bright ideas at a very high level of abstraction from the realities of art and literature, and can remind us, not at all of the vices and virtues of the old-fashioned dry-as-dust-scholar, but of something as up-to-date as W. H. Auden's criticism; it seems significant that in the present essay he can refer to Auden's *For the Time Being* as if he thought it a work of high distinction.

We need the breadth of view, the erudition, and the clarity of style of writers like Professor Frye; but it must be combined with the capacity to grasp the 'living hand, yet warm and capable / Of earnest grasping' of the great poets with whom he deals. Dare one say that this over-intellectuality, which one would have thought was as much out of place here as it could be in any period of literature, is a characteristic failing of American academic criticism? At any rate, Professor Trilling, starting from some interesting speculations on 'pleasure' as a key term in Wordsworth and Keats, and moving on to speak with sophisticated ease of Dostoevsky, Nietzsche, Kafka, St. Augustine. . . ., seems to operate at so high a plane above vulgar common sense that he can find himself speaking of 'the spirituality of modern literature' as its characteristic feature. Professor Trilling of course senses the inevitably ironic reaction of some of his readers, and goes on to qualify, and explain. But his perhaps not happily chosen phrase is useful in suggesting something that the great romantic poets had, and a sense of which it is vitally important that the modern critic should convey. One incidental merit of Professor Abrams's essay is that it brings out the spiritual need, to fulfil which the romantics evolved their figure of the poet-prophet. Ironically, again (ironically when we consider how this poet has become the touchstone for

academic orthodoxy), he shows how they identified the forerunner of the bard-saviour with Milton; and it may be suggested
that no amount of connoisseuring of Milton's style, and what he
has in common with the seventeenth-century *précieux*, will really
make *Paradise Lost* vibrate in our spirit, unless we can see in its
author what the romantic poets saw; in Raleigh's phrase, 'the
blazing and acrid visionary'.

1964

X

WORDSWORTH'S
RESOLUTION AND INDEPENDENCE

'*Resolution and Independence*,' says Coleridge, 'is *especially* characteristic of the author. There is scarce a defect or excellence in his writings of which it would not present a specimen.' It is also characteristic of the author in its method. Wordsworth chooses what would seem a slight episode. His success lies in convincing us of the significance *he* found in it, one essentially particular and personal. He imposes conviction by means of that characteristic medium *through* which we are made to see and judge all that Wordsworth wishes us to see and judge.

This medium is verse of a *timbre* we recognize at once as Wordsworthian: the medium of *The Ruined Cottage* and *Hart-Leap Well* and *Michael*. *Resolution and Independence* perhaps belongs more fully with the first of these than with the other two; Wordsworth (we can divine without knowing any external facts about the personal crisis that underlies it) is more deeply involved in the experience he offers for our contemplation. The point can be made by remarking on the quality of those poems. *Resolution and Independence* is, in an important sense, more profoundly personal than *Michael*; or, to say this in more strictly literary terms, it is more immediate; though it is on a larger scale, it has the same immediacy, as it has substantially the same method, as the 'Lucy' poems.

So I do not only mean that it has biographical value, though it certainly has, whether we judge its impulsion to have come chiefly from Wordsworth's worry about Coleridge, or about his own resolve to marry and settle down, or about his tendencies to recurrent depression. Certainly, too, it has its humanitarian aspect, as an example of poetic 'field-work among rustics'; and in this aspect also it is very typical of its author. But *Resolution and Independence* is not the anecdote related, in faithful detail, in Dorothy Wordsworth's *Journal*. For one thing, Dorothy is not there; and, though William of course is there, that sober, prosaic individual with the tradition-ally northern virtues, a child of the English eighteenth century, common-sensical, pious and *bourgeois* (while Dorothy, with her simple grace, is like the heroine of *Persuasion*), he is only fully asserted, and vindicated, at the poem's close; the core of the poem is the 'unknown modes of being': and in calling this poem per-sonal we are testifying primarily to an experience of them, and to Wordsworth's way of resolving and validating that experience. *Resolution and Independence* is a poem, self-sufficient and existing in its own right. It is a poem describing a psychological event which issued in a moral attitude. Our judgement that it is a 'public' poem follows closely upon the judgement that this moral conse-quence – this more general significance – is felt to spring rightly and naturally from Wordsworth's own interpretation of the psychological event. In *Strange Fits of Passion* Wordsworth comes very close to offering only the statement of a vividly evoked psychological curiosity: there is a tacit admission of limited significance ('But in the Lover's ear alone'). *Strange Fits of Passion*, nevertheless, is also a poem: but it is clearly a border-line case; 'border-line' between the private and the public, or (the dis-tinction is often much the same where Wordsworth is concerned) between the successful poem and the unsuccessful one. *Resolution and Independence*, which has a really similar method and subject-matter, implicitly claims more for itself than the shorter poem; it is conceived on a grander scale; and we are asked, in judging it, to apply to it – and apply it to – much more of our experience. Dorothy wrote gravely to an uncomprehending critic of the poem within the Wordsworth circle: 'When you happen to be dis-pleased with what you suppose to be the tendency or moral of any poem which William writes, ask yourself whether you have hit upon the real tendency and true moral, and above all never think that he writes for no reason but merely because a thing happened – and when you feel any poem of his to be tedious, ask yourself in what spirit it was written.' (Letter to Sara and Mary Hutchinson, June 1802.) The 'real tendency' and 'true moral' of *Resolution and*

Independence, together with the 'spirit in which it was written', make it clear that *Resolution and Independence* was meant to be important and general. If we cannot find it to be either, its failure must be judged to be more than technical; nothing in the poem will survive that failure of intention. However, I address myself here to readers for whom the poem does not so fail; wishing to examine more closely the grounds and conditions of its success.

The poem seems to begin artlessly enough, with a series of statements, in the specious present, that might be casual remarks introducing a very different kind of poem, 'lyrical' and careless of before and after. The shift to the past tense in III, going with the introduction of the poet (who brings in, though for the moment he has forgotten about them, 'all the ways of men, so vain and melancholy'), changes our sense of what the poem is to be; III, though so fully in the happy key of I and II, makes it certain that this key cannot honestly be maintained. Nevertheless, the opening stanzas play their part in our final impression. Their 'presentness' is quite right: as we can see if we turn them, for experimental purposes, into statements about the past. This *is* Nature is when Nature is happy; and there is, too, anticipatory contrast, not only between the happiness of Nature and the sudden sadness of Wordsworth, but between the bright light, the pleasant sounds, the gay movements of living creatures, and the sudden bareness, silence and stillness of the setting in which we see the leech-gatherer. (Compare the effect of 'Runs with her all the way, wherever she doth run' with 'And moveth all together, if it move at all'. Finally, when we go back to that opening having taken the poem as a whole, it seems a kind of proleptic clarification; Wordsworth, in 'laughing himself to scorn', laughs himself back to a happiness which is felt to be still there. The simple patterning of statements, then, turn out to be less artless than we might suppose from considering those stanzas in isolation. But the 'artless' effect is important; there is, we feel, no arranging; the objects of delight simply presented themselves so, freshly and naturally, in their innocent irresponsibility; their 'mirth' is not to be distinguished from the spectator's delighted motions of identification. The nature of *his* satisfaction is made explicit enough in one of Wordsworth's own pieces of 'practical criticism': 'The stock-dove is said to *coo*, a sound well imitating the note of the bird; but, by the intervention of the metaphor *broods*, the affections are called in by the imagination to assist in marking the manner in which the bird

reiterates and prolongs her soft note, as if herself delighting to
listen to it, and participating of a still and quiet satisfaction, like
that which may be supposed inseparable from the continous process of incubation.' (Preface to Poems, 1815.)

The satisfactions of I–III – those of Nature indistinguishable
from those of the poet ('with joy' in III can be taken indifferently
with 'the hare that raced about' or 'I saw') – are explicitly associated with childhood ('as happy as a boy')– so that we cannot say,
when we reach 'all the ways of men' at the end of III, whether the
'old remembrances' suggest to the poet the contrast between
'men' and Nature or the contrast between 'men' and boys;
clearly intending to remind himself of the former, he succeeds all
the more in reminding us of the latter. Thus in V the skylark, like
the hare, is no doubt a 'Child of earth' irrespective of its age; so
are human beings; but in view of what has gone we are inclined to
give a slight extra stress to 'Child'. It is a commonplace that
Wordsworth (as in *Tintern Abbey* and *The Prelude*) associates
Nature with the Child; but the association here, taken with the
emphasis laid on the problems of adult living in VI, introduces
a *kind* of contrast with the Man unusual in Wordsworth.
For *Resolution and Independence* sets forth the recognition of a
fact of moral experience without which there cannot be full
maturity; that is, a successful emergence from the world of the
Child.

But though the critical attitude towards a prolonged childhood
is felt in the gloomy anticipations of V ('Solitude, pain of heart,
distress and poverty') and the retrospect and self-searchings of
VI, the transition to the Poets in VII ('Poets' cannot be poets
without an ability to recapture the emotions of the Child) states it,
if not ambiguously, at any rate with some doubt. Chatterton – of
whom Wordsworth, in his prose moods, had no very high
opinion – was only a Boy ('It is wonderful,' said Johnson, 'how
the whelp has written such things') but 'marvellous'; 'The sleep-
less Soul' cannot mainly mean his insomnia due to guilt at being
found out, it is the Poet's eternal alertness that is relevant here;
'perished in his pride' might imply a doubt about the moral
legitimacy of Chatterton's suicide, but the line sounds triumphant
in itself, and it leads into the quite unequivocal 'glory and joy' of
Burns, which cannot be separated from his 'Following his plough'
as a child of Nature. The fifth line 'By our own spirits are we
deified' therefore comes in oddly – oddly when we ask ourselves

just what, for all its familiarity, it means. It serves its purpose, however; without it, the stanza would run the risk of smugness ('We Poets'); just being a Poet, and young, and glad, is enough to bring on eventually 'despondency' and 'madness' (why 'madness', we might ask?). 'Our own spirits', however, brings in the essential criticism, and, through 'deified', prepares the way for the surprising 'madness', while retroactively qualifying 'pride', 'glory', and 'joy'; one's spirits here are one's genius, or one's conviction of it, but 'spirits' also suggests the dispositional 'genial faith' and the more ephemeral 'high spirits'; the line condenses a fundamental criticism of Romantic poetry all the more effectively because embedded in a Romantic stanza.

The turning-point of the poem, VIII, gives us an immediate contrast, in its Wordsworthian tentativeness and embarrassed syntax, with the rhetorical, poetical verse of VII; the 'peculiar grace' and the 'eye of heaven', carrying a further criticism of 'deified'; the Poet has disappeared from the centre of interest in this stanza, with its characteristic starkness; in the next, there is nothing human at the centre at all. Of the two famous similes which occupy IX, Wordsworth observes: 'In these images, the conferring, the abstracting, and the modifying powers of the Imagination, immediately and mediately acting, are all brought into conjunction. The stone is endowed with something of the power of life to approximate it to the sea-beast; and the sea-beast stripped of some of its vital qualities to assimilate it to the stone; which intermediate image is thus treated for the purpose of bringing the original image, that of the stone, to a nearer resemblance to the figure and condition of the aged Man; who is divested of so much of the indication of life and motion as to bring him to the point where the two objects unite and coalesce in comparison.' (Preface to Poems, 1815.) Wordsworth indicates by what in such a context are themselves unusual metaphors ('stripped' and 'divested') the working here of his metaphoric technique. It achieves an effect, after the explicit emotionalism, the exhilarations and depressions ('joy' and 'dejection') in the first part of the poem, of an extraordinary dehumanization and spareness. 'Beside a pool bare to the eye of heaven' – that 'bare' is the key-word (cf. 'Couched on the bald top of an eminence'). Something existing by itself, obedient to its own mysterious laws, totally independent of the onlooker – this single figure now fills up the landscape that had formerly been so populous with 'blissful creatures'; that now, we realize for the first time, is a 'lonely place'. Instead of the meta-phoric language 'clothing' the thought (as we should normally say) it seems to operate by a process of 'stripping' and 'divesting'. Even what might seem merely an ungainly Wordsworthianism, 'The oldest man he seemed that ever *wore* grey hairs', perhaps helps, by the negative suggestion of 'wore', to reinforce 'bare to the eye of heaven'. It is the mere existence of the old Man which is so impressive (speaking of an earlier version of this stanza, in which Wordsworth indulged his 'mystical feeling for the verb "to be" – By which the old Man *was*', etc., the poet laid great stress on the importance, for his purposes, of the sudden unexplained appearance of this being in his primal simplicity). And it is this mere existence which the odd similes of IX co-operate to define. The first simile, indeed, if followed through strictly with an eye to its prose content, compares the old Man to something that only '*seems* a thing endued with sense'. The father-figure unquestion-ably is present, but we do not yet know in which of his embodi-ments; he seems certainly to be 'from some far region sent', but we do not yet know just what his 'apt admonishment' will be: it might be something terrifying. The 'huge stone', 'Couched on the bald top of an eminence', so that we don't know how it got there, and the 'sea-beast crawled forth', while serving, as Wordsworth says, to establish the intermediate status of the old Man, are themselves evocative of something nearer terror than awe.

In X the old Man is still impressive, but is now a recognizable, if very Wordsworthian, human being, a character of the *Prelude*, with the 'more than human weight' of his past upon him. That 'more than human', while seeming to make a greater claim on our capacity for awe than the non-human similes of IX, actually makes less; it prepares us for the transition to XII–XV, the part of the poem that has been adversely criticized, but which is none the less not only justifiable but essential. The simile which concludes XI, while reminding us of the extreme difference between Words-worth's sensibility and Shelley's, serves two purposes; its idio-syncrasy helps to reinforce the oddity of the pervious similes of the stone and the sea-beast, but in being so much less disturbing, it induces our acceptance of the old Man as a simple, dignified, and patient human figure, a 'resigned solitary'; and in 'That heareth not the loud winds when they call' we have both a direct evocation (again by negative suggestion) of the old Man, and a subtle hint of the imperious emotional demand of the poet (compare XVII, 'Perplexed, and longing to be comforted, My question eagerly did I renew'). The old Man is by now a recognizable old Man – however cloud-like, he has more than a figurative 'human weight': 'Himself he *propped*, limbs, body, and pale face, Upon a long grey staff of shaven wood' – 'propped', taken with the simile that closes the stanza, is an important word, helping as it does to counteract some part of the effect of 'cloud', and giving a prosaic grounding to the summing-up line, 'And moveth all together, if it move at all'.

The 'conversation' which follows brings forcibly to our attention the criticism levelled at *Resolution and Independence*. Coleridge, in illustration of his general thesis about Wordsworth, complains (in the *Biographia Literaria*) of the incongruities of style; citing the contrast between the diction of XVII and XIX on the one hand, and XVIII ('Yet still I persevere, and find them where I may') on the other. Admittedly, he had an earlier, and still more prosy version of XVIII in mind; as well as lines, later cancelled, such as

> Close by a pond, upon the further side,
> He stood alone; a minute's space, I guess,
> I watched him, he continuing motionless;
> To the pool's further margin then I drew,
> He being all the while before me full in view.

('The metre,' Coleridge had remarked a little earlier, 'merely reminds the reader of his claims in order to disappoint them.') But it seems a very unintelligent reading of the poem as it stands that merely finds in the manner of XII–XV and XIX-XX a Wordsworthian lapse into prosaicism. The awkwardnesses have point; but a point that cannot be brought out if one confines oneself to considering proprieties of diction. The mode of *Resolution and Independence,* as a whole has to be understood. *Resolution and Independence* is a poem which casts some doubt on the theory, made current by I. A. Richards in *The Principles of Literary Criticism,* that great poetry must in some way immunize itself to irony, by 'containing' or neutralizing unsympathetic reactions, or by anticipating them. The corollary to this theory, the great poems cannot be successfully parodied, is almost made to seem doubtful. For *Resolution and Independence* has been successfully parodied, by Lewis Carroll; and no doubt the parody, in its final form (in *Through the Looking Glass*), makes a pointed comic criticism of the poet's self-absorption and his tactlessness, and of the poem's superficial in-consequence. But when you enjoy the parody, and take its point, you cannot feel that it damages the original. To understand the mood and intention of *Resolution and Independence* is to see why it is not an adverse or qualifying criticism to admit that it contains no irony or humour, or that it is open to parody.

The justification for the banalities and gawkinesses of the central stanzas can be brought out by way of considering a parody of them that does not, on the whole, come off, though it is amusing; the earlier version (1856) of Lewis Carroll's *Looking Glass* parody. (Its author thought that its 'appearance' must be 'painful . . . to the admirers of Wordsworth and his poem of Resolution and Independence'.) The earlier version is much more severe on what, in speaking of the 'White Knight' parody, I called Words-worth's tactlessness; what is burlesqued here is patronizing snob-bery and a comically brutal egotism and self-preoccupation.

> I met an aged, aged man
>   Upon the lonely moor:
> I knew I was a gentleman,
>   And he was but a boor.

(Yet compare 'But now a stranger's privilege I took'); Words-worth's approach, and his handling of the spoken dialogue, are no doubt comically ungainly, but the whole point is that the old Man isn't a boor ('solemn order', 'lofty utterance', 'choice word and measured phrase', 'a stately speech', etc.). And Wordsworth shows no condescension towards him, rather a bewildered and at first only half-comprehending respectfulness.

> I did not hear a word he said,
>   But kicked that old man calm,
> And said, 'Come, tell me how you live!'
>   And pinched him in the arm.

This had more point, in so far as it fixes upon the inanity of Wordsworth's question. 'How is it that you live, and what is it you do?' *is* a flat line, and it does not cease to be flat when we see why it is there; but we need not find the poet's insistence ('My question eagerly did I renew') a complacent Wordsworthian in-dulgence of the kind here satirized. Wordsworth's personal need, his demand for reassurance, issuing in that oddly inappropriate question, is not so much for a reassurance *from* the old Man as for

a reassurance *about* the old Man. When this is realized, the pro-
saicisms seem quite justified; they perform an essential function, in
contrasting the public world of everyday human experience and
human endurance with the inner world into which Wordsworth
has taken the figure of the leech-gatherer, and made of it a quantity
which cannot be apprehended without uncertainty and dread.

> While he was talking thus, the lonely place,
> The old Man's shape, and speech – all troubled me;

'Troubled' is the key word here. The significance of the old Man –
one that is not finally grasped till the last stanza – is a very personal significance for the poet; there is no hint of anything like the
self-indulgence of

> I knew I was a gentleman,
> And he was but a boor.

– whatever we may think about some other short poems of
Wordsworth. And we might note that in the later version of the
parody (in *Through the Looking Glass*) the 'Wordsworth' figure becomes a sympathetic character (the White Knight) and many of
the satiric touches are softened into fantasy: so that many readers
have enjoyed it without realizing that it is a parody at all.

The movement of the later part of *Resolution and Independence*
may now be summarized. The old Man in XIII–XV, now seen in
close-up, is a credible figure, with his endurance, and his simple
dignity (the victim of 'an unjust state of society', Wordsworth remarked in a letter defending the poem). He stands for an important
element in Wordsworth's own temperament and character; Walter
Pater used the expression from XIV, 'grave Livers', to suggest the
social and moral habit of Wordsworthian verse. We might say,
indeed, that the poem as a whole gives us the two contrasting
aspects of Wordsworth himself: his strength of character and
prosaic simplicity in the leech-gatherer, his 'blank misgiving of a
creature' and sense of 'unknown modes of being' in the poet-
interlocutor. The conclusion of the poem gives us the reconciliation or 'resolution' of the two attitudes: an achieved integrity.

The way in which the resolution is effected is characteristic.
The mood of XVI – standing, as it does, in extreme and plainly
deliberate contrast with XV – is the reversion to the experience of
the stanzas in which the old Man first appears; he is an internalized
figure, of uncertain significance:

> And the whole body of the Man did seem
> Like one whom I had met with in a dream.

His voice is 'like a stream Scarce heard'; the simile associates him again with the non-human. But by now we have, as we had not in IX, an alternative estimate of him to set against that. Wordsworth, we know, attached great importance to the trance-like condition described in XVI; but, even if we agree with Mr. F. W. Bateson that he was mistaken in so doing, we can see the dramatic effect of the contrasting stanzas XV and XVI; the contrast, we note, is repeated in the juxtaposing of XVIII and XIX:

> While I these thoughts within myself pursued,
> He, having made a pause, the same discourse renewed.

The 'troubling' and uncertain significance of the old Man is one appropriate to the child's vision; the 'admonition' he represents to the child is morally ambiguous and disturbing. Recognition of the real nature of the 'admonition' – what the old Man really is and stands for – means achievement of 'so firm a mind'; the 'true moral' of the poem is not only that awareness of the greater suffering of others helps one to deal with one's own, but that *achieving* that awareness – that recognition of others' 'independence' of one's own fantasies, and of what one's fantasies make of them – is itself a moral discovery of the greatest importance: so that the last stanza comes with both a resolving and a validating effect. The old Man, existing in his own right, is himself a 'help' and 'stay' against the encroachments of fantasy; his solidity is guaranteed by the firmness and rectitude of that placid verse.

Resolution and Independence, then, has a structure, and it is this structure which makes it a successful and public poem. Properly viewed, the incongruities disappear, or seem to be functional; the artlessness and clumsiness serve to highlight, to dramatize a contrast which the poem intends to bring out (the 'Two Voices' in the same poem); they are intentionally set against a formal deliberateness of manner so noticeable that it suggests a stylization: one based upon a personal rehandling of the medium of Spenser.

The setting and presentation of the old Man may, indeed, show the influence of Spenser's Despair. But the significance of the leech-gatherer for Wordsworth is not only that he stands, of course, for something quite other than Despair, but that, in an important sense, he does not 'stand for' anything, but is just a normal and natural, though exceptionally dignified, patient, and resolute, human being. This is quite as important as the more obvious 'message' of the poem; and plays quite as large a part in the type-experience which the poem describes. But even if we take from it only the more obvious message (as Mr. Empson puts it, 'The endurance of the leech-gatherer gives Wordsworth strength to face the pain of the world') we are taking what is certainly there, and what, even stated abstractly, is by no means contemptible.

> He had also dim recollections
> Of pedlars tramping on their rounds;
> Milk-pans, and pails; and odd collections
> Of saws, and proverbs; and reflections
> Old parsons make in burying-grounds.

Shelley's smile is justified; but this element is essential to *Resolution and Independence*; it is part of Wordsworth's sanity and strength.

1955

XI

WORDSWORTH AFTER 1803

If the second volume of Mrs. Moorman's biography of Wordsworth,[1] dealing as it does with the poet's later years, is not in any
way dull, this must in part be credited to the biographer herself.
Scrupulous, dignified, yet often humorous, her narrative must
surely provide the standard life for our time. Completing it with
such satisfying serenity, Mrs. Moorman thus becomes the latest
and not the least distinguished of that band of devoted ladies, beginning with his wife and sister and sister-in-law, who first pro-
tected and ministered to Wordsworth during his years in the body,
and have continued to serve him faithfully in his life beyond. It is
quite in keeping that, like the Wordsworth ladies, Mrs. Moorman
should combine respect for the genius of the poet with a by no
means uncritical or solemnly reverent attitude towards the
crotchets of the man. This is family history at its best, appropriate
to a writer like Wordsworth, who is so personal, so rooted in the
familial, the domestic, the local.

The intensely personal quality of Wordsworth's poetry has its
problems for critics today. If we play it down, we are in danger of
being left with a Victorian-homiletic view of Wordsworth which
has little attractions for the modern: we cannot dwell with pleasure
on the belief, so profitable to hoteliers, that there is a close association between mountain scenery and moral uplift. On the other
hand, if we stress the intimate involvement of Wordsworth's best
poetry with his own private problems, we may find ourselves
handing him over to psychological biographers who, like Mr.
F. W. Bateson, seem to be rather unsympathetic with him and to

---

[1] (Mary Moorman,) *William Wordsworth: A Biography: The Later Years
1803–1850*, O.U.P., 1965.

K

feel that he offers us merely, or mainly, documentation of the case-history of a neurotic. We remember Mr. Bateson's insistence on the over-intense love of Wordsworth and Dorothy, and the crisis he believes it provoked in their lives, as crucially relevant to the interpretation of the 'Lucy' poems and to Wordsworth's later development.

The critical problem is clearly not a simple one. At any rate, we may observe that even the unsympathetic Mr. Bateson grants that the *tendency* of Wordsworth's genius – however much this tendency may have been diverted or obstructed – was towards sanity, gaiety, and health. And that the critical problem should be so interesting is itself a testimony to the power of Wordsworth's genius, his peculiar command over words.

It is true that when Mrs. Moorman resumes her narrative Wordsworth's poetic prime, the 'great decade', is almost half-way over. Most of her book is devoted to those long years during which Wordsworth wrote few great poems. But the later Wordsworth turns out not to be at all dull. One of the great themes of his poetry, as is well known, is the search for what gives unity and meaning to a human life; 'the child is father of the man'; and the essential unity of Wordsworth's life and character reveals itself again and again in these later, less poetically fruitful years. The total effect is not so much of a blaze of genius followed by a prolonged sad decline, but of a satisfying completeness. So it is with our memories of the poetry. At first Wordsworth's work might seem incomplete, amorphous; he left no central masterpiece about which the lesser things gather. It might be thought appropriate that his most considerable poem should be entitled (though not by him) *The Prelude*. And, recalling two of its finest lines:

> The ante-chapel, where the statue stood
> Of Newton, with his prism and silent face –

we might think of Wordsworth's own poetry as only the ante-chapel to the great cathedral he never built. We remember, too, the unfinished sheepfold with which *Michael* poignantly closes. But to think of *Michael* is not, after all, to think of failure. The poem finely realizes its Wordsworthian themes, based as it is, in the poet's own words, on two of the most powerful affections of the human heart; the parental affection, and the love of property, *landed* property, including the feeling of inheritance, home, and personal and family independence. We have thus something affirmative of Wordsworth's own achievement in the old man's struggle to build in that grey landscape, where the stone villages reflect that mysterious unity of man and his environment which was to afford Wordsworth his least forced perception of the enduring.

Mrs. Moorman's second volume opens with a scene of domestic happiness and creative activity.

> What want we? have we not perpetual streams,
> Warm woods, and sunny hills, and fresh green fields,
> And mountains not less green, and flocks, and herds,
> And thickets full of songsters, and the voice
> Of lordly birds, an unexpected sound
> Heard now and then from morn till latest eve,
> Admonishing the man who walks below
> Of solitude, and silence in the sky?

Even if the recovery from the mental suffering of the previous decade brought with it a decrease in poetic sensitivity, a temptation to the public rhetorical note, Wordsworth's poetry in these early years of the new century is still impressive. The year 1803 saw Wordsworth, happily married, at work on *The Prelude*, the 'Immortality' Ode, the *Ode to Duty*. The death by drowning of John Wordsworth (February 1805) came as an utterly shocking disaster to this contented recluse in his close-knit family group. It was not only a cruel blow to William as a brother; it brought home to him a certain hard, cold, self-centred quality in his sensibility as a poet. He became more fully conscious of how far his peculiar gift cut him off from other men; so that even tragic loss could be welcomed (as he suggests in his poem *Peele Castle*) in so far as it united him with them.

This family disaster also brought home to Wordsworth, as it does to the student of his poetry, the problem of his attitude to Christianity. That the attraction towards 'piety' in a traditional sense was a quite reasonable development of his 'natural piety', we need not doubt. But the characteristic doctrines of Christianity he may have recognized more as fulfilling a need for other men than for himself. He was to tell Crabb Robinson in 1812: 'I can feel more sympathy with the orthodox believer who needs a Redeemer and who, sensible of his own demerits, flies for refuge to Him (though perhaps I do not want one for myself) than with the cold and rational notions of the Unitarians.'

The parenthesis prompts a comment on something over and above the level of church-going: the profound *this-worldliness* of Wordsworth. Without that quality there could not have been Wordsworth's distinctive task, and his distinctive theme, as a poet: the attempt to locate, in *this* world, the 'very world', where happiness lies; to 'demythologize' the ancient conception of Heaven, by realizing it in poetry as a spiritual dimension in *this* life. But it is plain that tragic death, the apparently pointless destruction of the good, is the greatest possible challenge to this secular faith. And the death of John seems to have its bearings on Wordsworth's sporadic efforts to convince himself of another kind of 'immortality' and to make himself a Christian in more than a conventional sense.

For, if Wordsworth's theme of happiness is inseparable from his concern for spiritual health, we must also note that the latter is in turn inseparable, for him, from bodily vigour. No poet excels him in the power of rendering this; and when we are considering the religious question in Wordsworth, the question of ultimates, we should also remember passages like that in Book IV of *The Excursion*:

> Oh! what a joy it were, in vigorous health
> To have a body . . .
> And to the elements surrender it
> As if it were a spirit.

Raleigh drew attention to the stark contrast of this to Claudio's great speech in *Measure for Measure*. (. . . 'Or be imprisoned in the viewless winds . . .')

Wordsworth's self-reproach in *Peele Castle* has its relevance to the interpretation of *The Prelude*, and of his poetry generally. There does seem to have been something chilly and self-absorbed about the young Wordsworth. How powerful, then, we reflect, must have been that passionate love for Annette which drew him out of himself; which, with decent reticence, he could allude to only obliquely in *The Prelude*; but which must have been closely associated with that equally self-releasing impulse of generous idealism which *The Prelude* does record, the dawn of the French Revolution when it was bliss to be alive, and to be young was very heaven.

Mrs. Moorman does not shirk Wordsworth's reversion to self-centredness, nor the allied problem, which alternately puzzled, amused, or irritated his contemporaries: his egotism. This topic is not a simple one. Wordsworth's creative genius is intimately bound up with his way of using the word 'I' – a word so simple to use, so baffling to think about. His sense of the unfathomable depths of the mind, the ego, unforgettably stated in the opening of *The Recluse*, is pervasive in his best poetry. His greatness appears in the unmistakable note with which he speaks of

> Those forests unapproachable by death,
> That shall endure as long as man endures
> To think, to hope, to worship and to feel,
> To struggle, to be lost within himself
> In trepidation, from the blank abyss
> To look with bodily eyes and be consoled.

He would not be Wordsworth without it; and yet . . . Keats found a great phrase, summing up the blend of admiration and censure which we cannot but feel, in the presence of his unflagging solemn self-preoccupation: 'the egotistical sublime'. Censure there must be; we cannot ignore the ordinary moral meaning of the word egotism. But in mitigation we must remember that few original geniuses have ever been met with such derision and incomprehension. It persists to this day; in an English child of educated parents, to laugh at some of Wordsworth's simpler poems has almost become a criterion for the attainment of the age of reason. And this is understandable: Wordsworth is a *strange* poet. (Pater's essay brings out this strangeness better than Arnold's.)

The other chief human problem for the Wordsworth of the later years and for his admirers, is his relationship with Coleridge. Mrs. Moorman's second volume, in the nature of the case, cannot bring out, as the first could, how complementary Coleridge's genius was to Wordsworth's. Coleridge's poetic temperament was what Wordsworth's typically was not: warm, labile, prompt to respond emotionally. The sun often shines in Wordsworth's poetry, but it never seems warm; the atmosphere, if bracing, is cold. The different sensibilities, of course, go with different intellectual and moral qualities. In the great period it is difficult to say which of the two poets owed more to the other.

Yet Wordsworth always retained an inner independence. Meditative as he was, his mind was radically unphilosophical. We remember the beautiful emblem of the sea-shell in Book IV of *The Excursion*. The child there, applying the shell to his ear, hears it express 'mysterious union with its native sea'. So by analogy the universe itself, to the ear of faith, supplies

> Authentic tidings of invisible things,
> Of ebb and flow, and ever-during power;
> And central peace, subsisting at the heart
> Of endless agitation.

But the sounds one hears in a sea-shell are not really the waves of the sea but sounds in one's own head. Would this have invalidated his parable for Wordsworth? Surely not. To Coleridge's despair, Wordsworth would never take a firm stand on the 'realist/projective' issue. Forced into a corner, perhaps, he might have committed himself to the 'projective' view. But it did not really matter to him. Metaphysics was not his business.

The close association of those contrasting yet complementary geniuses was a great moment for English poetry. But in the period covered by Mrs. Moorman's second volume Coleridge is, inevitably, a disharmonious and tragic figure. The years 1806–7 already foreshadow the poets' estrangement of 1810–13. Coleridge ill in body and mind, was obsessed with Sara (the one he loved, not the one he married). His sick soul conceived a jealousy about Wordsworth's relations with her which he knew to be phantasmal, but which none the less tormented him. The old atmosphere of confidence and affection was gone. Coleridge was suspicious, irritable and resentful. Mrs. Moorman brings out how impossibly great were his emotional demands on that household – too great, for all their capacities for deep love. It is against this background that the famous breach between Wordsworth and Coleridge must be seen. Mrs. Moorman describes it with care and sympathy for all involved. All that need be said is that, if Wordsworth does not come 'perfectly' out of it, he comes out of it much better than it is common to suppose. Only those who are prepared to pronounce confidently on what would have been 'right', in this seemingly impossible situation, can dare to judge him.

Over the years we see Wordsworth still tinkering with *The Recluse*, the poem that Coleridge so much wanted him to write. Coleridge regarded Wordsworth's turning to prose, in the tract on the convention of Cintra, as a 'self-robbery' from the great philosophical poem. Yet this oracular impassioned prose is vitally and centrally Wordsworthian in thought and feeling, just as much as its prophetic-tragic idealism is Miltonic. Wordsworth, like Milton, with all his patriotism, felt that there was one great battle that had not been won by England: the battle against selfishness, materialism, spiritual obtuseness. The tract once again shows the unity of the later with the earlier Wordsworth. The poet, having once found it, never lost his insight into national feeling – in this case – the national feeling of the Spaniards – as one of the great basic human impulses.

The Cintra tract shows how superficial is the account of Wordsworth as a 'revolutionary' who became a 'reactionary'. It is still the work of the same man as he who, fifteen years before, had written so passionately against the smug complacency of the Bishop of Llandaff. Mrs. Moorman remarks that in his republican period Wordsworth was influenced by French political philosophers, who in their turn derived from seventeenth-century English Puritan republicans, After 1794 Wordsworth had given up republicanism; but his thought remained continuous with that of Milton and the thinkers close to him.

On Wordsworth's political thought in general Mrs. Moorman is shrewd and sensible. She does not attempt to explain away his reactionary politics, but she relates them to his deep convictions and his prophetic idealism as well as to his pessimism. Of his activities during the election of 1818 she says that: 'he knew the wine was new, but he refused to attempt to put it into anything but old bottles. The maintenance of the "landed interest" and an Anglican monopoly of education were his only remedies – and they were not enough'. One has the impression that Wordsworth's convictions about the ends of politics did not change much during his adult life; what changed was his feeling about means.

The Excursion, which reveals the fundamentally humane and decent intention of Wordsworth's political and social thought, unfortunately reveals also its failure to engage his profoundest poetic impulses. Prolix and repetitious, 'an eddying instead of progression of thought', as Coleridge said, it has no creative theme. The story of Margaret in Book I, written at Racedown and Alfoxden long before, is cruelly damaging to the Pastor's churchyard tales; it has that personal poignancy and simplicity which they have not. Wordsworth had once written;

Yet why repine, created as we are
For joy and rest, albeit to find them only
Lodged in the bosom of eternal things?

But what 'eternal things' he can or cannot render is not, for a poet, a matter of will and choice.

The completion of *The Excursion* (1812), felt then as now by Wordsworth's admirers to be a disappointment; the acquisition of Rydal Mount, and Wordsworth's becoming a civil servant; the deaths of two of his children – these were among the landmarks of the middle years. Wordsworth's opinions and character were by then thoroughly formed, not to say hardened. But they are still often misrepresented. Thus, it is not uncommon to find the man who had loved Annette described as having become, in later life, a vindictive puritan. Mrs. Moorman has some helpful material here. She recounts how shocked was the free-thinking Harriet Martineau at Wordsworth's ignoring the 'sensual vice' that abounded in rural districts. But the author of *Peter Bell* and *The Waggoner* had no illusions about the people of rural districts nor did he think 'sensual vice' necessarily the most soul-destroying of sins. And in this connexion it is interesting to read Mrs. Moorman's account of the great prose apologetic which Wordsworth was stirred to write in 1815 for the fame and character of Robert Burns: 'I pity him who cannot perceive that in all this [Burns's poetry], though there was no moral purpose, there is a moral effect'. It is this work which contains the astonishing remark that in Burns 'conjugal fidelity archly bends to the service of general benevolence'. This seems the moment to observe that Wordsworth, if a 'puritan', was very much in an English puritan tradition, humane and unprudish. This tradition differed from the puritanism of New England. It differed also from the Jacobin puritans of 1793 and 1794, for whose régime of Virtue and Terror Wordsworth felt nothing but repugnance.

The apologia for Burns was not, as Mrs. Moorman points out, merely a disinterested defence of a poet Wordsworth always loved. He was defending himself, getting back at his own impercipient critics, notably Jeffrey. This was perhaps unwise and undignified. Certainly Wordsworth was right to attack the obtuseness of his critics. But would not he have done better to ignore them and, instead, pay more attention to the latent critic within his own breast? True, the purity of Wordsworth's writing often suggests a wholly admirable innocence, an indifference to the pressure of social or literary conventionality, without which we could not have had the wonderful serene beauty of poems like *Ruth*. Yet much of *The Prelude* is dull because Wordsworth is not employing his critical faculty; not only in the obvious sense that, in his self-preoccupation, he is treating the banal in the same solemn tone as he treats the profound, but in a more important sense: the poetic manner he chooses prevents him from giving rein to the critical and satirical impulses within himself – which there is every reason to believe were quite strong.

Mrs. Moorman treats Wordsworth's old age with tact and dignity. The picture is not altogether mellow. For one thing, Wordsworth's already mentioned impatience with adverse criticism (even that of Coleridge in the *Biographia Literaria*), his far from harmonious relations with the younger generation of writers, combine with his dislike of the new industrial and commercial age to produce an effect of gloomy harshness. This is the Wordsworth that Carlyle saw: 'His face bore marks of much, not always peaceful meditation, the look of it not bland or benevolent so much as close, impregnable and hard.'

Then there are the illnesses and the deaths of those dear to him, inevitable misfortunes to a man who lives long, but none the less painful. Particularly sad to read about is the long-drawn-out living death of Dorothy, suffering from some form of arteriosclerosis, the nimble vital spirit of the *Journal* now an old woman, living in a timeless mental world of second childhood, crouched over a fire – Nature's cruel betrayal of the heart that loved her. By now we are looking at the old Wordsworth, famous, reciting sonnets to visitors, receiving the Poet Laureateship as a late coronal. This was in 1843; it was in 1835 that Wordsworth had written his last great poem, the *Extempore Effusion*, the dirge on Scott, Hogg, Coleridge, Crabbe, Lamb. He was to be spared for fifteen years more, till the quiet end.

All that can be said in criticism of Mrs. Moorman's work – if this *is* a criticism – is that it rarely brings out just why Wordsworth repays the composition of so long and full a biography. She could do this more easily in Volume I, with *The Prelude* to help her; in most of the period covered by Volume II there is no equivalent work to prop up with prose scaffolding. Her commentary is a little external. Mr. Salvesen's *The Landscape of Memory*,[1]

[1] *The Landscape of Memory*, Arnold, London, 1951.

in its own mode of commentary, is concerned with the inward life of Wordsworth, the life that matters most to readers of his poetry. He brings together the context of Wordsworth's preoccupation with memory, the continuity of the self, and the 'personal time' – the 'personal past' – of his poetry. The difference between the two books may be put like this: we are often moved in reading Mrs. Moorman, to remember the famous words about 'emotion recollected in tranquillity'; many of Mr. Salvesen's quotations bring to mind the less quoted words that come later: '. . . the tranquillity gradually disappears'. Memory, for the Wordsworth of the great period, was no mere idle reverie, but a mental discipline; almost a spiritual exercise.

Mr. Salvesen, having established his general approach in an introductory chapter, goes on to deal with the influence of Picturesque values and principles on Wordsworth's of seeing, more immediate, less literary; visual and sensuous still, perhaps, but not 'objective' or pictorial. His 'landscapes' reveal his sense of the unifying force of nature; they are not detailed; the feeling of a place is given through the emotions, rather than the senses. Wordsworth feels the landscape as a presence; *feels* it rather than *sees* it; he learnt to master what he came to think his over-dominant sense of sight. He *becomes* part of the landscape he is evoking. Wordsworth's 'descriptions', then, are of inner landscapes, countries of the mind. The Picturesque had been useful to him, as providing *some* sort of discipline of vision. But Wordsworth was to work out his own mode of disciplined contemplation. This was the 'wise passiveness' he cultivated, the passiveness dramatized in the story of the White Doe. And it was the poetic value of memory which provided the 'strength in what remains behind' for the aging poet of the 'Immortality' Ode. The vivacity of Wordsworth's memory is the subject of many anecdotes. It is closely connected with the 'physical' element in his poetic sensibility. Memories acquired a sensuous immediacy for him; he had a body-feeling for them as tangible things, things which impress and *press* upon us.

Mr. Salvesen describes well what came to be the ideal landscape for Wordsworth; the 'Hartleap Well' landscape, where every tree, every hillock, every pond, every mound of turf, every growth of moss, takes on an admonitory quality. Such is the landscape setting of a 'Michael' or a 'Brothers', 'out of time', outside the main stream of human activity; the 'hidden valley' of *Michael*, the re-

mote mountain churchyard of *The Brothers*. Whether one is looking to the past or to the future, the plot of earth on which one
stands remains important. So Wordsworth attributes a spiritual
value to Michael's feeling for his little bit of land; what he himself
felt about spiritual landscapes, he makes a Dalesman feel about
actual landed property.

Wordsworth is not only interested in the personal past but in
the historic past, as we see in *The Prelude* (especially Book VIII).
In London, he says, with characteristic imagery:

> A weight of Ages did at once descend
> Upon my heart; no thought embodied, no
> Distinct remembrances; but weight and power,
> Power growing with the weight.

But above all he relates a man's sense of his own living process to the great rhythm of nature, the circling of the earth;
finding an ultimate calm in the endless repetition, the assured
circle which is nature's time. Mr. Salvesen here shows convincingly that the object of Wordsworth's use of memory was
the release from time; the achievement through poetry of a
'passive stillness' which seems both to be within time and to
transcend it.

The question of literary criticism which Mr. Salvesen, if not
quite begging it, rather side-steps is: how much is Wordsworth's
personal poetry *limited* by its emotional vividness being usually
confined to these recollections of childhood and youth? It is a
commonplace that Wordsworth's longing for nature was closely
connected with his regret for childhood, as a lost world of
innocence and harmony. *The Prelude* might, with as much
appropriateness as Milton's poem, have been entitled *Paradise
Lost*. Do we feel that Wordsworth's poetry is less effective when
it deals with the adult world in which Wordsworth seeks to
persuade himself and others that he has found his paradise
regained? For this seems the case, on the evidence presented by
Mr. Salvesen. Mr. Salvesen's own uncertainties as a critic come
out here. He is too close to Wordsworth. Self-effacingness in
an interpreter is a real and a not too common merit. But Mr.
Salvesen is *too* unobtrusive. The exact 'hue' of Wordsworth's
poetry is not brought out when it is placed in a context of precisely
the same hue.

Yet *The Landscape of Memory*, in its quiet way, is a good book.

The self-effacement of its author allows the voice, or voices, of
Wordsworth to sound singularly pure:

> I stood . . .
> Within the area of the frozen vale,
> Mine eye subdued and quiet as the ear
> Of one that listens . . .
>
> O joy! that in our embers
> Is something that doth live,
> That nature yet remembers
> What was so fugitive!

We hear the poet himself, wandering about the road and fields
speaking his poetry aloud, 'like a river murmuring and talking to
itself', as he says in *The Prelude*. Even if we were to be more ruthless than Mr. Salvesen is about the elusive or woolly quality of
much of Wordsworth's meditative verse, we can never deny him
the power to fix for ever the glowing moments in a man's early
life, with a purity which a Rousseau or a Hazlitt, with whom Mr.
Salvesen compares him, could never have achieved.

Mr. Salvesen, with the tact which distinguishes his work
throughout, does not discuss anything later than the *White Doe*.
Few modern critics, with the exception of Mr. John Jones in *The
Egotistical Sublime*, have explored the large terrain of Wordsworth's later poetry. There is much more in it, we may agree with
Mr. Jones, than the 'old half-witted sheep' of J. K. Stephen's
parody. For one thing, it is more varied in style, ranging from re-
sumptions of various eighteenth-century modes, to effects which
curiously anticipate the artificialities of a modern poet like
Wallace Stevens. What is rare in it is the distinction and above all
the sensitiveness of the sonnet 'Surprised by joy' (the most moving of all Wordsworth's sonnets) or of the best in the 'Duddon'
series.

And bringing Mr. Salvesen's subject together with Mrs.
Moorman's we may regret, finally, that he says so little, about the
'Duddon' sonnets. These are comparatively late; yet they belong
to the essential Wordsworth. And one of them might have
provided the epigraph for Mr. Salvesen's book; showing as it
does Wordsworth's characteristic delicate sensitiveness to the
'low voice', 'the whisper from the heart', with its final lovely
image:

From her unworthy seat, the cloudy stall
Of Time, breaks forth triumphant Memory;
Her glistening tresses bound, yet light and free
As golden locks of birch, that rise and fall
On gales that breathe too gently to recall
Aught of the fading year's inclemency!

1966

XII

BYRON AS POET

So to entitle an essay presupposes that Byron is a subject for
literary criticism. But this is not self-evident. Byron's biographers,
whether they go to work in the spirit of Mr. Quennell and Sir
Harold Nicolson, or in that of Mr. Wilson Knight, use his poetry
quite freely as direct evidence for a biographical thesis. And they
are justified in doing so: that, indeed, is the first critical observation to be made about Byron's poetry. Whatever reservations may
accompany the judgement that Byron is not essentially a *dramatic*
artist, it will surely be agreed that his genius was not such as to
issue, characteristically, in self-sufficient works of art containing in
themselves (in Coleridge's phrase) the reasons why they are so
and not otherwise. No clear line of demarcation can be drawn between discussion of 'the man', and discussion of 'the work':
Byron's personality is as much the subject for a critical essay on
Byron, as it is for a biography. Our sense of the individuality of
the artist is inseparable from our sense of the human case that
underlies the art. But this is not to grant that the critic need
concern himself much with the latest details of pathological
excavation; or even with 'author-psychology' as that is ordinarily
understood; since he is concerned, not so much with the reasons
for the peculiarities of Byron's poetry, as with their nature. To
describe this permits of no freer or looser approach than should
be adopted with any poet. And to produce at the same time the
analysis and judgement which a correct description entails, is at
once the purpose of, and the justification for, reference to Byron's
personality in a critical essay, that is, which attempts to communicate with the reader whose interest is in poetry and not,
primarily, in *Kulturgeschichte*, psycho-pathology, or scandal.

Not that an interest in Byron's poetry needs justifying at present; it suffers neither from neglect, nor excessive depreciation; Byron is not only read about, he is read: as much, I imagine, as any other English poet. (I mean, read by others besides professional students of poetry.) But there seems to be missing, in current appraisals of Byron, a determination to define his peculiar qualities as a poet, and, still more, a recognition that the defining is difficult. Biographical studies of various aspects of Byron, and phases of his life, have been amply provided; and they are certainly needed, perhaps more in Byron's case than in that of any other English poet; but the extant ones fail, it seems to me, in a respect which is important even to the student of his life, as distinct from his poetry; they do not convey something essential to the understanding of this man, in that they do not record any first-hand perception of why he is worth discussing, or how he should be discussed, other than as a psychological problem or a fascinating 'period' subject. And perhaps this lack of concentrated critical interest in Byron's poetry, that is, in the precise character of what it has to offer to us here and now in the twentieth century, may be correlated (in Quennell's and Nicolson's books at any rate) with their seeming want of profound sympathy with Byron as a person, or a sense of him as a human force.

No one could accuse Mr. Wilson Knight of this last deficiency. And if the book he plans to bring out on Byron's poetry has the quality of his lecture on *Byron's Dramatic Prose* (University of Nottingham, Byron Foundation Lecture 1953), our inward understanding of the poetic/prophetic character of the Pilgrim of Eternity will be much increased. What worries me in what he has said so far, is that *his* Byron, existing so completely on an apocalyptic dimension to which most of us can have but little access, not only seems to be without some familiar Byronic traits, but apparently communicates with his interpreter quite as satisfactorily in what are surely inferior poems, as in impressive ones. We must wait for Mr. Wilson Knight's coming book, before passing judgement; but one is a little worried, when things so varied in character, substance, and artistic merit are used so confidently to establish a thesis; the argument incurs more suspicion from the judicious admirer of Byron, than it would if it had been presented with more constant regard to the varying quality, significance, and value of the evidence. To bring out this variety is to recognize the need to discriminate and distinguish; and this recognition is as necessary to the critic as the warm sympathy and fullness of response which Mr. Wilson Knight's work shows so abundantly. If he is going to ask us to swallow Byron whole, I hope he will serve him up well seasoned with the salt of criticism.

The ideal spirit in which the critic of Byron should set about his task is well suggested, in my opinion, by these two quotations from a critic enjoying the peculiar advantages, as a critic writing in English on English poetry, of a European point of view: I am thinking of George Santayana, who showed in his criticism all the Latin virtues, without many of the Latin limitations. I quote here two passages from his letters, apropos of Byron; the first written when he was young, the second in later life. In a letter of 1887 he writes:

> I always have found a great difficulty in feeling the glow of admiration and the glow of loyalty towards the same persons. Admiration comes from qualities, and loyalty from obligations. What one admires are abstractions and sides of character, but one is loyal to the whole man, as to one who is knit into one's own life. Perhaps I ought to confess that I worship one hero, although as a man out of history he oughtn't to count. I mean Byron. Towards Byron, I do feel a combination of admiration and loyalty. I admire what he is in himself, and I am full of recognition for what he has been to me. For you must know, Byron is my first friend among the poets, and my favourite.[1]

That, of course, is the voice of youthful enthusiasm; but coming from Santayana, it does bring home to us vividly the Latin, the European significance of Byron – one sees this in Santayana's own poetry – and the intensity and strength of Byron's European appeal. Many years later, however, having been 're-reading the whole of *Don Juan*', Santayana writes to Richard C. Lyon: 'Some parts bored me, the invectives especially; but, as you say, he is witty, and his rhymes sometimes surpassingly clever. *But he did not respect himself or his art as much as they deserved.*' (Italics mine.) It is that last sentence which condenses an essential criticism of *Don Juan*. And somewhere between this final attitude of critical reserve, and the earlier blend of 'admiration' and 'loyalty' towards 'one who is knit into one's own life', the critic's correct position seems

---

[1] Daniel Cory (Ed.), *The Letters of George Santayana*, Constable, London, 1955.

to me to be found; he must be capable of a real response to Byron's appeal, which does not preclude, or leave finally in abeyance, a sense of dissatisfaction, disappointment, and disillusion. He must, in fact, be prepared to recapitulate, in his experience of Byron's poetry, something of that general process of maturing, often painfully and with loss as well as gain, which parts of *Don Juan* itself unforgettably record; a development necessarily implying the renunciation of much that delighted our youth.

The doubt that afflicts us, after we have mentally gone over our impressions of Byron's poetry, crystallizes into the question: how much of it *is* poetry? And this leads to the further question; has Byron as poet enough self-knowledge and command of his experience to be judged a *great* poet? These questions remain to trouble us, even if we confine our attention to the things that, by general agreement, constitute – at any rate for the modern reader – the main body of Byron's achievement in verse: *Don Juan*, the *Vision of Judgment*, and *Beppo* (and, I would add, the later cantos of *Childe Harold*). Of these, the *Vision of Judgment* comes the nearest to being a thing done and complete, an object for criticism by itself and in itself; and the *Vision of Judgment* is hardly a great creative work. *Don Juan* is naturally what most of us would cite in support of a high estimate of Byron's poetic genius; but one's established impression of it is ominously coloured by that sense of dissatisfaction recorded by Santayana. The casualness, or irresponsibility, of its procedure may be the condition for the poem's virtues, but it is not itself always, or even often, a virtue. One feels in reading much of *Don Juan* that it must have come very easily, and this feeling shades into the judgement '*too* easily'; a great work of art must contain themes which have offered a resistance to the artist, as well as being attractive to him. I do not dispute that *Don Juan* is very entertaining, one of the most readable of long poems; I am concerned at the moment only with the very high claims for it which are made by some of its admirers. I do not think the justice of these claims is by any means self-evident.

Santayana is surely right to link his dissatisfaction with the 'art' of the poem, to his dissatisfaction with the recurrent attitude of self-contempt – the basis perhaps of the intermittent disrespect for humanity in general – which is so striking a feature of Byron's case. This mood bears a relation to the equally typical habit of self-assertion, in that famous rhetorical attudinizing; a relation which is not one of simple antithesis. All that matters to the critic, of

course, is what is *made* of these moods and habits, and the relationships between them, by the creative force of the poet; but he
would be a very bold critic who would argue that the moral and
emotional predispositions which these moods reflect, are everywhere and uniformly in Byron impersonalized, absolved, or
transcended. The case is more complex: everywhere in Byron we
find assertion, and the contrasting, yet complementary, abjectness.
But when we find too in the mature work, the beginnings of a
power to diagnose them; to see his pride, and its less harmful (if
less dignified) accompaniments of vanity and conceit, for what
they are. And these insights appear often in close quarters with the
ignorance of oneself and other people which egotism always entails. Similarly, there are obtusenesses and blindnesses, the more
disturbing because they will often occur in the midst of a display
of notable sensitiveness, intelligence, and imagination. An
example from life here will not mean a wanton digression, since in
Byron's case (it is not so, of course, with many other artists) either
the art, or the man, will testify in a fairly straightforward way what
each other is like. How akin to the art of the good novelist is the
moral delicacy, evincing and articulating itself in that constant
play of representation and perception – at once witty and profound – which determines the whole presentment in those letters
to Lady Melbourne of his 'affair', if such we must call it, with
Lady Frances Webster! What insight into milieu, situation, and
character, his own (as the star of the drama) included! And yet,
what a limitation of moral outlook, what a lack of awareness
of self and the people concerned, is there as well! Now it is a real
tribute, if a paradoxical one, to Byron as a responsible being and
a born creative writer, and to what he makes thereby of that little
episode in writing of it, that we speak of these disablements as we
might in criticizing a novelist; that we are tempted to speak in
moral terms, rather than in terms of a neurotic condition. It is just
because of the very great degree to which Byron is obviously in
command of his experience here, that we are led to ask for evidence of a still fuller and finer control. The apparent absence of
this in life is closely related to the undoubted absence of it in
Byron's writings. But to suggest that Byron's judgement is sometimes blurred by egotism, of one kind or another, is not at all to
contradict the assertion that 'he did not respect himself, or his
art, as much as they deserved'. On the contrary, a lack of true
self-respect, so far from being incompatible with self-love, often

accompanies it. Similarly, the luxury of self-abasement may well be a corollary of the will to assert oneself.

Attitudes such as those characteristic of Bryon are not uncommon; although the opportunity to strike them on so large a stage, and to act out so completely their consequences, is not granted to many. At any rate, whatever view we take of Byron's own character, there can be no doubt that much of the cult of Byron, in his own time and later, was merely the gratification, in fantasy, of numerous petty egotisms; the magnifying to heroic proportions of one's own easy angers, tears, and surrenders; the indulgence of *saeva indignatio*; and that sense of injured merit which provides so many occasions for the release of a vindicated self-pity. Which of us cannot see himself as the hero-victim of that *besoin de la fatalité* which M. du Bos declares to be the dominant force in Byron's life? And who does not also see, in his more veracious moments, that this vision is but an illusory enlargement of his own pettiness? But to see that constantly; and yet to be unable to resist the recurrent temptation thus to indulge oneself; and to have also the power to give truly classical expression to both sides of that state of mind and soul – this is Byron's own case, as distinct from that of many of his admirers and would-be imitators, and it is a very unusual one. The Byronic predicament may not be simply or wholly what it purports to be; but to give both its illusion of itself, and its reality, is a remarkable achievement. It is the achievement of a robust, if not often very fine, creative intelligence. And so either to castigate Byron's self-indulgences as an artist, or to condone them, is equally irrelevant; he himself having done both, with incomparable power, in his own poetry: since the wish or need to do both was very likely a necessary condition for his creative effort.

We must therefore be sedulous, in reconsidering Byron's achievement in poetry, to keep the general human judgement in suspense; by way of a recognition that it is not a simple one. It is impossible not to be constantly incited to commit ourselves to it, because of the frankly and insistently personal quality of Byron's characteristic poetry, as shown in both its manner and its matter. But at least we can avoid that *parti pris* which is derived from a (very understandable) anti-romantic prejudice. Mr. Eliot has given us an excellent essay on Byron (in *From Anne to Victoria*, edited by Bonamy Dobrée). Yet it is to my mind weakened by the constant intrusion of this prejudice. Thus, having affirmed that Byron's being a Scot is the most significant single clue for the student of his poetry, Mr. Eliot is inevitably led to a comparison with Byron's greatest Scots contemporary. And the reminder of the human qualities of Walter Scott – on which Byron himself generously insisted to Stendhal – only serves to strengthen the critic's initial prejudice against Byron's disorder. But this kind of human judgement, made at the outset, and always felt in the background, means the deflection of criticism. The assessment of Byron's poetry – this truism is particularly worth repeating and emphasizing in his case – must begin and end with the poetry.

As the popularizer of Romanticism, Byron the poet has important European affinities, as well as being a pervasive (if not always obvious) influence in nineteenth-century English poetry; and therefore he demands more critical attention in this role than the poetry it gave rise to perhaps merits intrinsically. No doubt it is the cine-camera passage of *Childe Harold* that accounted for part of its sensational and immediate success, with a public starved of travel; but a more important attraction was the offer of metaphysical and spiritual profundities, the dark hints of hidden depths of sin and guilt, associated – as they are also in the verse-tales which followed – with the impressive and sombre, if somewhat histrionic and self-conscious, *persona* of Byronic legend. The evaluation of this, in its relation to Byron's literary personality as a whole, is not simple. It cannot be dismissed as merely the striking of an attitude.

> With all that chilling mystery of mien,
> And seeming gladness to remain unseen,
> He had (if 'twere not nature's boon) an art
> Of fixing memory on another's heart:
> It was not love perchance, nor hate, nor aught
> That words can image to express the thought;
> But they who saw him did not see in vain,
> And once beheld, would ask of him again;
> And those to whom he spake remember'd well,
> And on the words, however light, would dwell;
> None knew nor how, nor why, but he entwined
> Himself perforce around the hearer's mind;
> There he was stamp'd, in liking, or in hate,
> If greeted once: however brief the date
> That friendship, pity, or aversion knew,
> Still there within the inmost thought he grew.

You could not penetrate his soul, but found,
Despite your wonder, to your own he wound;
His presence haunted still; and from the breast
He forced an all unwilling interest:
Vain was the struggle in that mental net,
His spirit seem'd to dare you to forget!
(*Lara*, I, xix)

No doubt there is some attitudinizing here, but there is also something genuine. One cannot, however, agree with certain French critics that such passages represent a profound self-study, the result of prolonged self-analysis. The effect is either of a man speaking with the conviction of one who is the greatest living authority on a subject, because he has invented it; or of one trying himself out in a role, and discovering as he goes along that it suits him. And the success of this role depends on the awareness of a public predisposed to be impressed by it. Such a public is not likely to notice, or care of it did, the contradictoriness of his apologia, pointed out by Mr. Eliot: the Byronic sinner, the Giaour for example, alternately excuses his wickedness by proclaiming that it is not wickedness, since he has transvalued his values, and by pleading that it is not his fault, but the fault of circumstances. Both the contradictoriness, and the popularity, of the Byronic sinner in this attitude, testify to its origin in rebellious Protestantism; in this case, in the consciousness of a rakish patrician with the emotional habit-pattern of a Presbyterian minister. (Even in Byron's Venice period we are reminded that he was brought up in Aberdeen.)

But it is not as the precise summing-up of an attitude, even a contradictory one, that such Byronic figures are finally significant and influential. Their power lay in the indefiniteness of their *Weltanschauung*: they could be the ready receptacle for the vague emotions of a great variety of temperaments. There is today a prejudice against poetry which expresses only vague emotion; but it should be noted that in Byron's verse, while the emotion may be vague, the statement of it is explicit. And here of course is the unsatisfactoriness of this kind of poetry. Byronism is better expressed in music; there is something about words which is alien to it, their obstinate tendency to particularize. The Byronic mood at its most intense consists of desire and sadness in their simplest, their most general character; to specify what the sadness is about, or what object could satisfy the desire, can only dissipate the mood by recalling those very particulars of experience which it was its consolation to transcend.

And there is not only something unsatisfactory about Byron's Romantic poetry, there is something false. The declamatory style of the 'profound' passages in *Childe Harold* III and IV is at odds with the simultaneous attempt at an inward treatment of the themes. This discrepancy, producing a typical effect of externality, we diagnose as the result of derivativeness; the main source being Wordsworth[1] – though we should probably add Coleridge and Shelly to the list of tributaries. Indeed, the whole of *Childe Harold* is an interesting study in what 'influence' really means – influence of the wrong kind, of course, since Byron's relation to Wordsworth's poetry is not the less but the more parasitic for being probably not conscious. The Romantic element in the poem is an instructive example of how the process of popularization – *vulgarization* – inevitably denatures what it touches. And we still have to note this, even when Byron's materials are most his own, when he is taking his bleeding heart to the tourist-places of Europe in a most un-Wordsworthian fashion.

And yet there is something impressive about the strength and conviction with which Byron does what he does, and one cannot copy out a famous set-piece like the Dying Gladiator without feeling admiration.

> I see before me the Gladiator lie:
> He leans upon his hand – his manly brow
> Consents to death, but conquers agony,
> And his droop'd head sinks gradually low –
> And through his side the last drops, ebbing slow
> From the red gash, fall heavy, one by one,
> Like the first of a thunder-shower; and now
> The arena swims around him – he is gone,
> Ere ceased the inhuman shout which hail'd the wretch who
>   won.
> He heard it, but he heeded not – his eyes
> Were with his heart, and that was far away . . .

This of course is rhetorical writing, but it is a very distinguished rhetoric; there is a great Latin and European tradition behind it, and a national poetry which is not adorned by such things is the

---

[1] Wordsworth himself noted Byron's debt to 'my poem on the Wye'.

poorer, the more provincial. No living poet could write this kind of verse with that degree of strength and conviction; poetry which is both good, and popular, in the way this is, I cannot imagine appearing in the twentieth century. Byron speaks here in the accents of a great European tradition of the public style. But he none the less speaks with his own voice: Arnold, indeed, cited the last two lines of the passage I have quoted, as illustrating Byron's specific quality as a poet; and, in justice to that quality, I will quote again what seem to me two still finer lines:

> He leans upon his hand – his manly brow
> Consents to death, but conquers agony.

If we are compelled, in considering the whole undertaking of *Childe Harold*, to lay stress on the limitations of the rhetorical manner, it is only fair to bring out at the same time what that manner, at its most impressive, can do.

The limitations, of course, were inherent in Byron's conception of poetry when he began *Childe Harold*. The poem contains that striking rhetoric on grand 'public' themes; and even when Harold's philosophical rhapsodizing are in full swing, they are not unimpressive; yet a casual fragment of Byron's prose will often contain more of the true poet's quick, alert, immediate report of experience, than any of the personal declarations of *Childe Harold*, and the reflective moments are in keeping.

> Woke, and was ill all day, till I had galloped a few miles. Query – was it the cockles, or what I took to correct them, that caused the commotion? I think both. I remarked in my illness the complete inertion, inaction and destruction of my chief mental faculties. I tried to rouse them, and yet could not – and this is the *Soul*!!! I should believe that it was married to the body, if they did not sympathize so much with each other. If the one rose, when the other fell, it would be a sign that they longed for the natural state of divorce. But as it is, they seem to draw together like post-horses.

It would be hard to divine from *Childe Harold* the variety, range, and above all the intellectual mobility (evinced in the quality of the perceptiveness) of the Byron of the letters and journals.

But this brings us back to Byron's conception of form and style in poetry. *Childe Harold* is unquestionably the work of a very intelligent man; but in poetry the quality of intelligence is the quality of perceptiveness; and the quality of the perceptions in *this* poetry is affected by the mode they are expressed in. And here we have the other way in which Byron is a representative voice of his age; he is not only a popularizer of Romanticism; he is also a poet of the Regency. The living poet and critic to whom he most deferred was Gifford; and, though he has greater scope and force even in his earlier work, he is there the same *kind* of poet as Rogers, Campbell, or Moore, whom he backed against Southey and Wordsworth to 'try the question' with posterity. His staple language, though characterized, even in his earlier work, by the tones of his natural voice, acknowledges an eighteenth-century poetic. And it is afflicted everywhere with the effeteness of a verse-idiom in decline. The style of the earlier eighteenth-century poets, though it seems restricted in comparison with Shakespeare's freedom, gets its vitality partly from one's feeling of its perpetual effort to *hold back* concreteness. The spirit in which those poets wrote is shown in Johnson's rationalizing analysis of *To be, or not to be* . . . And the extrusion of Shakespearianism in this verse appears, not as a mere absence of concreteness, but as a positive sense of tension in the effort to reject it. In later eighteenth-century poetry this pressure has relaxed; so that the diction is choked with the accumulated dry husks of a style designed to restrain, which now restrains nothing. And here we have the explanation of Byron's prolixity, his habit of never using one word when three will do. Even in his more mature work, he cannot rely on the single word or phrase to carry any potency of charge; his poetic effects must be cumulative, since they cannot be concentrated. He is capable of, and indeed cultivates, the shape, lucidity, and *ordonnance* of Augustan poetry, but he cannot achieve its distinction of style. Compare any passage of *English Bards* with the best of Dryden or Pope.

We should recall that the Regency is pre-eminently a period of 'good bad poetry' – if we may so designate a species of composition which is neither good, nor bad, nor, in any important sense, poetry. It is the period of *Ye Mariners* and *Hohenlinden*, of *The Stately Homes* and *Casabianca*; a genre to which Byron himself contributes, with his *Destruction of Sennacherib* and other things. To write such poems, with their terrible memorability, requires, together with complete conviction, absolute banality of sentiment, and obvious rhythm, a poetic diction on the point of death. And, varied as are the kinds of badness in Byron's poetry: the schoolboy rhetoric which can be found everywhere in his work, from

Hours of Idleness to *Don Juan*; the leading-article declamation of *Napoleon's Farewell*; the drawing-room romanticism of *Tambourgi, Tambourgi*; the Regency album sentiment: the Augustan platform manner; the modes ranging from the histrionic-profound of *Darkness: a Fragment* at one extreme to the squib and lampoon at the other; all these have in common, besides the invariable energy of Byron, a lack of verbal distinction. Byron is the poet and stylist of a linguistic nadir.

And other discrepancies and falsities can be blamed in part on the period of English literature, of which this diction was the habit. The Regency in literature was a moment of interruption; a time when Romantic feeling had not yet found its social, moral, and religious bearings in the consciousness of the community, or united itself with other new trends in the national life. Romanticism in its first phase was only alive in the experience of a few individuals; there was thus an effect of externality and falsetto when, like Byron, they sought to express the new development of feeling in an idiom which did not grant, in poetry, such primacy to the experience of the individual. And the liberation achieved in the first place by Robert Burns, and in the second by Wordsworth and Coleridge, did not affect the texture of Byron's verse until he had reached a stage when Romantic feeling was not primarily what he had to express.

Byron's earlier poetry, then, apart from its purely biographical significance, has on the whole only a representative importance. All the same, his work even in its later and greater developments, never loses touch with the eighteenth century. Bertrand Russell was wrong in thinking that Byron's cult of Pope, as the supreme poet, was an affectation. (See the chapter on Byron in *A History of Western Philosophy*.) Nothing is clearer or sincerer in Byron's poetry than his admiration for the eighteenth-century order and rationality, for its limpidity and pattern. The pre-eminence of *Don Juan* among his poems is in one respect unfortunate: in that it causes critics to forget that usual concern of Byron's for method, arrangement, and structure, a concern from which *Don Juan*, like its predecessor *Beppo*, is a deliberate exception. It is in diction and rhythm that Byron's earlier poetry shows a difference, and a deterioration, from the best eighteenth-century work. In his verse tales, which are very entertaining, this may be partially compensated by the energy and easy movement; as in the opening of *The Corsair*:

> O'er the glad waters of the dark blue sea,
> Our thoughts as boundless, and our souls as free,
> Far as the breeze can bear, the bollows foam,
> Survey our empire, and behold our home!
> These are our reals, no limits to their sway –
> Our flag the sceptre all who meet obey.
> Ours the wild life in tumult still to range,
> From toil to rest, and joy in every change.

The *élan* of the movement is characteristically Byron's; but the language is merely politician's English. Where anything in the nature of a concentrated effect is wanted, this is painfully obvious; Byron's very forcefulness only accentuates the poverty of the style. We become aware, not so much of the lack of ear which Swinburne complains of in Byron, as the lack of *mouth* (so to speak); delivery of Byron's verse neither liquefies the palate, nor tightens the jawbone; he has no sense of words as physiological facts, more or less subtly co-operating when we pronounce them to create the illusion of meaning-analogues modifying the vocal organs. Where he is successful in more concentrated pieces, as in the bitter *Ode to Napoleon* (1814), verse-form serves merely the purpose of adding emphasis, regularity, and outline to the virtue of discourse. The distinction of Byron's more interesting poems is not that he attained, or even moved towards, a greater plasticity of language; but that, in admitting a fresh range of feelings into his poetry, he introduced new shades and inflexions of the speaking voice; and so, while his staple language is not altered – being still a mixture of conventional poeticism, formal prose qualities, and his own colloquial accent – its effect is different, since it moves with more interesting and more personal rhythms.

By looking at the relation between diction and movement, then, we may study the evolution of Byron's most truly personal and original poetry, the core of his work. A very early poem like *When we two parted* (1808) already shows the close association, in Byron, between the depth or quality of a poem's sentiment and the individuality of its verse-rhythm. The perpetual slight un-expectedness of the measure, the continuous small uncertainty that the reader-aloud must feel as to where a break or pause is coming, testifies to the genuineness of the poem's impulse. Where its rhythm approaches regularity, as in the second and third stanzas:

> The dew of the morning
> Sunk chill on my brow –
> It felt like the warning
> Of what I feel now

a vulgarity in the writing becomes more obvious; and we have a sense of the extreme precariousness, the fragility, of this mode of expression, in what is after all a work of immaturity.

A comparison between this poem and *Ae fond kiss* is instructive. (The comparison is suggested, though not elaborated on, by I. A. Richards in *The Principles of Literary Criticism*.) The four famous lines of the latter poem:

> Had we never lov'd sae kindly,
> Had we never lov'd sae blindly,
> Never met and never parted,
> We had ne'er been broken-hearted

– these, as Arnold says, are beyond Byron's reach. But after re-peated readings of Burns's poem they stand out oddly from the hubbub of stock emotionalism which surrounds them (the 'dark despairs' and all the rest of it). This contrast, taken with the flaccid, overweight character of the stanza form, suggests an im-purity in the poetic impulse; a suggestion which is confirmed (not that confirmation is necessary) by what we know of Burns's atti-tude in life towards the importunities of 'Nancy'. In Byron's poem, on the other hand, there is no such impurity. It springs from a situation which is felt by the reader as real (whatever the bio-graphical facts may be). And this feeling of reality, together with the immaturity which conditions it, is conveyed in the varying character of the rhythm.

An equal, though different, success is the later lyric *There be none of Beauty's daughters*. Here the constituent of the poem is no more than a gravely conventional compliment, in the Regency manner. The imagery:

> And the midnight moon is weaving
> Her bright chain o'er the deep

is of the same quality as Byron's friend Tom Moore's. The dis-tinctiveness is again in the rhythm and tempo. It is not just in the subtle abrogations of regularity:

> There be none of Beauty's daughters
> – With a magic like thee;

(Everything is lost, if we make the semantically insignificant change to 'With a magic *like to* thee'.) The charm lies most in the way in which, while the phrasing pays the most graceful homage possible to Miss Clairmont's singing (by announcing that it has made Lord Byron's spirit bow before her, and lulled to rest that oceanic, tempestuous bosom), at the same time those light but subtle changes of tempo acknowledge with an equal grace the essential slightness of the theme. ('A full *but soft* emotion.') It is in ways like these that Byron's short lyrics at their best may be said to achieve their own kind of decorum, a decorum not deriving from any impersonal convention or established mode. In a piece like *She walks in beauty* we have the nearest that this decorum, while remaining quite personal to Byron, comes to a stylization.

> . . . And all that's best of dark and bright
> Meet in her aspect and her eyes;
> Thus mellow'd to that tender light
> Which heaven to gaudy day denies.
> One shade the more, one ray the less,
> Had half impair'd the nameless grace . . .

This last line quotes Pope, and the manner in general is plainly near to one of Pope's manners:

> So, when the sun's broad beam has tir'd the sight,
> All mild ascends the moon's more sober light;
> Serene in virgin modesty she shines,
> And unobserved the glaring orb declines.

But this air of graceful conformity to a tradition is rare in Byron's lyrics. They are perfectly complete in themselves; but, as a rule, they excite an interest in the poet over and above our admiration of his skill; we feel them to be parts of a whole which is both greater and different. Reading an exquisite poem of Thomas Campion may make us want to read other poems of Campion; but wider reading, while it increases our respect for the poet by revealing the scope of his art, adds nothing to our appreciation of the poem with which we started. And to appreciate that poem rightly is to realize that there is no point in trying to go behind or beyond it. This is not because Campion is 'minor'; we have the same feeling about that fine lyric of Dryden *Ah, fading joy*. A lyric of Byron, on the other hand, a lyric like *So we'll go no more a-roving*, the best one he wrote, differs from *Ah, fading joy* or *Rose-cheekt Lawra*, not only in gaining in life and meaning from our sense that it is the culmination of a poet's whole work, but in being on the face of it a dramatic utterance: the voice of an individual.

'Sincerity and strength', was the judgement of Swinburne, endorsed by Arnold; and it brings us again to that personal question, which can never be long postponed, or dodged, in the discussion of Byron. The 'strength', of course, needs little commentary. An athletic buoyancy is the most noticeable, and often the redeeming, feature of Byron's poetry, tempering our exasperation after a long session with the Poetical Works, some of which are bad, and many of which are not very good. He has the extra zest, the record-breaker's enthusiasm, of the lame man exulting in his ability to ride and swim. Sometimes, indeed, this immortal velocity of Byron's causes a comic incongruity between his movement and his matter:

> Though wit may flash from fluent lips, and mirth distract the
> breast,
> Through midnight hours that yield no more their former
> hope of rest;
> 'Tis but as ivy-leaves around the ruin'd turret wreath,
> All green and wildly fresh without, all worn and grey
> beneath.

And a poem like the one that begins:

> Oh, talk to me not of a name great in story;
> The days of our youth are the days of our glory;

offered as a poignant utterance of the ageing Byron, is an exhilarating gallop. The strength of Byron, then, can show itself in uninteresting or undistinguished ways; but it is an indispensable quality of his best poetry: while it prevents his lesser things from being at any rate tame or dull. Even where the strength is consciously measured and restraining itself, as in the sonnet to George IV ('To be the father of the fatherless'), we see its power when we compare it with Shelley's sonnet *England in 1819*.

'Sincerity', however – that difficult but indispensable concept –

is a more complex matter; all readers of Byron know how awkward is its application to him. For the moment, its reference may be limited to the felt identification of the poet with the emotion expressed. Now it is an interesting, and peculiar, characteristic of some of the greatest things that Byron wrote, that their impressiveness derives partly from our feeling that there is *not* this complete identification. I am thinking particularly of poems associated with the Separation Drama. The explicit emotion – or commotion – is expressed powerfully enough. Byron is much more deeply disturbed than in his earlier poems; there is no question of his acting a part, as in the verse-romances; the expression comes from the centre. And yet we register some consciousness of the writer that there are features of the experience which his present state of mind compels him to leave out, but which will reassert themselves later. Faced with these poems of Byron, poems which have a human and poetic character for which I can think of no parallel, we cannot call them insincere; we are forced, therefore, to revise our notion of sincerity. Consider the *Lines on hearing that Lady Byron was ill*, perhaps the most impressive poem that Byron wrote; since it is not very well known, and I wish to comment on some details, I will quote the whole.

> And thou wert sad – yet I was not with thee;
> And thou wert sick, and yet I was not near;
> Methought that joy and health alone could be
> Where I was *not* – and pain and sorrow here!
> And is it thus? – It is as I foretold,
> And shall be more so; for the mind recoils
> Upon itself, and the wreck'd heart lies cold,
> While heaviness collects the shattered spoils.
> It is not in the storm nor in the strife
> We feel benumb'd, and wish to be no more,
> But in the after-silence on the shore,
> When all is lost, except a little life.
> I am too well avenged! – but 'twas my right;
> Whate'er my sins might be, *thou* wert not sent
> To be the Nemesis who should requite –
> Nor did Heaven choose so near an instrument.
> Mercy is for the merciful! – if thou
> Hast been of such, 'twill be accorded now.
> Thy nights are banish'd from the realms of sleep! –

Yes! they may flatter thee, but thou shalt feel
A hollow agony which will not heal,
For thou art pillow'd on a curse too deep;
Thou hast sown in my sorrow, and must reap
The bitter harvest in a woe as real!
I have had many foes, but none like thee;
For 'gainst the rest I could myself defend,
And be avenged, or turn them into friend;
But thou in safe implacability
Hadst nought to dread – in thy own weakness shielded,
And in my love, which hath but too much yielded,
And spared, for thy sake, some I should not spare;
And thus upon the world – trust in thy truth,
And the wild fame of my ungovern'd youth –
On things that were not, and on things that are –
Even upon such a basis hast thou built
A monument, whose cement hath been guilt!
The moral Clytemnestra of thy lord,
And hew'd down, with an unsuspected sword,
Fame, peace, and hope – and all the better life,
Which, but for this cold treason of thy heart,
Might still have risen from out the grave of strife,
And found a nobler duty than to part.
But of thy virtues didst thou make a vice,
Trafficking with them in a purpose cold,
For present anger, and for future gold –
And buying other's grief at any price.
And thus once enter'd into crooked ways,
The earthly truth, which was thy proper praise,
Did not still walk beside thee – but at times,
And with a breast unknowing its own crimes,
Deceit, averments incompatible,
Equivocations, and the thoughts which dwell
In Janus-spirits – the significant eye
Which learns to lie with silence – the pretext
Of prudence, with advantages annex'd –
The acquiescence in all things which tend,
No matter how, to the desired end –
All found a place in thy philosophy.
The means were worthy, and the end is won –
I would not do by thee as thou hast done!

Even without knowledge of the personal situation, the *Sitz im Leben*, we recognize this as a poem coming straight out of life; the command of form and expression that makes it a poem being obviously sustained by an impulse to self-justification *in* life. And a proper reading could only be done by a reader who grasped that situation. At the same time, different readings – though they would all have to be dramatic ones – could well be effective. Thus, the substance of the poem *appears* to be the expression of a feeling of vindictiveness, together with a demonstrative grounding and rationalization of that feeling. And so it could be plausibly rendered. It develops dramatically, from an anguished effort of self-justification before the 'moral Clytemnestra' to a concentrated and merciless analysis of her character, of which the impulsion is manifestly Byron-Agamemnon's incredulous resentment. It is this impulsion which gives their remarkable force to the closing lines, where the prose-like precision of the writing only heightens our sense of the agonized animosity which pervades the whole:

> Deceit, averments incompatible,
> Equivocations, and the thoughts which dwell
> In Janus-spirits – the significant eye
> Which learns to lie with silence – the pretext
> Of prudence, with advantages annex'd –
> The acquiescence in all things which tend,
> No matter how, to the desired end, –
> All found a place in thy philosophy.

This animosity is the *apparent* substance of the poem. But in its true character, which the proper dramatic reading could bring out, it is surely not so much an expression of hatred, as an expression of the will to feel hatred. That there is, indeed, no conscious criticism of the self-indulgence, is evident in the tense inflexibility of the accent. And it might be protested that, while we know that the vindictiveness is not the whole of the poem, we have to go outside the poem to justify that reading. However, there are signs in the poem itself of good, restorative feelings which are trying, though not successfully, to sustain themselves against the overmastering waves of destructive emotion. Let us imagine that we read the opening, without knowing anything of the situation behind the poem, or guessing what is coming; certainly it is a remonstrance, but could it not sound like a tender one? –

And thou wert sad – yet I was not with thee;
And thou wert sick, and yet I was not near;
Methought that joy and health alone could be
Where I was *not* – and pain and sorrow here!
And is it thus? –

With 'It is as I foretold' the vindictiveness asserts itself. Yet the generalized reflection that follows, 'It is not in the storm nor in the strife', etc., again suggests, if not sympathy, at least a recognition of the common humanity of Lady Byron, with a latent sadness that comes to the surface in 'I am too well avenged!' But once again comes the insistence, this time with a significant extra emphasis: 'I am too well avenged! – *but 'twas my right*!' From then on, irritation at the strain of sustaining this implacable attitude of angry righteousness seems to increase the volume and destructiveness of the negative emotions, the indulgence of which is what one's memory chiefly carries away from the poem. And yet, read again with an ear for its true music, does it not convey a Byron who both wants, and does not want, to feel like this? It is a remarkable human document.

As such it prompts us, as Byron's work so insistently does, to biographical conjecture. But it seems to me sufficiently a poem, despite the 'character' terms which analysis of it must require, to be discussed without passing into appraisal of the rights and wrongs of the Separation Drama. So does another poem of this period, the *Epistle to Augusta*, which makes an interesting contrast: here we have a different note:

The fault was mine; nor do I seek to screen
My errors with defensive paradox;
I have been cunning in mine overthrow,

The careful pilot of my proper woe.
Mine were my faults, and mine be their reward.
My whole life was a contest, since the day
That gave me being, gave me that which marr'd
The gift – a fate, or will, that walk'd astray . . .

That 'fate, *or will*', is a relevant comment on the lines on Lady Byron, and 'I have been cunning in mine overthrow', with its suggestion of insight into the nature of masochistic gratification, also suggests something of what has been kept out of the earlier poem, the keeping of it out being possibly the reason for that

M

curious effect of willed inflexibility noted there. True, we can still hear the Byron of *Childe Harold*:

> Kingdoms and empires in my little day
> I have outlived, and yet I am not old;
> And when I look on this, the petty spray
> Of my own years of trouble, which have roll'd
> Like a wild bay of breakers, melts away;
> Something – I know not what – does still uphold
> A spirit of slight patience . . .

But there is a difference; in spite of 'Something, I know not what . . .', Byron is not offering vagueness as profundity; his uncertainties are frankly uncertainties:

> Surely I once beheld a nobler aim.
> But all is over – I am one the more
> To baffled millions who have gone before.

And correspondingly, his self-knowledge seems deeper and more genuine:

> Had I but sooner learnt the crowd to shun,
> I had been better than I now can be;
> The passions which have torn me would have slept;
> I had not suffered, and *thou* hadst not wept.

> . . . I have had the share
> Or life which might have fill'd a century,
> Before its fourth in time had pass'd me by.

> . . . not in vain,
> Even for its own sake, do we purchase pain.

And comparing the manner with that of the lines on Lady Byron, as well as *Childe Harold*, we notice another difference; the *Epistle* is unmistakably by the same poet, but unlike them it is not declamation; it is, on the whole, restrained and circumstantial. It might be called Byron's *Tintern Abbey*, the nearest he comes to 'emotion recollected in tranquillity' – his affairs usually allowing him little tranquillity to recollect in. And like *Tintern Abbey* it associates the renewal of strength for living with the emotion of love, towards Nature – the 'Nature' of Romantic poets – and towards a sister for whom he has more than the conventional affection of a brother. The comparison with Wordsworth of

course reminds us that the two poets are extremely, almost ab-
surdly, unlike: in spite of such lines as these in the *Epistle*:

> Perhaps a kinder clime, or purer air,
> (For even to this may change of sould refer,
> And with light armour we may learn to bear,)
> Have taught me a strange quiet, which was not

> The chief companion of a calmer lot.
> I feel almost at times as I have felt
> In happy childhood; tree, and flowers and brooks,
> Which do remember me of where I dwelt
> Ere my young mind was sacrified to books,
> Come as of yore upon me . . .

> The world is all before me; I but ask
> Of Nature that with which she will comply –

> . . . Nor shall I conceal
> That with all this I still can look around,
> And worship Nature with a thought profound.

But, as the last quotation suggests, Byron's 'Nature' is a shade
perfunctory, and he has not earned, as Wordsworth has, his right
to the word 'profound'. We feel the 'strange quiet' to be indeed
strange, to be but a breathing-space amid storm and stress. The
reassurance and reorientation promised by the Alps is felt even in
the poem as merely temporary; *caelum non animum mutat* is as true
of Byron's wanderings, as of D. H. Lawrence's.

Compared with any passage of *Childe Harold* or the lines on
Lady Byron, the *Epistle* has some variety of tone; but it is still
only the expression of one side of Byron's nature; we feel that
another tone is wanting, and at one moment it seems to be almost
there:

> But now I fain would for a time survive,
> If but to see what next can well arrive.

Contemplating that rueful humour (*what next?!*) we are reminded
at this point that the *Epistle* is written in the stanza of *Don Juan*.

But though neither the *Epistle*, nor the *Lines*, are fully representative of Byron's mature genius, they show a great advance in
reality compared with anything he had written earlier; and, though
I have criticized this and that point in their composition, I should

not like to leave them without recording my opinion that they are
the work of a great (if not fully developed) poet. Stylistically, they
have one striking feature. The Regency quality, associated in
Byron's verse and prose with an air of aristocratic recklessness,
has disappeared. An urgent personal pressure has transformed
Byron's characteristic way of writing into a style of no particular
'period' flavour, dateless. It is at this time that the emancipation
effected by 'Wordsworth's trash' first appears at all decisively in
Byron's verse; there is the trace of a changed sensibility here and
there in *The Dream*, which also belongs to this period (1816):

> And he stood calm and quiet, and he spoke
> The fitting vows, but heard not his own words,
> And all things reel'd around him; he could see
> Not that which was, nor that which should have been –
> But the old mansion, and the accustom'd hall,
> And the remember'd chambers, and the place,
> The day, the hour, the sunshine, and the shade,
> All things pertaining to that place and hour,
> And her who was destiny – came back
> And thrust themselves between him and the light:
> What business had they there at such a time?

The last line, with its brusque directness of speech, is Byronic,
not Wordsworthian; but Wordsworth certainly counts for something in the general manner.

The Regency quality which is so unlike Wordsworth, the
aristocratic recklessness of a poem like *English Bards*, returns to
Byron's verse in the serio-comic poems which are by common
consent his most solid achievement: *Beppo*, the *Vision of Judgment*,
and *Don Juan*. But it appears now in a context which, for all its
high spirits and geniality, is charged with that fuller sense of the
actual world. Mr. Eliot, making the point that a great poet's forms
cannot be repeated, remarks that 'you cannot write satire in the line
of Pope or the stanza of Byron'. 'Satire' seems as good a word as
any to describe these extravaganzas, but 'the stanza of Byron'
needs further commentary; everything that needs to be said about
Byron's later poetry can be said in terms of what he does with that
'stanza'. The great technical freedom of his comic poems corresponds to the spirit in which they were written, one which
allowed for great variety of moods, whose swift changes and
oscillations now for the first time find expression in Byron's verse.

It is usual to account for the manner of *Beppo* and *Don Juan* by referring to Byron's attachment to Italy; first as the English milord enjoying – perhaps not so much as he sometimes claims – his Venetian emancipation from English stuffiness; and then as the *inglese italianato* in the milieu of Teresa Guiccioli, a participator not only in the patriotic conspiracies of Italy, but in Italian domesticity. (See *The Last Attachment*, by Iris Origo.) And these new associations, together with his interest in the comic poetry of the Italian Renaissance, certainly colour the lively and pictur-esque surface of those poems. But the core of *Don Juan* is still Byron's preoccupation with England, and with himself as he was, and might have been, and might still be, in England. And with this particular preoccupation there goes a general concern for truth and reality, expressed either as an impatient moral and social criticism, or as a literary protest: he uses poetry for the expression of anti-poetic sentiments. What is often in itself gay story-telling, or down-to-earth humour, or sentimental inconsequence, or Romantic bravura, or brusque sarcasm, or just pure fun and high spirits, is underlined and given point by this constant appeal to a standard of truth in life and literature. There is an incidental com-parison and contrast here between Byron's development and that of Shelley and Keats. In their later work, in *The Triumph of Life* and the revised *Hyperion*, there are signs that the acceptance of a stricter criterion of reality is associated with a need for greater technical control in the versification. They turn, not to the comic Italian poets, but to Petrarch and Dante. Now in Byron – though he too wrote his *Prophecy of Dante*, in *terza rima* – a contrasting process occurs. The new development is not so much a technical development, as a disdain of technique in the ordinary sense. But the purpose likewise is to secure the maximum directness and realism of presentation.

However, it must be granted that the reality in which Byron was interested was sometimes of a more mundane order than that which concerned Keats and Shelley. Byron can be preoccupied with the actual at quite a humdrum level. For instance, he had a love of literalness, and a passion for facts; he rebukes Bacon and Voltaire for their historical inaccuracies, which he demonstrates in detail; and he is imaginatively moved when in Venice, not at all by the thought of Shylock or Othello, who are fiction, but only by the history of the Republic. The literal-mindedness can show itself in odd ways, and at surprising moments. 'They mean to *insurrect* here, and are to honour me with a call thereupon,' he broods in his *Journal* of 9 January 1821, 'I shall not fall back; though I don't think them in force or heart sufficient to make much of it.' Now, as often in Byron, the misgivings of practicality are overcome by a calling up of emotional reserves.

> But, *onward*! – it is now the time to act, and what signifies *self*, if a single spark of that which would be worthy of the past can be bequeathed unquenchedly to the future? It is not one man, nor a million, but the *spirit* of liberty which must be spread. The waves which dash upon the shore are, one by one, broken, but yet the *ocean* conquers, nevertheless. It overwhelms the Armada, it wears the rock, and, if the *Neptunians* are to be believed, it has not only destroyed, but made a world. In like manner, whatever the sacrifice of individuals, the great cause will gather strength, sweep down what is rugged, or fertilize (for *seaweed* is *manure*) what is cultivable.

This impassioned meditation, on a cosmic theme, into which the personal preoccupation develops, comes from the grand, the European Byron, the great human force in the world, who is well qualified to command that admiration and loyalty of which Santayana speaks. But the point I want to make is that that last touch ('for *seaweed* is *manure*'), in such a context, is equally characteristic, and equally admirable. It is a quality without which we would not have had *Don Juan*.

But of course the truthfulness of *Don Juan* is not so much this literalism, and still less the intenser, higher-order truth to life which preoccupied Keats and Shelley; it is man-of-the-world realism; and as such Byron defends the poem, with suitable frankness, in a letter to Kinnaird.

> As to 'Don Juan', confess, confess – you dog and be candid – that it is the sublime of *that there* sort of writing – it may be bawdy but is it not good English? It may be profligate but is it not *life*, is it not the thing? Could any man have written it who has not lived in the world? – and fooled in a post-chaise? – in a hackney coach? – in a gondola? – against a wall? – in a court carriage? – in a *vis-à-vis*? – on a table? – and under it?

Yet even here, in that proximity of 'life', 'the thing', 'lived in the world', to 'good English', there is a literary manifesto. And in the general attitude there is a moral intention, which Arnold perceived in Byron, though he did not explicitly refer to *Don Juan*. 'The truth is,' Byron wrote to Murray during the Pope controversy. 'that in these days the grand *primum mobile* of England is *cant*; cant political, cant religious, cant moral; but always *cant*, multiplied through all the varieties of life. It is the fashion . . .' That the fashion does not change so very much, is one reason why *Don Juan* is still lively reading. There are still enough shabby smugnesses at home, and tyrannies abroad, to preserve its astringency and ensure its tonic effect. In this moral attitude, and in the tone of voice in which it is conveyed, Byron reminds us of Burns, with whom indeed he felt an affinity. 'Burns,' he says, comparing him to the Cockney School, 'is often coarse, but never vulgar.' And again: 'Read Burns today. What would he have been, if a patrician? We should have had more polish – less force – just as much verse, but no immortality – a divorce and a duel or two, the which had he survived, as his potations must have been less spirituous, he might have lived as long as Sheridan.'[1] But this last comment also registers Byron's sense of his difference from Burns. For all they have in common, in their man-to-man appeal, their amatory inflammability, their satiric bent, and their invocation of the universal human heart – and also, it may be, a national characteristic which comes out in all these traits – Byron remains the 'patrician', speaking from the plane of Sheridan, not that of Burns; there is something dignified about his dissipation, even while there is something of *l'homme sensuel moyen* about his dignity.

It is not, then, from his admiration for Burns, nor even from his interest in the Italian poets, that Byron's comic poetry derives its inspiration and sanction; but from the use of resources in Byron himself, which he had not previously exploited in poetry. The Byron of the letters and journals, of the world in which he was worried and was bored, and sneered and gossiped, comes into the verse; to provide the standards by which Wordsworth or Wilberforce, George IV or the Duke of Wellington, are judged. In the *Vision of Judgment* it is the demeanour of Wilkes, besides that of Junius ('I loved my country, and I hated him'), that attracts Byron; while in *Beppo* the viewpoint is that of the amused and amusing cosmopolitan Englishman, observing Venetian sexual *mores*, with their matter-of-factness and good sense. The extension of range appears poetically as that ability to modulate, or to pass

[1] *Journal*, 16 November, 1813.

from key to key without modulation, which constantly appears in the letters; here, for example, is the conclusion of a letter to Moore (Venice, 19 September 1818):

> I wish you good-night, with a Venetian benediction, *Benedetto te, e la terra che farà*! 'May you be blessed, and the earth which you will *make*!' – is it not pretty? You would think it prettier still, if you had heard it, as I did two hours ago, from the lips of a Venetian girl, with large black eyes, a face like Faustina's, and the figure of a Juno – tall and energetic as a Pythoness, with eyes flashing, and her dark hair streaming in the moonlight – one of those women who may be made anything. I am sure that if I put a poniard into the hand of this one, she would plunge it where I told her – and into *me*, if I offended her. I like this kind of animal, and am sure that I should have preferred Medea to any woman that ever breathed. You may, perhaps, wonder that I don't in that case . . . I could have forgiven the dagger and the bowl, – any thing, but the deliberate desolation piled upon me, when I stood alone upon my heart, with my household gods shivered around me. Do you suppose I have forgotten it? It has comparatively swallowed up in me every other feeling, and I am only a spectator upon earth, till a tenfold opportunity offers. It may come yet. There are more to be blamed than ———, and it is on these that my eyes are fixed unceasingly.

Here the accent of the final sentences strikes us, not as a sudden reversal of feeling, but as the disentangling of a feeling that is already a constituent of the half-humorous, half-Romantic description of the Venetian girl. A finer example is what follows an impassioned defence of Sheridan's character, as a type of the gentleman-adventurer of genius; when there emerges, in a beautiful way, the general sense of life, at once melancholy and admiring, which gives depth to it.

> Were his [Sheridan's] intrigues more notorious than those of all his contemporaries? and is his memory to be blasted, and theirs respected? Don't let yourself be led away by clamour, but compare him with the coalitioner Fox, and the pensioner Burke, as man of principle, and with none in talent, for he beat them all *out* and *out*. Without means, without means, without connexion, without character (which might be false at first, and

make him mad afterwards in desperation), he beat them all, in all he ever attempted. But alas, poor human nature! Good-night, or rather, morning. It is four, and the dawn gleams over the Grand Canal, and unshadows the Rialto. I must to bed; up all night – but, as George Philpot says, 'it's life, though, damme it's life!'

It is a way of life that Byron is defending here, and the reference to it is one of the positive criteria of judgement in *Don Juan*. The other, of course, is Byron's Romanticism; the Romantic self which Byron had not so much outgrown, as come to see for one acting-part among others. And the success of *Don Juan* is mainly a matter of Byron's success in effecting a positive relation between the two. The poem is a triumph of personality.

The relation between the Romantic-tragic and the sophisti-cated-cynical appear in a simple form in the story of Juan's father. This is the conclusion:

> It was a trying moment that which found him
> Standing alone beside his desolate hearth,
> Where all his household gods lay shiver'd round him;
> No choice was left his feelings or his pride,
> But death or Doctors' Commons – so he died.

The predominant effect is of the Byronic obsession; Byron is still mowing the aftermath of the Separation Drama. But the effect is of course qualified by the manner of its introduction ('It was a trying moment . . .'), which invites the attitude of ironic detach-ment; and the astringent terseness of the last couplet is reminis-scent of George Crabbe, whose poetry Byron admired. This man-ner of dealing with his troubles is obvious; but often, especially in the digressive passages, the effect is more complex. Consider the celebrated outburst towards the end of Canto I. Here Byron has been alluding to the adverse reception he expects to get, as a 'dissenting author', from the *Edinburgh* and *Quarterly*, and quoting Horace (*Non ego hoc ferrem calida juventa Consule Planco*) adds that in his 'hot youth' he 'would not have brooked at all this sort of thing', 'being most ready to return a blow'. Now we see Byron's way of picking up a theme for extensive development; the interest of such passages is partly that we do not know *which* element will be picked up. 'Hot youth', in its Horatian context, here becomes the theme, and is developed, at first with a little irony:

> But now at thirty years my hair is gray –
> (I wonder what it will be like at forty?
> I thought of a peruke the other day),
> My heart is not much greener; and in short, I
> Have squander'd my whole summer while 'twas May,
> And feel no more the spirit to retort; I
> Have spent my life, both interest and principal,
> And deem not, what I deem'd, my soul invincible.

We notice the off-hand rhymes, 'forty', 'short, I', 'retort; I'. Then the irony vanishes, in a full-volumed Romanticism; as usual in *Don Juan*, the modulation is signalized by a change in the character of the rhymes, and the general sonority: the voice, though remaining a speaking voice, takes on an underlying singing tone:

> No more – no more – Oh! never more on me
> The freshness of the heart can fall like dew,
> Which out of all the lovely things we see
> Extracts emotions beautiful and new;
> Hived in our bosoms like the bag o' the bee.
> Think'st thou the honey with those objects grew?
> Alas! 'twas not in them, but in thy power
> To double even the sweetness of a flower.

It is Byron's equivalent to *Dejection: an Ode*. But the stanza just quoted is followed by a partial return of the common sense, the reasonable, the Augustan, emerging ruefully in a still predominantly Romantic context:

> No more – no more – Oh! never more, my heart,
> Canst thou be my sole world, my universe!
> Once all in all, but now a thing apart,
> Thou canst not be my blessing or my curse:
> The illusion's gone for ever, and thou art
> Insensible, I trust, but none the worse,
> And in thy stead I've got a deal of judgment,
> Though heaven knows how it even found a lodgment.

None the worse: the very unsonorous rhyme of judgment/lodgment' is typical of the manner. This returning reasonableness takes on a colour of light irony:

My days of love are over; me no more
The charms of maid, wife, and still less of widow
Can make the fool of which they did before –
In short, I must not lead the life I did do;
The credulous hope of mutual minds is o'er,
The copious use of claret is forbid too;
So, for a good old-gentlemanly vice,
I think I must take up with avarice.

The Horatian regret (*nec spes animi mutua creduli*) appears as a foil
to middle-aged matter-of-factness; the stanza running out into
flippancy.

The return to the general manner of the poem is effected in an
interesting way. There is first a surprise turn: a blast on the trom-
bone of *Childe Harold*:

Ambition was my idol, which was broken
Before the shrines of Sorrow, and of Pleasure;

But this leads into four lines, neither ironic nor Romantic, though
serious enough:

And the two last have left me many a token
O'er which reflection may be made at leisure;
Now, like Friar Bacon's brazen head, I've spoken,
'Time is, Time was, Time's past':

and these serve as a bridge passage to the conclusion, or culmination:

. . . a chymic treasure
Is glittering youth, which I have spent betimes –
My heart in passion, and my head on rhymes.

This culmination is Romantic in feeling; but the Romanticism is
subtly qualified by the reversion to a completely Augustan manner, a Popean neatness:

. . . glittering youth, which I have spent betimes –
My heart in passion, and my head on rhymes.

The general nature of the effect is obvious, but analysis perhaps
serves to bring out the peculiar significance, the dramatic force, of
that closing couplet. The Romantic and the Augustan come together with an air of momentary reconciliation; nostalgia for lost
youth, for the loss of the emotional spontaneity and power of

empathy that belong to youth, is accommodated to a practical acceptance of reality; giving the effect of a resolution (*Aufhebung*) of the two contrasting attitudes on which the passage is built. This dialectic is the life of *Don Juan*.

It may be worth adding that neither the Romanticism, nor the irony, nor their coming from the same poet, is specifically Byronic. There is such a thing as Romantic irony, as in Heine or Musset. What *is* highly personal to Byron, is the temporary stabilization of conflicting emotions, in a manner which is neither Romantic nor ironical. There is no calculation, of course, in this effect, but in all the wayward progress of the verse there is an internal control which is lacking in other semi-serious poetry, Auden's for example.

In range and variety of emotional tone, as in other respects, *Don Juan* is the antithesis of *The Prelude*. One difficulty in reading the latter is Wordsworth's habit of moving placidly on from dull passages, or passages of fair to middling interest, to inspired passages, without break, transposition, or change of gear. In *Don Juan* Byron has solved for himself and his purposes, as Wordsworth in my opinion did not, the problem of the long poem. His solution is to come forward frankly as an improviser.

> I don't know that there may be much ability
> Shown in this sort of desultory rhyme;
> But there's a conversational facility,
> Which may round off an hour upon a time.
> Of this I'm sure at least, there's no servility
> In mine irregularity of chime,
> Which rings what's uppermost of new or hoary,
> Just as I feel the *Improvvisatore*.

One need not dwell on the dangers and temptations of the *Improvvisatore* in poetry. Perhaps his most tiresome characteristic is Byron's recurrent self-satisfaction that, without taking any pains, he is writing better poetry than his fellow poets who do. This makes him the victim of a technique, or lack of technique, which permits him not only to tolerate second-rateness but elaborate it with gusto.

> Who holds the balance of the world? Who reign
> O'er congress, whether royalist or liberal?
> Who rouse the shirtless patriots of Spain?

(That make old Europe's journals squeak and gibber all),
Who keep the world, both old and new, in pain
Or pleasure? Who makes politics run glibber all?
The shade of Buonaparte's noble daring?
Jew Rothschild, and his fellow-Christian, Baring.

The nullity of the writing appropriately accompanies the sentiment of a writer in *Gringoire*. At the other extreme, there are many lapses into the histrionic-profound, from which Byron is never free in any of his work, 'Between two worlds life hovers like a star' and all the rest of it; unimaginable from a poet like Leopardi, beside whom, with all his bookishness, Byron often seems an essentially uneducated spirit.

But the aplomb of the improviser, and the reader's awareness of it, are essential to the art of a poem which Hazlitt described, felicitously, as 'a poem about itself'.

But Adeline was not indifferent: for
(*Now* for a commonplace!) beneath the snow,
As a volcano holds the lava more
Within – *et caetera*. Shall I go on? No,
I have to hunt down a tired metaphor,
So let the often-used volcano go,
Poor thing! How frequently, by me and others,
It hath been stirred up till its smoke quite smothers!

I'll have another figure in a trice –
What say you to a bottle of champagne?
Frozen into a very vinous ice,
Which leaves few drops of that immortal rain,
Yet in the very centre, past all price,
About a liquid glassful will remain;
And this is stronger than the strongest grape
Could e'er express in its expanded shape.

Byron's improvisation here, after the hit at conventional poetry, his own included, is a justification in practice of figures drawn from 'Art', rather than 'Nature', Pope's use of which he defended against Bowles. But the important point about it is this: the false start shows not only the slip into commonplace which he notices, but an inability which he was perhaps not conscious of, to concentrate his effects; he needs space to be a poet. This of course has bearings on the lack of a distinctive diction, noted earlier. A poet like Keats might have done something with that 'volcano'; Byron could not, but he turns his incapacity into a virtue by rejecting the figure in full view of the reader.

And in fact Byron is perpetually aware, unlike Wordsworth, or the Tennyson of *In Memoriam*, that he has a reader. Then, his sociable tone, his friendship with the reader, is founded on the tacit agreement that he too is a fellow sinner.

> They the sailors vow to amend their lives, and yet they don't;
> Because if drown'd they can't; if spared, they won't.

And Malthus does the thing 'gainst which he writes. We know what human nature is like, and have not too exalted a conception of it; since we ourselves are the examples that we know most intimately. The air of nonchalant familiarity, which finds its sanction in this fellow-feeling, is not un-Augustan; but it is nearer to Dryden than to Pope. And this is not the only way in which the Regency, as illustrated by Byron, reminds us of the Restoration. But Byron's true analogue in Restoration poetry is not Dryden but Rochester.

> Without, or with, offence to friends and foes,
> I sketch your world exactly as it goes.

'Without, *or with*' is the touch of recklessness typical of Byron; but it reminds us also of the isolated, anarchic flouting of society which we often find in Rochester, and never in Dryden. There are interesting social and political parallels, as well as personal and poetic ones, between these two rebellious patricians of different epochs; quite apart from their aristocratic anarchism and will to *épater le bourgeois*, there are likeness between the Rochester seen by Bishop Burnet, and the Byron seen by Dr. Kennedy.

But this debonair freedom, and the ease with which Byron manages his transitions and expatiates at whatever length he pleases, and on whatever occasion, about anything which interests him – none of these vivacities convince us that the poet is always enjoying himself. He is not always letting himself go with such satisfaction as he shows in the flyting of Southey. His success in elevating drunken inconsequence to the status of art, is itself as much a product of the unhappy libertine's trying to persuade himself that he is cheerful, as of the half-earnest moralist's ambition to be serious. Even his fun is more the evidence of a gay, than of a cheerful, temperament. It is not hard to see a desperately un-

comfortable man in the author of *Don Juan*; the very writing of it is
part of the attempt to cheer himself up.

> And if I laugh at any mortal thing,
> 'Tis that I may not weep.

The switches and reversals of mood are not so much the result
of a critical check upon his emotion, as a flinching away from it; he
hastens to a superficial kind of self-revelation, for fear of a deeper
self-betrayal. Sometimes he seems actually frightened by a thought
that has arisen in composition. The strange opening of Canto
XIV, with the typical change between stanzas vi and vii, is a case
in point; and earlier in the poem, after a moving rendering of the
madness and death of Haidee, he intervenes with:

> But let me change this theme, which grows too sad,
> And lay this sheet of sorrows on the shelf;
> I don't much like describing people mad,
> For fear of seeming rather touch'd myself –

And a similar fear seems to spring up, when he has let himself go
in some tender sentiment, of a kind which he will commit to
verse, though rarely to prose; but will be quick to abandon, if he
thinks he is being caught out, or 'placed' in any single attitude.
Indeed, one of his unpleasant traits of character, the caddishness
that he showed in the Guiccioli episode (in his letters to friends),
seems to be due, not merely to an obvious dislike of ridicule, but to
this fear of being 'typed', thought of as committed to any one part –
especially if it is undignified: among the Christian virtues which
Mr. Wilson Knight has found in Byron, indifference about one's
personal dignity was not included.

But the great self-release Byron gets in *Don Juan* is only possible
when he gives up his dignity as a poet. This is interestingly shown
in the *ubi sunt* passage in Canto XI. Juan's presence in England
leads Byron to moralize, in a gruesome-cum-humorous manner,
on 'the life of a young noble'. After an epigrammatic stanza describing this (lxxv) the thought of the personal application of these
lines provokes him to an exercise in the histrionic-profound:

> 'Where is the world?' cried Young, at *eighty* – 'Where
> The world in which a man was born?' Alas!
> Where is the world of *eight* years past? '*Twas there* –
> I look for it – 'tis gone, a globe of glass!

> Crack'd, shiver'd, vanish'd, scarcely gazed on, ere
> A silent change dissolves the glittering mass.

These lines, and there are many like them in *Don Juan*, incite us to
a use of Goethe's comment; 'When he reflects, he is a child.' The
inability to think is as evident as the jerky, straining motion, and,
as the italics betray, Byron is trying to compensate by an imposed
emphasis and gesture for his failure to realize his elusive subject.
Against his excited gesticulating we may place two lines from a
Shakespeare sonnet:

> Ah, yet doth beauty, like a dial-hand,
> Steal from his figure, and no pace perceived.

In Byron's lines, it is the generality of the concept of Time that
defeats him; his poetic gift only appears when he gets down to
particulars.

> Where is Napoleon the Grand? God knows;
> Where little Castlereagh? The devil can tell:
> Where Grattan, Curran, Sheridan, all those
> Who bound the bar or senate in their spell?
> Where is the unhappy Queen, with all her woes?
> And where the Daughter, whom the Isles loved well?
> Where are those martyr'd saints the Five per Cents?
> And where – oh, where the devil are the Rents?
>
> Where's Brummel? Dish'd. Where's Long Pole Wellesley?
>   Diddled.
> Where's Whitbread? Romilly? Where's George the Third?
> Where is his will? (That's not so soon unriddled.)
> And where is 'Fum' the Fourth, our 'royal bird'?
> Gone down, it seems, to Scotland to be fiddled
> Unto by Sawney's violin, we have heard:
> 'Caw me, caw thee' – for six months hath been hatching
> This scene of royal itch and loyal scratching.
>
> Where is Lord This? And where my Lady That?
> The Honourable Mistresses and Misses?
> Some laid aside like an old Opera hat,
> Married, unmarried, and remarried (this is
> An evolution oft performed of late),
> Where are the Dublin shouts – and London hisses?
> Where are the Grenvilles? Turn'd as usual. Where
> My friends the Whigs? Exactly where they were.

The spacious movement ('. . . queens, patriots, kings, And dandies, all are gone on the wind's wings') is broken up into staccato, as with a crash of cymbals. His pen then runs away from him; the freedom of the *ottava rima* is exploited to the full; the incoherence of the stanza on Time returns, but this time incoherence has a dramatic effect – the random snatching at names evocative of grandeur and gossip, heroes and faded dandies, scandal and tragedy, triviality and History, which gives such a hop-skip-and-jump to the movement, only enhances the amusing reversal at the close: the exemption of the Whigs, with their permanence of *vis inertiae*, only adds extra sparkle to the whirligig. Byron has here made a virtue out of his inability to concentrate his thoughts, to realize the idea of Time either in a telling image, or a pregnant abstraction; we are to feel his resilience to the solemn commonplace, in his capacity to organize a movement of so prodigiously long a wave-length; we ride the thought not knowing when the next lift or bump is coming, and emerge exhilarated at the place from which we started.

The whole performance is admirably dramatic. And here we have a word that must, after all, be used of Byron. An agreement between Mr. Wilson Knight and Byron's more conventional biographers, is their common recognition of this quality in his behaviour and life-style. 'And each man in his life plays many parts.' On that question of Byron's sincerity, touched on earlier, the comparison with a dramatic performer throws some light. It is possible, in watching a great actor, to respond simultaneously in two ways: 'How moving!' and 'How well he plays his part!' And we should not feel the actor's greatness less, were we to infer a corresponding duality of consciousness in him. There is no question of insincerity; the performance is successful or unsuccessful, good or bad, but it is not sincere or insincere. Success is a matter of being able to mobilize emotions which one has either had, or can imagine having, without necessarily having them at the moment. This is in a sense a commonplace about Byron. But not all his critics have recognized, as Mr. Wilson Knight clearly has, that there are distinctions to be made here between great acting, attitudinizing, and 'putting on an act'. To judge Byron fairly we have to set aside what is mere theatricality, or neurosis, the reduplication of an already existent pattern, and recognize what is in effect a *new* emotion, in responding to which we are appreciating a conscious art. Some of Byron's worst attitudinizing occurs when he is least conscious of it; greater consciousness means greater sincerity, but not in the sense of a fuller identification of the poet with the explicit state of feeling; it shows itself rather in an unusual *directness*, which gives an exceptional artistic distinction to the familiar show of strength. (I am thinking here of passages like Canto XIV, stanzas i to xii.)

It is relevant here to mention Byron's interest in the theatre (he was on the management committee of Drury Lane for a time) and to say a word about his plays. When we look at these, a likely expectation is not fulfilled. We shall be surprised, if we turn to *Marino Faliero* or *Sardanapalus* in the desire, or dread, of an emotional debauch. The objection to these plays is quite otherwise; they are too analytic, too schematized; we are offered the analysis of dramatic characters and situations, whose presence is a mere intellectual postulate. The plays none the less have some interest, as a serious and conscious attempt at classical strictness in English drama; they consist in a dramatic rhetoric of ideas belonging to the nineteenth century, but presented in conformity with canons of taste that Corneille might have approved. The intention is worth study: but few will agree with Mr. Wilson Knight that the achievement is that of a great dramatist. The idea, the situations, and the characters are of a piece with the quality of the verse, and the verse is the verse of Byron. True, there is no necessary connexion between dramatic effectiveness and the Elizabethan stage tradition which Byron refused to revive in his own plays. Nor is there an *a priori* objection to the lucid explicitness of his language, and the severe formality of his dramatic structure. The objection refers to their compatibility with Byron's genius as a whole. In order to subdue his matter to his purpose, and find matter which would suit such a purpose, Byron has to leave out nearly everything that makes him interesting. His genius needed, besides a frame of strictness, rationality, and restraint to enclose it, a world of landscape, disorder, and 'hamming' in which to let itself go. We can go from some letters of Byron to the prose speeches of Hamlet without a jar or sense of transition; we may feel that Byron could have been a character in Shakespeare's plays; but he could not have been a character in one of Byron's. The dramatic gift of Byron is not in his plays, but in his letters and journals; and in the dramatic monody of *Don Juan*.

About the narrative and action of *Don Juan*, it is not necessary to go into detail; their attractions are obvious; and the most original feature of Byron's enterprise is well suggested in this quotation from Halévy's Preface to his *History of the English People in 1815*:

To an Englishman, English society is the whole of society, the ideal society. Buckle, in a work celebrated half a century ago, avowedly treated all forms of human civilisation as so many deviations from the true norm of civilisation, the civilisation of Great Britain. Very different is the attitude of the observer from abroad. A great number of characteristics which, being familiar to the natives from birth, have come to form part of their intellectual and moral nature, are for him matter of astonishment – whether of admiration or disapproval is indifferent – and demand from him an explanation. Indeed, of all the nations in Europe, it is perhaps the English whose institutions must, in many respects, be regarded as being, beyond the institutions of other people, paradoxical, 'unique'.

The later cantos of *Don Juan*, and especially the description of the house-party, owe their excellence to Byron's ability to be both inside and outside the people, the institutions, and the social falsities and absurdities, which supply his material. At home in no civilization himself, he responds the more keenly to the comic aspect of people who are at home in theirs. In serious moods, he reveals himself as a *déraciné* who cannot forget 'Society' and his triumphs and disasters in it, but who dreams of another kind of society in which the standards of success or failure are different. That there is an element of daydream in his fondness for the viewpoint of a Tartar chieftain, or a levelling radical, does not mean that he cannot thereby project a lively criticism of the unrealities, fallacies, and inhumanities of the established fact: his knowledge of 'life' and 'the world' projects him from many illusions; and his indulgences in misanthropy do not preclude a real and generous humanity. The anger and horror of the war sections of *Don Juan* owe the power of their expression to their being the correlates of positive feelings; just as the force of the irony, in the frivolous parts of the poem, derives from Byron's unfailing capacity to discriminate between the 'human' values and the 'social 'ones. And thus it is that *Don Juan*, which in one aspect is licentious, cynical, antinomian, in another aspect is a most edifying and improving work.

As to the nominal hero of the poem, objections have been made to his general colourlessness, passivity, and silence; but he plays the part that is allotted to him. He seems in his love-affairs to represent that willingness of Byron to be *used* by women, which is so curious a quality of Byron's own *vie amoureuse*; but he never evinces the reaction against that role, and against the Regency gentleman-amorist in general, which is equally characteristic and significant. So his performance, as a dramatization of Byron's own relations with women, is always simplified and partial. Thus, if we judge that his relationship to Catherine II reflects – as it probably does – Byron's affair with Lady Oxford, we must add at once that the fiction leaves out something essential to the understanding of the life-situation: Byron's need for, or intermittent conviction of his need for, a woman who would be motherly without moralizing. There are two reasons, one technical, and one biographical, for this two-dimensional character of the hero. In so far as the traditional Don Juan is part of the conception, Byron the narrator has taken over his functions; and in so far as he stands for the young Byron, the older man is too remote from him (except in the early cantos) to be willing, or perhaps able, to re-capture either his foolishness or his charm. The Byron of *Don Juan* does not give us, as does Stendhal, that re-creation of the follies of youth which is done from within, but which we none the less feel to be always under the eyes of maturity. For Byron, the contemplation of the past is too painful; he has too much a sense of loss, and of tragic waste, to accept it as a condition of the present. *Don Juan* is the work of a mature mind, but not one with an integral vision.

And this is, finally, why we cannot rank it very high among the creative works of literature. 'He did not respect himself, or his art, as much as they deserved'; great art cannot be made out of a boredom with oneself, which is expressed as a boredom with one's subject-matter; and the later cantos of *Don Juan*, which are the finest and most mature parts of the poem, are also, significantly, the parts in which that distate, that boredom, is becoming a settled attitude.

> But 'why then publish?' – There are no rewards,
> Of fame or profit when the world grows weary.
> I ask in turn, – Why do you play at cards?
> Why drink? Why read? – To make some hour less dreary.
> It occupies me to turn back regards

On what I've seen or ponder'd, sad or cheery;
And what I write I cast upon the stream,
To swim or sink – I have had at least my dream.

(XIV, xi)

Byron may get relief from his boredom by writing about it;
but this state of mind is incompatible with a sustained creative
art. His desire and will to ground Romanticism on reality cannot
be satisfied with the attempt to do this in art; he feels that it must
be done in life, and it must be done in spite of that nagging fear
(exceptionally poignant in one who makes a cult of the spontaneous) of emotional inadequacy. This comes out, not only in
the grumbling passages of *Don Juan*, but, with a very pathetic
accent, in the very late poem, *On this day I complete my thirty-sixth
year*; which was written in Greece.

That reminder of Byron's last service, in the flesh, to the cause
of national freedom, induces the suitably sympathetic spirit in
which to ask: what is the value of Byron's poetry? what does he
leave us with? It is not a question of ranking him among poets; as
Byron himself says in his 1813 *Journal*, 'Surely the field of thought
is infinite; what does it signify who is before or behind, in a race
which has no goal?' But whether we are to revere him as an oracle,
or regard him, dispassionately or sympathetically, as a human
case, is not a question that can be lightly dismissed. Byron's personal predicament is certainly there:

> . . . I am one the more
> To baffled millions who have gone before.

And it certainly accounts for many of the weaknesses of his work;
the egocentricity, the grandiloquence, the failures in self-knowledge, the lack of balance and perspective, the ensuing monotony.
But I have tried to show that even in his morose or destructive
moods, even in works that reveal his spiritual malaise most
clearly, there is an opposite movement towards restorativeness and
health. He is a poet not only in that (to use a convenient vul-
garism) he 'gets across' his egoistic passions; he conveys along
with them, though doubtless unwittingly, a sense that his vehement
indulgence in them is, deep down, against the grain. And our
recognition of this ultimate probity is allied to our pleasure in
Byron's vitality. Whether one should go further than that, and
find in Byron the poet a moral hero, a religious and spiritual force,

I am doubtful; is he coherent enough to command that kind or degree of reverence? I should prefer to say that at his best he leaves us with a heightened realization of the value of *personality*, in the sense in which this is distinguished from *character*. But of course the two are not to be finally separated. And to admit this is also a tribute to Byron. His human and poetic sins are many; but, as with some characters in the *Inferno*, we dare not view them with patronage, any more than we wish to mitigate them with pity. He wrings a paradoxical victory out of defeat.

> Poi si rivolse, e parve di coloro
> che corrono a Verona il drappo verde
> per la campagna; e parve di costoro
> Quegli che vince e non colui che perde.

1957

PART FOUR

PART FOUR

XIII

THE DILEMMA OF TENNYSON

I begin by quoting one of the most familiar passages of nine-teenth-century English poetry.

> The lights begin to twinkle from the rocks:
> The long day wanes: the slow moon climbs: the deep
> Moans round with many voices. Come, my friends,
> 'Tis not too late to seek a newer world.
> Push off, and sitting well in order smite
> The sounding furrows; for my purpose holds
> To sail beyond the sunset, and the baths
> Of all the western stars, until I die.
> It may be that the gulfs will wash us down:
> It may be we shall touch the Happy Isles,
> And see the great Achilles, whom we knew.
> Tho' much is taken, much abides; and tho'
> We are not now that strength which in old days
> Moved earth and heaven; that which we are, we are;
> One equal temper of heroic hearts,
> Made weak by time and fate, but strong in will
> To strive, to seek, to find, and not to yield.

That is the close of Tennyson's *Ulysses*. It is a very beautiful poem; and I think it will be agreed that those closing lines derive part of their beauty from a sense we have of a whole history of European imagination and aspiration to which Tennyson is giving voice through the lips of Ulysses. For although he speaks with the accent of Tennyson, the speaker is unmistakably for the Ulysses of Dante. In the eleventh book of the *Odyssey* it is foretold to Ulysses that, after his return to Ithaca and the slaying of the suitors, he is to set off again on a mysterious voyage. This voyage, and its sequel, is described by the tragic figure in Dante's *Inferno*. His most famous lines are these, which exhort his companions on his last voyage, beyond the Pillars of Hercules:

> 'O brothers', said I, 'who are come despite
> Ten thousand perils to the West, let none,
> While still our senses hold the vigil slight
> Remaining to us ere our course is run,　　'
> Be willing to forgo experience
> Of the unpeopled world beyond the sun.
> Regard your origin, – from whom and whence!
> Not to exist like brutes, but made were ye
> To follow virtue and intelligence'.

> (Considerate la vostra semenza:
> fatti non foste a viver come bruti,
> ma per seguir virtute e conoscenza.)

Tennyson's Ulysses is Homer's Odysseus felt through Dante; but the vibration of this poem of Tennyson is not due merely to a modern poet's response to the Renaissance. The emotion to which it gives this dramatic expression is something personal to the poet, as a man alive in his own time. What the poem meant to Tennyson we know. He tells us that *Ulysses* was written soon after Arthur Hallam's death. 'It gives the feeling [he says] about the need of going forward and braving the struggle of life more simply than anything in *In Memoriam*.' As so often in Tennyson, the resolve, the will, to undertake responsible public action and effort, is linked with the need to find release from an overwhelming personal sorrow. This message, then, about 'the need of going forward and braving the struggle of life', is the point of juncture between the poet as a private individual, with his private sorrows, and the poet as a responsible social being, conscious of a public world in which he has duties. The poet in the first place is exhorting himself, to seek consolation in 'going forward'; but he exhorts himself as a responsible social being, and his exhortation – as the tone of the verse so plainly indicates – is equally aimed at a whole moral community of which he is one member.

And it found a response in that community. *Ulysses* seems to have been what converted Carlyle to a belief in Tennyson. Edward Fitzgerald tells us:

This was the Poem which, as might perhaps be expected, Carlyle liked best in the Book. [The 1842 volumes.] I do not think he became acquainted with Alfred Tennyson till after these Volumes appeared; being naturally prejudiced against one whom everyone was praising, and praising for a *Sort* of Poetry which he despised. But directly he saw, and heard, the Man, he knew there was A Man to deal with: and took pains to cultivate him; assiduous in exhorting him to leave Verse and Rhyme, and to apply his Genius to Prose and *Work*.

This exhortation of Carlyle, the amusing starkness of the antithesis between 'Poetry' and 'Work', helps us to bring into focus a curious anomaly in *Ulysses*. It is an anomaly which in various forms must often trouble the reader of Tennyson – the reader whose interest is in poetry as poetry, and not merely in the explicit intentions of the poet or the paraphraseable conten. No one can doubt that that admirable Victorian seriousness, which Carlyle saluted in *Ulysses*, is really there; the desire to express it is manifestly an important part of the poem's inspiration. And yet, when we restore that heroic close of the poem to its context – and even when we examine the passage I quoted by itself – there is something to be said about the quality of the verse, the poetic texture, which is striking at odds with the judgement – so obviously true – that Tennyson is here at one with an aspiration of his age.

> The lights begin to twinkle from the rocks:
> The long day wanes: the slow moon climbs: the deep
> Moans round with many voices . . .

That slow movement, still further retarded by the characteristic lingering on the vowel sounds ('. . . mouthing out his hollow o'es and a'es,) pervades the poem.

> Yet all experience is an arch wherethro'
> Gleams that untravell'd world, whose margin fades
> For ever and for ever when I move.

Matthew Arnold said of these lines that they take up as much time as a whole book of the *Odyssey*. And it seems to me that even at the point where Tennyson's Ulysses rouses himself finally from his lethargy, and sounds the call to action, the effect of the verse as verse is not radically different.

> Come, my friends,
> 'Tis not too late to seek a newer world.
> Push off, and sitting well in order smite
> The sounding furrows; for my purpose holds
> To sail beyond the sunset, and the baths
> Of all the western stars, until I die.

There is not here the same obvious preoccupation with a decorative effect that we see in 'The long day wanes: the slow moon climbs', and so on, but the prevailing quality, as it were of a language or medium that is too conscious of itself, is not really different. T. S. Eliot has remarked on the contrast, in one important respect, between Tennyson's Ulysses and Dante's; Dante's character, whatever else he may be, is certainly in the first place a seaman telling a yarn; Tennyson's speaker is a self-conscious poet. This contrast considered by itself does not imply that Tennyson's poem is inferior; there is no critical rule about the degree of transparency permitted to a poet's *persona*. But the contrast remarked by Eliot does bring out the effect of which, I think, Tennyson's attitude to his language is the cause. There is a radical discrepancy between the strenuousness aspired to, and the medium in which the aspiration is expressed.

This discrepancy points to no insincerity here, at any level, in Tennyson. It is not true to say, as is sometimes said – and I think in Tennyson's own time, Edward Fitzgerald at least implied something like this – that Tennyson was essentially a lyric poet, with a true gift only for the decorative, the evocative, and the elegiac, who made himself express the attitudes of his age to large public subjects not because he really wanted to do this or was capable of doing it but because he felt he ought to. This is not, I think, a true account of Tennyson's development in general, and it is certainly not fair to *Ulysses*. The unsatisfactoriness – if there is unsatisfactoriness – in *Ulysses* is more interesting than that. My point is this: there is a real ring of conviction in those last lines of the poem:

> . . . that which we are, we are;
> One equal temper of heroic hearts,
> Made weak by time and fate, but strong in will
> To strive, to seek, to find, and not to yield.

If Tennyson was expressing here a feeling that can be called 'typically Victorian', it was a feeling in which he himself shared to the full; we do not need biographical evidence in order to see that the theme is personally felt. But the more we recognize this, the more strongly are we conscious of that anomaly I spoke of: how could a Tennyson who is so deeply concerned with what he is saying – and we will be making a big mistake if we underrate the scope and reality of Tennyson's intellectual and moral preoccupations – how *could* a poet of that intelligence have been content with the style of a minor poet?

The incongruity of *Ulysses* may be summed up like this: 'Tennyson, the responsible social being, the admirably serious and "committed" Victorian intellectual, is uttering strenuous sentiments in the accent of Tennyson the most unstrenuous, lonely, and poignant of poets.' That this incongruity does not spoil the poem, that it remains very beautiful and, in its way, perfect, I infer from my own experience and the attested experience of generations of readers. But to appreciate its beauty – and at the same time to recognize its limitations – that is useful in reminding us of how complex the 'poet-public' relationship is in Tennyson's more interesting verse. There is plenty of evidence that Tennyson felt himself compelled, as Laureate and mouthpiece of Society, to write things in which his peculiar genius was not involved; we dismiss those things, or put them in their place – they are dated – just because the 'poet-public' relationship, in their case, so plainly is a simple one: the 'public' addressed is external, Tennyson is speaking from a platform. The poems – *Ulysses*, for example – that concern the literary critic and the lover of poetry, allow no such easy analysis of ends and means.

In *Ulysses* the 'public' in the first place is Tennyson himself: and its exceptional interest lies in the fact that both Tennyson the responsible social being, and Tennyson the depressed private poet, are really there in the poem: while its limitation, I think, lies in there being no conscious relationship, manifested at the poetic level, between them. But there is no crude antithesis. In the obviously unsatisfactory or bad poems of Tennyson – I mean, such of them as are more than mere official utterances or popular anthology-pieces – there is a patent disharmony. Indeed, it often looks as if Tennyson the moralist and Tennyson the artist are functioning on entirely separate planes. Certainly it is possible for the reader to take an interest in the skill, the technique, which is quite distinct from any interest he may have in what is being said. I am thinking of things like the bad parts of *Maud*. Technique, in a

sense, and in a sense that was important to Tennyson, never fails
him in those parts; it can be analysed and appreciated, indepen-
dently of one's sense of the value of what is being done; but that
this should be so is a comment on the quality of the technique –
which in the good parts can so perfectly serve the emotional and
moral purposes of the poet. And the presence of this technique,
cultivated apart from the particular demands of any particular
subject-matter, is perhaps what makes the bad parts of *Maud* seem
so desolatingly bad:

And the vitriol madness flushes up in the ruffian's head,
Till the filthy by-lane rings to the yell of the trampled wife . . .
And Sleep must lie down arm'd, for the villainous centre-
　　bits
Grind on the wakeful ear in the hush of the moonless nights,
While another is cheating the sick of a few last gasps, as he sits
To pestle a poison'd poison behind his crimson lights.

It is true that in *Maud* the narrator is not avowedly Tennyson,
but a dramatic figure who is supposed to be hysterical and
neurotic. But there is no evidence in that poem that the poet has
firm criteria by which the hysteria and neurosis are judged to be
so. The hero of *Maud* is sometimes a dramatic figure, and sometimes a mere subterfuge; he is, and is not, Tennyson. The result is
that such passages as 'And the vitriol madness flushes up in the
ruffian's head etc.' strike us, not as the product of dramatic imagination, but as a self-indulgence, and (because the show of
drama is there to protect it) they strike us as self-indulgence of
an exceptionally disagreeable kind.

These things are disagreeable, I think, because of the insistent
presence of that technique – a technique practised everywhere in
the poem – which compels us all the time to recognize, as some
more ragged imprecation would not, that all this violence is being
willed. But the critical interest of such things is more than that:
they make us begin to wonder whether some of the exasperation
they proclaim so stridently is due to the poet's own partial awareness that something is going wrong: his skill is not producing the
effect which, at one level of his being, is what he wants. I would
like to consider this further in its bearings on the whole critical
problem of Tennyson's poetry.

The decline of Tennyson is to me a much more painful spect-
acle than the decline of Wordsworth. This is because, in Tennyson's

case, the difference between his living work and the work of his decadence is not simply the difference between life and death. There is often a curious unpleasant life in the later Tennyson that compels some reaction from the reader, as the later Wordsworth so rarely does.

I would like to look at one of the poems produced by the elderly Tennyson, *Locksley Hall Sixty Years After*. This is a poem that was famous in its day. Nowadays, I think it can safely be said, there is no poem in the whole Tennyson canon which is more damagingly and damningly dated; and yet, looked at without prejudice, can it be denied to have considerable power?

> Effects like this are not at all uncommon:
> ... war will die out late then. Will it ever? late or soon?
> Can it, till this outworn earth be dead as yon dead world the
>   moon?
> Dead the new astronomy calls her ...
> Poor old Heraldry, poor old History, poor old Poetry,
>   passing hence,
> In the common deluge drowning old political common-
>   sense!

Tennyson is writing with unusual power, when he is able, as he is here, to get his intellectual and scientific interests into poetry. And yet *Locksley Hall Sixty Years After* is disastrously bad, and in the same way as *Maud* is bad where it is bad: this is a representative bit:

> It is well that while we range with Science, glorying in the
>   Time,
> City children soak and blacken soul and sense in city slime?
> There among the glooming alleys Progress halts on palsied
>   feet,
> Crime and hunger cast our maidens by the thousand on the
>   street.
> There the Master scrimps his haggard sempstress of her
>   daily bread,
> There a single sordid attic holds the living and the dead.
> There the smouldering fire of fever creeps across the rotted
>   floor,
> And the crowded couch of incest in the warrens of the
>   poor.

We cannot mistake the genuine anguish of the agonized social conscience; these horrors are realities to Tennyson, and he labours to render them with all he can summon of dramatic (and melo-dramatic) power. But – that tone of voice, and that movement:

> There among the glooming alleys Progress halts on palsied feet,
> Crime and hunger cast our maidens by the thousand on the street.

It is like bad Dickens. I expect no one now would dispute either of two judgements: Tennyson is deeply stirred here; and here Tennyson is not a poet; the verdict on the later Tennyson is pronounced by the almost total neglect of him. But I am surprised how unquestioningly both literary historians and amateurs of his poetry accept this failure as a matter of course. The meaningless judgement that Tennyson was 'outside his range' is all the critical help one is given. But Tennyson was one of the most intelligent and morally concerned men of his time, and I cannot see why it should be so complacently granted that he could not, in the nature of the case, write poetry about these things.

I think the main value of contemplating *Locksley Hall Sixty Years After* is that it shows us in an extreme and crude form what went wrong with the poet-public, or public-private, relationship in Tennyson's poetry. There were no doubt many reasons why this went wrong, some of them lying quite outside Tennyson's personality or the short-comings of the Victorian poetic tradition, but I am concerned here only with what bears on the essential, the individual Tennyson. What I trace as a growing awareness in his poetry that he could not meet the needs of the public which he had helped to create, and to which, as a social being, he himself belonged – this awareness becomes open and complete in this poem. The *persona* here is in no such equivocal relation to Tennyson as the hero of *Maud*: he *is* Tennyson in all that matters, and it is significant that he relapses at last openly into what he has been essentially throughout: a futile old reactionary, half-pathetic, half-defiant in his sense of his futility:

> Poor old voice of eighty crying after voices that have fled!
> All I loved are vanish'd voices, all my steps are on the dead.
> All the world is ghost to me, and as the phantom disappears,
> Forward far and far from here is all the hope of eighty years.

There is, of course, a special poignancy in remembering the closing lines of *Ulysses* when one reads this poem of the old Tennyson. But it is not merely that Tennyson is old and embittered; a certain violent irresponsibility about the writing suggests that he is getting a kind of gloomy satisfaction out of his feeling of powerlessness: while expressly admitting his final inability to engage his talents upon these themes that both fascinate and horrify him, he produces a picture of the 'public' world which has a queer nightmare life; the nightmare in his own; public and private are neither separate, as in some of his earlier poetry, nor consciously and critically related, but just confused.

In *Locksley Hall Sixty Years After* we have an extreme case of the breakdown of relation between Tennyson's 'art' and his 'social conscience'. But this breakdown had occurred, in milder forms, long before. I think the difference at the end is merely that Tennyson was more aware of it, and this gave him a paradoxical energy of despair. His true greatness lay elsewhere; but, in concurring with the judgement that things like the lyrics in *Maud*, the lyrics in *The Princess*, are among his supreme achievements, we must recognize that without the earnestness, the sense of responsibility towards the world outside the poet, they could not have been written; while at the same time their peculiar sadness seems tacitly to acknowledge the inability of their author to confront that world as a poet.

1957

o

XIV

THREE VICTORIAN POETS

The poets of the Victorian Age were numerous, and they included people of talent and even of genius. But it is now almost a commonplace to remark that the greatest imaginative writers of the period are novelists, not poets. The reasons for this decline of poetry are disputable, but the fact of the decline itself is rarely questioned. Perhaps Matthew Arnold had it in mind when he made his celebrated formulation: 'Poetry is at bottom a criticism of life.' Certainly he was the opponent, in his critical propaganda, of a tendency which he discerned in the work of the great Romantic poets: a separation between poetry and life. It is these poets whose joint influence constitutes the Victorian poetic tradition. And the influence of none of them – not even Wordsworth's – was such as to counteract the trends which Arnold saw. One of them indeed, was virtually the discovery of, and a chief inspiration and sanction to, some poets in the phase of Victorian Romanticism succeeding that of the earlier Tennyson; the high priest of their religion of beauty was John Keats.

This religion of beauty is today unpopular. The work of the Pre-Raphaelites (like that of their successors in the Aesthetic Movement) is now commonly judged to be not only inferior to, but in some ways essentially unlike, the 'priest-like task' of Keats. Pre-Raphaelite poetry is felt by many readers to bear a derivative and subordinate relation to that of the great Romantics, and even to the contemporary poetry of Tennyson and Browning. Its relation to Tennyson I shall discuss presently; I merely note here that the influence of Browning on Rossetti (as in *Jenny*) has not always been emphasized; and, correlatively, there is a 'Pre-Raphaelite' element in Browning:

Only, they see not God, I know,
Nor all that chivalry of his,
The soldier-saints who, row on row,
Burn upward each to his point of bliss.
(The Statue and the Bust)

And this may be the place to mention a related symptom of the
modern change of taste: the enlistment of Hopkins as a 'modern'
poet, alongside Eliot and the later Yeats; and the consequent
exalting of him above Tennyson and Browning, the official great
poets of the Victorian period. Hopkins himself remains unmistakably a Victorian; but his work is obviously unlike theirs,
especially unlike Tennyson's. Pre-Raphaelite poetry, on the other
hand, though not exactly like Tennyson's, contains less that is
likely, in manner if not in matter, to disturb the admirer of Tennyson – although it is obvious that they were trying to do something
very unlike Tennyson. And so it has suffered the neglect which
has befallen other Victorian poetry of which the same could be
said. My purpose here is not to suggest reasons for reversing the
general verdict on Victorian poetry, not to discuss whether other
poets – notably Hopkins, but perhaps also Beddoes, Darley, or
Davidson – or writers who are not verse-poets at all – have better
claims to be regarded as the true heirs of the great Romantics. I
wish rather to consider what kind of interest Pre-Raphaelite
poetry can yield to the reader who shares Arnold's view of the
relation between poetry and life.

By Pre-Raphaelite poetry I mean the poetry of Dante Gabriel
Rossetti, of his sister Christina, and of William Morris. There are
lesser figures associated with the movement, and other important
poets, from Swinburne to Yeats, have Pre-Raphaelite connexions.
But D. G. Rossetti, the strongest personality and effective organ-
izer of the group, deserves the chief critical attention. However,
his picturesque life and habit of confession have proved a biographical lure too strong for most critics. The 'cult of personality'
existed among the Pre-Raphaelites themselves and their followers;
and the flood of autobiography, memoirs and letters has not yet
subsided. I am not of course saying that Rossetti's private life is
ultimately irrelevant to the study of his poetry; any more, or
any less, than the relation between devoutness and morbidity in
Christina Rossetti, or the activity of Morris as designer, printer, or
propagandist of Socialism, is irrelevant to the study of theirs.

These things have their importance, but they must be recalled in their due place as ancillaries, not as substitutes for the study of poetry.

But at this point an obvious objection must be met. Is it proper, or useful, to discuss Pre-Raphaelite poetry without discussing Pre-Raphaelite theory and practice in painting? The term 'Pre-Raphaelite' itself, as is well known, came to be used when the young Holman Hunt and the young J. E. Millais adversely criticized Raphael's *Transfiguration*, challenged the 'classical' doctrines expounded by Sir Joshua Reynolds, and extolled the superior purity and simplicity of the Italian primitives. And the movement began, at the close of the 1840s, as an attempt to introduce into visual art, not only the qualities of medieval Italian painting, but the naturalistic accuracy of detail thought appropriate to the dawning age of science. But by the 1850s what is now associated with Pre-Raphaelite painting – the merely decorative neo-medievalism, the subjectivity, the dreaminess – had become its dominant style. Painters were turning their eyes away from a contemporary industrial and urban world which was *ipso facto* hideous and hence, on Ruskin's principles, intractable to treatment in art. In any case, Rossetti himself seems to have had no very intense interest in the philosophical basis of the early naturalism of Hunt and Millais. (The general lack of wide intellectual interests in the circle of Rossetti and Morris comes out clearly in contemporary accounts.) And that dogmatic concern with precision of detail, which excited the admiration of Ruskin and the scorn of Dickens, appears in Rossetti – the Rossetti of *Ecce Ancilla Domini* – only as a transient phase of style. He was always essentially a literary painter, and the Pre-Raphaelite Brotherhood was fundamentally literary and preoccupied with literature. A literary approach, therefore, seems to be possible.

The adjective 'Pre-Raphaelite' in literary history suggests certain idiosyncrasies of style – sometimes they are hardly more than tricks – associated with the Rossettis and the early Morris. Yet many of them are to be seen in earlier poetry: in Tennyson's *Mariana* poems; in Coleridge's *Christabel* (which might be called the first Pre-Raphaelite poem); or in Keats's *The Eve of St. Mark*. There is the deliberate simplicity (or *simplesse*) of manner, often found in conjunction with that curious trick of particularizing, e.g. numbers:

> She had three lilies in her hand,
> And the stars in her hair were seven.
>
> (Rossetti, *The Blessed Damozel*)

> There were five swans that ne'er did eat
> The water-weeds, for ladies came
> Each day, and young knights did the same,
> And gave them cakes and bread for meat.
>
> (Morris, *Golden Wings*)

There is the particularity of sensory detail; visual detail, as here:

> Without, there was a cold moon up,
> Of Winter radiance sheer and thin;
> The hollow halo it was in
> Was like an icy crystal cup.
>
> (Rossetti, *My Sister's Sleep*)

Or auditory detail:

> Twelve struck. That sound, by dwindling years
> Heard in each hour, crept off, and then
> The ruffled silence spread again,
> Like water that a pebble stirs.
> Our mother rose from where she sat;
> Her needles, as she laid them down,
> Met lightly, and her silken gown
> Settled: no other noise than that.
>
> (*My Sister's Sleep*)

There is the archaizing and medievalizing, the cultivation of the ballad-mode and similar archaic forms, accompanied (especially in Morris) by a liking for archaic technical vocabulary:

> 'They hammer'd out my basnet point
> Into a round salade,' he said.
> 'The basnet being quite out of joint
> Natheless the salade rasps my head.'
>
> (Morris, *Old Love*)

There is a characteristic Pre-Raphaelite taste in decoration, as in:

> Raise me a dais of silk and down;
> Hang it with vair and purple dyes;
> Carve it in doves and pomegranates,
> And peacocks with a hundred eyes;

> Work it in gold and silver grapes,
>   In leaves and silver fleur-de-lys;
>   (Christina Rossetti, *A Birthday*)

But these are superficial traits. More important is the recurrence of certain habits of feeling; especially a mood associated with autumn, regarded as the season of listlessness, decay, desolation, death; never, in Pre-Raphaelite poetry, the 'close bosom-friend of the maturing sun', but Tennyson's 'spirit' that 'haunts the year's last hours, Dwelling amid these yellowing bowers'; as in

>   . . . the sere
> Autumnal springs, from many a dying year
> Born dead;
>
>   (Rossetti, *The Stream's Secret*)

>   . . . the year grown old
> A-dying mid the autumn-scented haze,
> That hangeth o'er the hollow in the wold,
> Where the wind-bitten ancient elms enfold
> Grey church, long barn, orchard, and red-roofed stead,
> Wrought in dead days for men a long while dead.
>   (Morris, *The Earthly Paradise: October*)

> [Life's] very bud hangs cankered on the stalk,
>   Its very song-bird trails a broken wing,
>   Its very Spring is not indeed like Spring,
> But sighs like Autumn round an aimless walk.
>   (Christina Rossetti, *Later Life*)

Finally, there is the habit suggested by such passages as these:

> O thou who at Love's hour ecstatically
> Unto my lips does ever more present
> The body and blood of Love in sacrament;
> Whom I have neared and felt they breath to be
> The inmost incense of his sanctuary;
>   (Rossetti, *Love's Redemption*)

> This feast-day of the sun, his altar there
>   In the broad west has blazed for vesper-song;
>   And I have loitered in the vale too long
> And gaze now a belated worshipper.
>   (Rossetti, *The Hill Summit*)

This appears to be the use of religious language for evocative purposes, by a man to whom real religion means nothing. But with this example we have left the Pre-Raphaelite group as a whole and become aware of the need to make distinctions; religiosity is not a characteristic of Morris's poetry: formal religion meant little to him, and he was not tempted to exploit its language in this way; neither was Christina Rossetti – though for an opposite reason. But it is significant that the last two passages quoted from Rossetti could be endlessly paralleled in other Victorian poetry.

One feature all these examples have in common with each other, and with mid-Victorian poetry in general: their obvious literariness. In Rossetti especially, whether in his simple or his elaborate manner, one is conscious all the time of the artifice, the sophistication, of a poet using a diction and movement which he well knows to have been used before by other poets. There is little that is fresh, spontaneous, unliterary, immediate. The contrast with another poet-painter, William Blake, is illuminating. In reading Blake's successful poems (*O Rose, thou art sick*, for example) we do not merely hear, we see, and our seeing is not confined to mere visualization ('In my mind's eye, Horatio'); since Blake's own seeing is an activity of the intelligence, manifesting itself in an almost clairvoyant power of notation of mental and spiritual realities. In a Rossetti sonnet – to show the contrast with Blake at its most extreme – our response is predominantly a response to *words*, words heavily charged with literary association and reminiscence; there is nothing that is strong in imagery or definite in evocation:

> So it happeneth
> When Work or Will awake too late, to gaze
> After their life sailed by; and hold their breath.
> Ah! who shall dare to search through what sad maze
> Thenceforth their incommunicable ways
> Follow the desultory feet of Death?
>
> (*Known in Vain*)

This seems so much written for the sake of the adjectives that, if we are reading critically, we cannot but focus on them; and when we do, they do not seem particularly appropriate. Rossetti and his circle liked to call beautiful women 'stunners', and he seems to expect from the reader a similar attitude to his strutting polysyllables.

A care for finish of style has taken the place of a scrupulous effort at truth of feeling. And when we inspect the phrasing of lines like

> Thenceforth their incommunicable ways
> Follow the desultory feet of Death?

and try to characterize more exactly the spirit of Rossetti's manipulation of the language, it is tempting to recall his Italian connexion. But this use of English is an important part of *English* poetic history from Spenser and Milton to Keats and Tennyson. And it has clear drawbacks. It is not merely that the Italianate use of English tends to deprive it of the typically English energy of the verbs. The great limitation of the music cultivated by Tennyson and Rossetti is that it is a medium unsuited to the clear expression of thought. This, no doubt, could be said to some extent of its earlier phases of development. But it would be easy to find passages from Spenser or Milton in which the thought is vigorous; whereas the Victorian development of this use of English, even in an earnestly didactic poet like Tennyson, tends towards confusion, vagueness, and emaciation. Thus, while Swinburne has his own music, which is not Tennyson's or Rossetti's – it is often cruder than either – his well-known sacrifices of sense to sound, his rhythmic self-intoxication, his hypnotic cadences, his phantasms of meaning dissolving inextricably into one another, may be considered as an exotic variant of the same tradition.

What is most distracting, and so not enjoyable, in this verbal music appears, not in frankly incantatory poetry like much in the early Morris (*The Blue Closet*, for example) but in passages where the poet is making a sustained offer of thought. It will be noted that the passage previously quoted from Rossetti is sententious. And though Rossetti makes a special point of not coming before us as Tennyson sometimes does, as moral and didactic, but rather as a fellow-sufferer, his mature poetry is quite as sententious as Tennyson's, and stakes quite as much on the reader's thoughtful acceptance of an utterance solemnly delivered. And the admirer of Rossetti discovers 'fundamental brainwork' even in the more lush and mannered specimens of his later style (*The Stream's Secret*, for example, a poem Yeats admired). But to those who wish to verify the attribution of fundamental brainwork, may be recommended a close study of that attitudinizing poem in which Rossetti offers a deliberated and credal affirmation of his religion of beauty; I mean the famous sonnet *Sibylla Palmifera*, of which this is the sester:

> This is that Lady Beauty, in whose praise
> Thy voice and hand shake still, – long known to thee
> By flying hair and fluttering hem, – the beat
> Following her daily of thy heart and feet,
> How passionately and irretrievably,
> In what fond flight, how many ways and days!

The poem is written with great aplomb, but so vague is the imagining that only the general effect matters; the admirer must be predisposed to admire the attitude struck by the poet, otherwise there is nothing. The tone combines grandiloquent expansiveness with unction, and even the most sympathetic reader of this sonnet will find it hard to play down its unctuous rectitude:

> The allotted bondman of her palm and wreath.

Does this merely articulate a prejudice against the subject? But this poem seems to be nothing but 'subject'; what is approved of or disapproved of, by one reader or another, is something outside the poem which the poem itself merely motions towards; what is found impressive or unimpressive is nothing more specific than a manner and a tone of voice. Detailed fault-finding is not necessary; it will hardly be contended that either sestet or octave offers anything distinguished in the form of thought or imagery.

It is time now to say something more positive. Rossetti wrote much better things than *Sibylla Palmifera*, typical though it is. His most remarkable poem is his best known, written very early: *The Blessed Damozel*. It is so well known that detailed discussion is not needed. In the present context I find it hard to avoid treating the poem as a document of the decadence of Victorian poetry; to point to its relationship with poems like Keats's *La Belle Dame sans Merci* and Tennyson's *Mariana*; to comment on the misunderstanding, or misrepresentation, of medieval art and literature which it helped to foster, and to talk about nineteenth-century pseudo-medievalism and arty-craftiness. But if we look at *The Blessed Damozel* as a poem rather than as a document, it has some curious and individual features. One of these I will mention is the 'spatial' effect, the movement from the brooding poet-narrator on earth to the Damozel in heaven, and how this is brought out by the parenthetical method illustrated at the end:

> (I saw her smile.) But soon their path
>   Was vague in distant spheres:
> And then she cast her arms along
>   The golden barriers,
> And laid her face between her hands,
>   And wept. (I heard her tears.)

This stanza is a miniature of the framing effect characteristic of the whole poem. By this means something that seems personal and inward is made out of what otherwise might have been merely an arty and mannered Victorian variation on certain motifs of Dante.

Another kind of success in Rossetti's early work is a vein of sensibility, shown especially in *Jenny*, which suggests an affinity this time with Baudelaire: the imaginative response to modern city life:

>   you stare
> Along the streets alone, and there
> Round the long park, across the bridge,
> The cold lamps at the pavement's edge
> Wind on together and apart,
> A fiery serpent for your heart.

Had Rossetti developed this vein he would, like Baudelaire, have claims to be an important forerunner of what we think of as distinctively twentieth-century kinds of poetry.

But Baudelaire might have avoided the insensitive complacency and self-indulgent moralizing which mar *Jenny*. And to deal justly with Rossetti it is necessary to examine those qualities which may be said to make him, for twentieth-century poets, not a forerunner, but an awful warning of what to *avoid* in poetry, the embodiment of the Victorian anti-poet. These qualities are to be found in his turbid, mannered love-poetry, with its alternation of the hectic and the languid, of overripe voluptuousness and the chill of desolation.

> Stand still, fond fettered wretch! while Memory's art
> Parades the Past before thy face, and lures
> Thy spirit to her passionate portraitures:
> Till the tempestuous tide-gates flung apart
> Flood with wild will the hollows of the heart,
> And thy heart rends thee, and thy body endures.

Over-sophisticated as this is, it has a certain power, if not of a very pleasing kind, the power of

> 'O ye, all ye that walk in Willowwood,
> That walk with hollow faces burning white;' . . .
> Alas! the bitter banks in Willowwood,
> With tear-spurge wan, with blood-wort burning red.
>
> *(Willowwood)*

But without conceding anything to the nauseous canting of Rossetti's contemporary Buchanan, who attacked the poet in his *Fleshly School of Poetry*, it still has to be said that Willowwood is everywhere in this poetry; romantic idealization, but, half-glimpsed behind it, the incapacity for a mutually respecting relationship with another; ahead of it, the nemesis of inevitable disappointment, weariness with oneself, a sense of irretrievable waste and loss. The Rossetti of *Barren Spring*, of *Lost Days*, of 'Retro Me, Sathana!', could have echoed Baudelaire's:

> Mais mon coeur, que jamais ne visite l'extase,
> Est un théâtre ou l'on attend
> Toujours, toujours en vain, l'être aux ailes de gaze!

Yet the comparison with Baudelaire reminds us that the Rossetti of such poems is still the Rossetti of *Sibylla Palmifera*. They reveal a temptation, yielded to by the poet, to find in spiritual sickness the occasion for suggesting a spiritual superiority. The temptation is insidious, and I do not say Baudelaire always overcame it; he was much given to rhetorical self-pity; but his greatness is surely that he succeeded, in his finest poems, in diagnosing his own malady, and thereby making himself and us see his own very special case in relation to more common feelings and more general principles of health. Rossetti's guilt, remorse, and sensation of spiritual bankruptcy remain egocentric. The result is that doom of the emotionalist: monotony; the monotony which so soon afflicts the reader of his poetry, small in bulk though it is. Worse still is its pretentiousness:

> Because our talk was of the cloud-control
> And moon-track of the journeying face of Fate.
> Her tremulous kisses faltered at love's gate
> And her eyes dreamed against a distant goal:

> But soon, remembering her how brief the whole
> Of joy, which its own hours annihilate,
> Her set gaze gathered, thirstier than of late,
> And as she kissed, her mouth became her soul.

This manages to be both pompous and vulgar, in the way Meredith sometimes is in *Modern Love*.

Where Rossetti is good, and most individual, he shows something very different, a freshness and directness of perception. It sometimes takes an experienced ear to distinguish his personal accent when he is being heavily Victorian-literary, but there is no mistaking it in things like *Song IV* in *The House of Life*, the poem called *Sudden Light*, which begins:

> I have been here before,
>   But when or how I cannot tell,
> I know the grass beyond the door,
>   The sweet keen smell,
> The sighing sound, the lights around the shore.

From the first line onwards we have an unusually direct presentment of a sensitively particularized experience. It reminds us of that element in poems like *The Woodspurge* or *The Blessed Damozel*, an element that fascinates many readers of Rossetti's poetry; a particularity working to re-create that peculiar state, at once one of bewilderment and of clarity, which he here calls 'sudden light'. There is a lightness, a fresh air, here, 'the sweet keen smell', which we think of as un-Rossettian and un-Pre-Raphaelite. And we note how the 'sighing', which elsewhere is a dangerously 'poetical' word, is not so in this poem. But the stanza in its context tends to reinforce the view I have taken of Rossetti's poetry in general. For the poem modulates back into a familiar mid-Victorian or Pre-Raphaelite key; the static dreamy atmosphere has not the transitory vividness of real dreams, but rather the insubstantiality of a waking dream or reverie:

> Shall we not lie as we have lain,
> Thus for Love's sake,
> And sleep, and wake, yet never break the chain?

Full critical justice would require more attention to the strong side of Rossetti's sensibility, shown in poems like *Dante in Verona* or the ballads. This appears also in his translations of early Italian poetry, which attracted the young Ezra Pound, (the Pound of *The Spirit of Romance*) and suggest an interesting if minor link between this Pre-Raphaelite speciality and the preoccupation of Pound and Eliot with the revival of Dante. There is little doubt, either, that the stronger work of Rossetti also helped the last great poet of the romantic tradition, Yeats, to find his own way of coping with the problem of all later nineteenth-century English poets: how to write differently from Tennyson. But Rossetti's historically representative work is closely related to the weaknesses and limitations on which he himself seems to be implicitly passing judgement in characteristic lines:

> Look in my face: my name is Might-have-been;
> I am also called No-more. Too-late, Farewell.
>
> > (*A Superscription*)

So hard is it to over-praise the beauty and purity of Christina Rossetti's writing that there must be a strong temptation to over-exalt her as a poet. For she shows those qualities of sensitiveness and intelligence, in dealing with matters of deep and intimate concern to men and women, which we expect from a poet, and which we often sadly miss in the work of her larger contemporaries. After so much Victorian literariness and elaborateness (and the fundamental inhumanity which they reflect) amid the hothouse atmosphere of the mid-century, her poetry comes like a spring of fresh cool water. Here is a woman speaking to a man:

> Pardon the faults in me,
> > For the love of years ago:
> > > Good-bye.
> I must drift across the sea,
> > I must sink into the snow,
> > > I must die.
>
> You can bask in this sun,
> > You can drink wine, and eat:
> > > Good-bye.
> I must gird myself and run,
> > Though with unsteady feet:
> > > I must die.
>
> Blank sea to sail upon,
> > Cold bed to sleep in:
> > > Good-bye.

> While you clasp, I must be gone
> For all your weeping;
> I must die.
>
> (*Wife to Husband*)

> Yet come to me in dreams, that I may live
> My very life again though cold in death:
> Come back to me in dreams, that I may give
> Pulse for pulse, breath for breath:
> Speak low, lean low,
> As long ago, my love, how long ago.
>
> (*Echo*)

That speaking voice, tinged with the characteristically elegiac quality, could be endlessly illustrated. So also could the deprived quality which goes with her sectarian religion, and must tempt her admirers to use her work for the augmentation of an impressive case against the latter. But the one poem to exhibit fully the strong sensuousness which must have corresponded to her intensity of denying asceticism is *Goblin Market*, the poem that helped so much to make the Pre-Raphaelites known; inadvertently it became a sort of advertisement for them, as an attractive poem for children. Perhaps its being a poem for children helped her, by giving her the sense of a sanction to describe the tempting goblins:

> Curious Laura chose to linger
> Wondering at each merchant man.
> One had a cat's face,
> One whisked a tail,
> One tramped at a rat's pace,
> One crawled like a snail,
> One like a wombat prowled obtuse and furry,
> One like a ratel tumbled hurry skurry.
> She heard a voice like voice of doves
> Cooing all together:
> They sounded kind and full of loves
> In the pleasant weather.

They are the strange, probably naughty, but – or therefore? – fascinating children in the next street. What the adult enjoys in *Goblin Market* is what the child enjoys, though he may be more consciously appreciative. (He will remark, too, how often the distinguished Victorian writers are more natural, and so more truly profound, when writing for children.) The suggestion (it is no more) of allegory in *Goblin Market* is the more acceptable for being unpretentious. To read the poem in an adult way is to recognize that the temptations have to do with sex; but its limpid candour makes attempts to press that kind of analysis seem boorish. To read it properly is to recover, as best one can, the spirit in which it is read in childhood – which is to admit that it is not an *Ancient Mariner*.

Christina's poetry has the Rossetti skill and the careful concern with form and design, and it has a Pre-Raphaelite vocabulary and colouring. But it has none of the over-sophistication and artificiality of her brother's poetry; it is never lush or mannered; nor does it succumb to the temptations, gross or subtle, which beset a poet seeking, as becomes a devotional poet, to express an attitude of humility and self-forgetfulness. Yet it must be significant that one finds oneself appraising her work in these negative terms. For negation, denial, deprivation are the characteristic notes of her religious poetry; and it must be admitted that an extensive reading of it is depressing. There is a sadness, often morbidity, which is felt even in her delightful poetry for children, even in *Goblin Market*, certainly in *The Prince's Progress*. There is also the felt absence of any outlet for aggressive impulses, deepening into depression or resignation. And there is the compensating yearning for death imagined as an anodyne, an eternal anaesthetic. We do not need to turn from her poetry to Donne's divine poems, to bring out how little her verse (unlike his) quickens to the theme of resurrection. 'Resurrexi: et adhuc tecum sum, alleluia!' – even when that is the explicit note, her real weight of feeling is in lines like:

> O Earth, lie heavily upon her eyes,
> Seal her sweet eyes weary of watching, Earth.

There are occasions – but these are rare – when her poetry speaks of revival and refreshment, as in *A Pause*:

> They made the chamber sweet with flowers and leaves,
> And the bed sweet with flowers on which I lay;
> While my soul, love-bound, loitered on its way.
> I did not hear the birds about the eaves,
> Nor hear the reapers talk among the sheaves:
> Only my soul kept watch from day to day,
> My thirsty soul kept watch for one away: –
> Perhaps he loves, I thought, remembers, grieves.

> At length there came the step upon the stair,
> Upon the lock the old familiar hand:
> Then first my spirit seemed to scent the air
> Of Paradise; then first the tardy sand
> Of time ran golden; and I felt my hair
> Put on a glory, and my soul expand.

The simplicity and naturalness of this writing are not artless, but show a craftsmanship none the less effective for being unobtrusive; the plain manner does not preclude the turning of so beautiful a phrase as 'the tardy sand / Of time ran golden'. There is a spiritual good taste here (if the expression may be permitted) in the way the religious and secular are related. This is the point at which to mention Hopkins, who admired her poetry. A comparison of her little poem *Spring Quiet* with his well-known *Heaven-Haven* ('I have desired to go') will bring out a certain community of temperament between the two poets – though even the latter, slight as it is, has Hopkins's idiosyncrasy: 'sharp *and sided* hail.' And we should reflect also that *Heaven-Haven*, unlike *Spring Quiet*, by no means represents a high point of its author's achievement: Christina Rossetti is not a major poet.

This can be brought out, not by producing specimens of her weaker work, but by considering her where she is characteristically good, as in her often quoted poem, the sonnet *Remember*.

> Remember me when I am gone away,
> Gone far away into the silent land;
> When you can no more hold me by the hand,
> Nor I half turn to go yet turning stay.
> Remember me when no more day by day
> You tell me of our future that you plann'd;
> Only remember me; you understand
> It will be late to counsel then or pray.
> Yet if you should forget me for a while
> And afterwards remember, do not grieve:
> For if the darkness and corruption leave
> A vestige of the thoughts that once I had,
> Better by far you should forget and smile
> Than that you should remember and be sad.

This appears to be a touching personal variation on Shakespeare's 71st sonnet ('No longer mourn . . .'), and as we read over the closing lines, with their epigrammatic turn of phrasing which sends us back to the Shakespeare sonnet, the modest wistfulness begins to sound, if not mawkish, a little thin. Not that the Shakespeare sonnet is overpoweringly better; indeed in another context it might be used to justify our sense of uneasiness about the distinction – which certainly *is* distinction – of his writing in this and some other of the Sonnets; the distinction which makes him *seem* to be offering more in the way of content than the sonnet, on critical inspection, proves to carry; the *manner* suggests the presence of an attacking vigour of thought which I cannot find in the poem. But it is much crisper than Christina Rossetti's poem, and the only explanation I can find for this is Shakespeare's awareness in it of 'the world' – the 'vile world' which is always there, ready to mock this loving self-abnegation. We believe more in the latter because of the sharp emphasis in the poet's rejection of the former. Christina Rossetti's poem shows nothing corresponding to this.

But what we are more inclined to comment on is another lack in it, a very welcome one; the absence of anything like the overcharged manner (somewhat incongruous in being at the same time declamatory and intimate) which we associate with poets like Mrs. Browning or Dame Edith Sitwell. It is a frequent vice in poetry written by women, and Christina Rossetti's distinction might well be indicated by remarking how entirely free from it her poetry is.

The deprived, depressed, monotonous quality of her writing is to be accounted for, we know, very largely by the circumstances of her life and her renunciations. But in one form or another this quality is a common feature of Victorian Romantic poetry. And if we ignore the personal accent of Christina Rossetti, and the devotional vocabulary and setting of her poems, their moods and tones are immediately recognizable as moods and tones of the period. This is certainly not because of any affectation of fashionable melancholy on her part. No poet could be more movingly sincere and disinterested. Yet we may wonder if, had she been in contact with a tradition allowing the exercise, in serious verse, of her sharp wits and her astringency, the substance of her work might not have been more considerable and its variety and play of mind more evident. Certainly after reading her poetry we are keenly reminded of the advantages enjoyed by some seventeenth-century devotional poets.

P

William Morris's most immediately compelling work as a verse-poet is to be found in the early *Defence of Guinevere* volume, especially in the title-poem. Here Guinevere is speaking:

> 'It chanced upon a day that Launcelot came
> To dwell at Arthur's court: at Christmas-time
> This happened; when the heralds sung his name,
>
> '"Son of King Ban of Benwick", seemed to chime
> Along with all the bells that rang that day,
> O'er white roofs, with little change of rhyme.
>
> 'Christmas and whitened winter passed away,
> And over me the April sunshine came,
> Made very awful with black hail-clouds, yea
>
> 'And in the Summer I grew white with flame,
> And bowed my head down – Autumn, and the sick
> Sure knowledge things would never be the same,
>
> 'However often Spring might be most thick
> Of blossoms and buds, smote on me, and I grew
> Careless of most things, let the clock tick, tick,
>
> 'To my unhappy pulse, the beat right through
> My eager body; while I laughed out loud,
> And let my lips curl up at false or true,
>
> 'Seemed cold and shallow without any cloud,
> Behold my judges, then the cloths were brought;
> While I was dizzied thus, old thoughts would crowd,
>
> 'Belonging to the time ere I was bought
> By Arthur's great name and his little love,
> Must I give up for ever then, I thought,
>
> 'That which I deemed would ever round me move
> Glorifying all things; for a little word,
> Scarce ever meant at all, must now I prove
>
> 'Stone-cold for ever? Pray you, does the Lord
> Will that all folks should be quite happy and good?'

The last line and a half gives us the kind of thrill we rarely if ever get from Tennyson's *Idylls of the King*, and in gratitude for the speaking voice, the clear outlines and the distinct colours, the cool quiet atmosphere in which we can hear the bells chime or the clock tick, we may be prepared to overlook the troubling oddities of a style which manages to be at once careless and slightly mannered. But things like the constant overrunning of the metrical frame, justifiable perhaps in the passage quoted, are so persistent throughout that it is difficult, eventually, to see any special function in them.

Of the other poems in the volume, the natural temptation is to say that they are charming, and much in Morris invites that patronizing word. Surely it is a damning thing to say of a poetic tradition that it should have confined a man like Morris to charming minor poetry. How did this come about? Arnold, regretting Burns's background, remarked that it was a great advantage to a poet to live in a beautiful world; but many readers have found Morris's beautiful world, being a world from which everything harsh or disagreeable is excluded, to be daydream and so, in the long run, uninteresting. It is easy to quote, in illustration of this, passages like the pleasant opening of *Golden Wings*, which also illustrates his typical colour-effects and arty simplicity:

> Midways of a walled garden,
> In the happy poplar land,
> Did an ancient castle stand,
> With an old knight for a warden.
>
> Many scarlet bricks there were
> In its walls, and old grey stone;
> Over which red apples shone
> At the right time of the year.
>
> On the bricks the green moss grew,
> Yellow lichen on the stone,
> Over which red apples shone;
> Little war that castle knew.
>
> Deep green water fill'd the moat,
> Each side had a red-brick lip,
> Green and mossy with the drip
> Of dew and rain . . .

Fairness requires, however, that we also quote the close of the poem, which is somewhat different in effect:

> The apples now grow green and sour
> Upon the mouldering castle-wall,
> Before they ripen there they fall:
> There are no banners on the tower.
>
> The draggled swans most eagerly eat
> The green weeds trailing in the moat;
> Inside the rotting leaky boat
> You see a slain man's stiffen'd feet.

The grim side of life, and a hard-bitten quality which makes it easy to see why Morris was attracted by the Sagas, are more represented in his poetry than is sometimes realized; we should remember things like *The Haystack in the Floods*, in which this famous idealizer of medieval life renders with force its brutality and cruelty. Another qualifying element in the happiness which Yeats noted as characteristic of Morris's work is pathos; and even the happier poems may be said to imply the sadness from which they withdraw. But in his poetry Morris's protest against the nineteenth century tends to be confined to the protest of ignoring it. We do not demand that he write about industrialism and the 'six counties overhung with smoke' which his poetry asks us to forget; an artist has the right to choose his own *données*. But it is reasonable to expect from a man of Morris's calibre that his sensibility should have been modified by his involvement in the human problems of his own time.

Morris's art seems to lack this preoccupation. Thus *The Life and Death of Jason* shows little sign that the poet has glimpsed the tragic power of the story he is telling; the sin of Jason seems to have little religious significance. Perhaps to deny it *moral* significance also is going too far, but the poet's activity does not seem to be directed towards the making real of the moral issues, but rather into rendering charming incidentals of visual observation, of costume and landscape. In *The Earthly Paradise* – however much Morris may have felt himself to be the successor of Chaucer – there is none of Chaucer's vigorous interest in life in so many of its forms, the sense of *nihil humanum a me alienum puto*. Morris's interest is always in the picturesque, the decorative, in the romantic 'feel' of the legends, as in the 'northernness' of *Sigurd the Volsung*. When men and women are the ostensible centre of interest there is an odd externality, difficult to illustrate convincingly because it is so pervasive. Hence it would be futile to enter the controversy about *The Earthly Paradise* – is it not really poetry of escape, but a sociological sermon in the form of an allegory? This kind of question may be real for the student of Spenser; but whatever Morris's aim, no effective message of the kind he is credited with could be delivered in his verse.

We often have the sense in reading Morris's poetry – and in his prose romances too – that what he is doing is quite marginal to the main activities of his life. Outside his poetry we know Morris as an energetic, strenuous figure and strong character, the last of the great Victorian 'prophets', but more than a 'prophet', a man of action and a maker. But in his poetry – even after the Pre-Raphaelite phase – we observe in an extreme and a naïve form the Pre-Raphaelite separation of art from life. For Morris art tended to be a relaxation, an amusement, something to do; writing poetry came easily to him, and he was not the poet to resist the temptations of profusion and careless workmanship inherent in being one's own publisher and printer.

> The fascination of what's difficult
> Has dried the sap out of my veins, and rent
> Spontaneous joy and natural content
> Out of my heart.

Morris the poet could not have applied to himself these words of Yeats. And it is significant that there is no real parallel between his development and that of Yeats – who also began as a Pre-Raphaelite, born out of due time. Why this is so is suggested by Yeats's remark in his *Autobiographies* that 'the dream-world of Morris was as much the antithesis of daily life as with other men of genius, but he was never conscious of the antithesis and so knew nothing of intellectual sufferings'.

Yeats's view of course need not be accepted as final; nor, in so far as it is valid, can its validity be solely accounted for by the shortcomings of the Victorian poetic tradition in which both he and Morris began. A hard vigour and a delicate sensibility to *some* things – these qualities are contrasting and complementary in Morris's best work; but there is also a hollowness, an impercipience, even a denseness, about the mind behind the work, which are somewhat baffling. The work does not lend itself as easily as might be supposed to assignment to a particular niche of cultural history; as do, for example, Gilbert Murray's translations from Euripides, which show obvious marks of inspiration from Morris.

Morris is not to be simply 'placed' as merely representing a certain phase of late-Romantic sensibility. It is important to stress that in the history of England he has an honourable place in the line that runs from Ruskin's *Unto this Last* to the welfare state.

But the robuster side of his nature he seems to have reserved for the Anti-Scrape Society, the settlement-house, and the socialist meeting; for the attempt, in short, to put Ruskin's ideas into practice in the world of Victorian industrialism, Karl Marx, and Mr. Podsnap. Morris's poetry (and there is no point here in distinguishing between his verse and his prose) seems to strive, at its best, to fulfil something that was not fulfilled in his life. I am not thinking here of a book like *News from Nowhere*, which seems arty and feeble. (Though in making this kind of criticism we should bear in mind that Morris, unlike some later extollers of a mythical golden age, was never under any illusion that he was evoking *was* mythical.) The striving for fulfilment seems rather to appear in the expression of *personal* longing. What was this longing for? C. S. Lewis, in an otherwise not very convincing essay on Morris in *Rehabilitations*, suggests that it was in the last analysis the longing for personal immortality. There would be then a disharmony in Morris's imagination: on the one hand, he insists as a socialist on the subduing of the individual personality and its needs in the interest of the tribe, the community, the corporate; on the other hand, at some other level of his being he evinces an intense and dream-like longing for a lost beauty, which is of its essence private, inward, and solitary.

Whatever the truth about this, it would be a truth so delicate that it may be convenient to stop here by remarking that Morris's art is not usually strong or compelling enough to impel us into so difficult a discussion. Morris, then, (though not so substantially) succeeded, like the Rossettis, in writing differently from Tennyson. His *literary* distinction should be sought less in the great rivers of his prose and verse, than in a thin but very pure channel of a certain kind of feeling; rather the 'old, unhappy, far-off things' which Wordsworth speculates that the Solitary Reaper sang of, than the 'familiar matter of today, / Some natural sorrow, loss of pain / That has been, or may be again', which he gives more space to, and which were the subject-matter of so many of his own best poems. Morris expresses another kind of 'Romanticism', but in an extremely and poignantly, specialized form.

'Do you know where it is – the Hollow Land?

'I have been looking for it now so long, trying to find it again – the Hollow Land – for there I saw my love first.

'I wish to tell you how I found it first of all; but I am old, my memory fails me; you must wait and let me think if I perchance can tell you how it happened.

'Yea, in my ears is a confused noise of trumpet-blasts singing over desolate moors, in my ears and eyes a clashing and clanging of horse-hoofs, a ringing glittering of steel; drawn-back lips, set teeth, shouts, shrieks, and curses.

'How was it that no one of us ever found it till that day? for it is near our country: but what time have we to look for it, or any good thing; with such biting carking cares hemming us in on every side – cares about great things – mighty things: mighty thing, O my brothers! or rather little things enough, if we only knew it.

'Lives past in turmoil, in making one another unhappy; in bitterest misunderstanding of our brother's hearts, making those sad whom God has not made sad, – alas! what chance for any of us to find the Hollow Land? what time even to look for it?

'Yet who has not dreamed of it? Who, half miserable yet the while, for that he knows it is but a dream, has not felt the cool waves round his feet, the roses crowning him, and through the leaves of beech and lime the many whispering winds of the Hollow Land?'

1958

PART FIVE

PART FIVE

XV

HENRY JAMES'S *THE TRAGIC MUSE*

It is strange that *The Tragic Muse* should be the most neglected of James's longer novels. For of all of them it comes the nearest to being what the ordinary novel-reader requires of a good novel; it is a comedy of manners and a piece of social history; it manifestly is the work of 'a delicate observer', 'a wit', 'a great narrator and plot-constructor'. (I am quoting from Mr. John Betjeman's review of Mr. David Garnett's selection from James's shorter stories.) One might say that it does a good deal better – certainly, for the modern reader, much more readably – what George Meredith is supposed to have done. But it does not seem to be among the novels that even James's admirers often talk about.

For the comparative unpopularity of this novel Mr. Edmund Wilson (in his essay included in *The Triple Thinkers*) has an explanation. He remarks of the first part of *The Tragic Muse* that it '. . . makes us think that it must be James's best novel, so solid and alive does it seem. Here are areas of experience and types of a kind that James has never before given us: a delicately comic portrait of a retired parliamentarian, which constitutes, by implication, a criticism of British Liberal politics; a really charged and convincing scene between a man and a woman (Nick Dormer and Julia Dallow) in place of the mild battledore and shuttlecock we are accustomed to getting from James; and in Miriam Rooth, the Muse, a character who comes nearer to carrying the author out of the bounds of puritan scruples and prim prejudices on to the larger and more dangerous stage of human creative effort than any other he has hitherto drawn. . . . Then suddenly the story stops short: after the arrival of Miriam in London, *The Tragic Muse* is

almost a blank. Of the two young men who have been preoccupied with Miriam, one renounces her because she will not leave
the stage and the other doesn't apparently, fall in love with her'.
And Mr. Wilson goes on to give his explanation of this story's unpopularity, in the nineties and since: 'You will particularly damp
your readers with a story . . . which deals with two men and a girl
but in which neither man ever gets her. There is, as I have said, in
The Tragic Muse, one of his more convincing man-and-woman
relationships. Julia Dallow is really female and she behaves
like a woman with Nick Dormer; but here the woman's political
ambitions get between Nick and her, so that this too, never comes
to anything; here the man, again, must renounce.' It was not
merely the grundyism of the period (referred to by James in his
Preface) that prevented the relationship between Nick and
Miriam – in Mr. Wilson's phrase – 'coming to anything'; after all,
Hardy, whatever the public's reaction, did write *Jude the Obscure*,
and Meredith wrote of Lord Ormont and his Aminta. It is some
inner refusal or evasion of James's own – and this is a main subject of Mr. Wilson's whole essay, which is psychological in
emphasis – that we must see as explaining the lamentable tailing-off
of a distinguished novel.

Mr. Wilson reads the story very differently from the way in
which I read it. But to debate details about this reading, or about
the merits of Mr. Wilson's general thesis ('The ambiguity of
Henry James') seems less important than giving a positive account
of the book in one's own terms. James's book is about the relation
between Art and Life, or the relation between the 'aesthetic' and
the 'moral' judgement, and here is one side of it expounded by
Gabriel Nash, a representative of the Oscar Wilde phase of the
Aesthetic movement.

> 'My dear fellow,' said Gabriel Nash, 'we have only one life
> that we know anything about: fancy taking it up with dis-
> agreeable impressions! . . .
> The great thing is to . . . encourage the beautiful.'
> 'You must be very sure you get hold of the beautiful,' said
> Nick.
> 'Ah, precisely, and that's just the importance of the faculty of
> appreciation. We must train our special sense. It is capable of
> extraordinary extension. Life's none too long for that.'
> 'But what's the good of the extraordinary extension if there

is no affirmation of it, if it all goes to the negative, as you say? Where are the fine consequences?' Dormer asked.

'In one's own spirit. One is one's self a fine consequence. That's the most important one we have to do with. I am a fine consequence,' said Gabriel Nash.

The kind of Art and Style represented by Gabriel Nash are not as the remarks of Nick Dormer suggest, what interest James himself. They are in the novel very largely to provide opportunities for critical comedy. Consider the way in which the comically banal high-mindedness of the shabby-genteel Mrs. Rooth, Miriam's mother, complements the attitude of Gabriel: '"I feel the responsiblity of what she [Miriam] shall find in the life, the standards of the theatre," Mrs. Rooth explained. "Where is the purest tone – where are the highest standards? that's what I ask," the good lady continued, with a persistent candour which elicited a peal of unceremonious but sociable laughter from Gabriel Nash.' James himself is asking these questions, but with a very different accent. The paradoxical affinity between the respectable Mrs. Rooth and the sophisticated aesthete lies in their disjunction of 'style' from 'subject-matter' – a notion which James exposes to severe criticism in the novel (as in so many of his explicit critical pronouncements). At a more serious level, though still in the tone proper to comedy, we have Gabriel's clash with Mrs. Dallow, when she asks seriously:

'Are you an artist?'
'I try to be,' Nash replied, smiling, 'but I work in such a difficult material!'
He spoke this with such a clever suggestion of unexpected reference that, in spite of herself, Mrs. Dallow said after him:
'Difficult material?'
'I work in life!'
At this Mrs. Dallow turned away, leaving Nash the impression that she probably misunderstood his speech, thinking he meant that he drew from the living model, or some such platitude; as if there could have been any likelihood that he drew from the dead one. This, indeed, would not have explained the abruptness with which she dropped their conversation. Gabriel Nash, however, was used to sudden collapses, and even to sudden ruptures, on the part of his interlocutors, and no man had

more the secret of remaining gracefully with his ideas on his hands.

Gabriel Nash is not held up to derision; he is intelligent – some of the most interesting conversation in the book comes from him – and he can recognize intelligence in others. But of course he has our sympathies very little. Yet, without our being very perplexed by any problem of valuation where he is concerned, he stands for something reputable enough for us to enter quite sympathetically into Nick Dormer's perplexity: 'I say, my dear fellow, do you mind mentioning to me whether you are the greatest humbug and charlatan on earth, or a geniune intelligence, one that has sifted things for itself?' But Nick at one point makes the decisive criticism:

> 'By never, never making the concession Nash says one may end by becoming a perceptible force for good.'
> 'What concession are you talking about?' asked Nick Dormer.
> 'Why, that we are only here for dreariness. It's impossible to grant it sometimes, if you wish to withhold it ever.'
> 'And what do you mean by dreariness? That's modern slang, and it's terribly vague. Many good things are dreary – virtue and decency and charity and perseverance and courage and honour.'

Nick himself is aspiring to be an artist, so that there is an especial significance in the contrast between the two men shown in the account of their reactions to Notre-Dame:

> The lamplight of the great city washed its foundations, but the towers and buttresses, the arches, the galleries, the statues, the vast rose-window, the large, full composition, seemed to grow clearer as they climbed higher, as if they had a conscious benevolent answer for the upward gaze of men.
> 'How it straightens things out and blows away one's vapours – anything that's *done*!' said Nick; while his companion exclaimed, blandly and affectionately:
> 'The dear old thing!'

The response of Nick, as the note of the narrative passage suggests, is not fully adequate either; but his sense of vocation does not go with this conception of the good life proposed by the self-styled 'artist in living': 'Life consists of the personal experiments of each of us, and the point of an experiment is that it shall succeed. What we contribute is our treatment of the material, our rendering of the text, our style.' The dramatic answer to this is provided when Nick says:

> 'I wish very much you had more to show for it.'
> 'To show for what?'
> 'Your little system – the aesthetic life.'

Nash hesitated, tolerantly, gaily, as he often did, with an air of being embarrassed to choose between several answers, any one of them would be so right. 'Oh, having something to show is such a poor business. It's a kind of confession of failure.'

Nick's reply is significant: '"Yes, you're more affected than anything else," said Nick impatiently.'

But the part that Gabriel Nash plays in the drama is not, as might have been expected from the passage quoted, a merely negative or stultifying one. We are not invited to dissociate ourselves altogether from Nick Dormer's eventual tribute to him: 'You rescued me; you converted me from a representative into an example.' But we cannot accept as expressing the novelist's own view the general judgement implied in other phrases of Nick's:

> 'The only thing he [Nash] really takes seriously is to speculate and understand, to talk about the reasons and the essence of things: the people who do that are the highest. The applications, the consequences, the vulgar little effects belong to a lower plane, to which one must doubtless be tolerant and indulgent, but which is after all an affair of comparative accidents and trifles.'

For the James of *The Tragic Muse* – of the period of his greatest work – there is no such easy kind of opposition of the contemplative to the practical. His own judgement lies in the enacted parable, (notice the reference to Hawthorne) which occurs after Nick's abortive attempt to paint Gabriel's portrait: 'The picture . . . had a singular air of gradually fading from the canvas. He couldn't catch it in the act, but he could have a suspicion, when he glanced at it, that the hand of time was rubbing it away little by little (for all the world as in some delicate Hawthorne tale) making the surface indistinct and bare – bare of all resemblance to the model.' Gabriel's personality, like his aestheticism, is a will-o'-the-wisp. When we consider all the Gabriel Nash part of the book, with its obviousness – and in places over-obviousness – of intention, it seems odd that people still liken James's art to Pater's – see, for instance, Mr. Connolly in *Enemies of Promise*, or Stuart P. Sherman, 'The Aesthetic Idealism of Henry James'.

This part of the novel, which belongs most obviously to the 'thesis', is not, however, the most interesting; we have a surer sense of the presence of the essential James in Lady Agnes, Nick's mother; who has a totally dissimilar, indeed a quite contrary, role to that of Gabriel Nash, and yet brings out the same kind of discriminations and judgements. She too is a minor figure, but, though she contributes to the comedy, one who makes demands on our sympathies which he does not. Lady Agnes represents the impoverished governing class, and her 'sense of reality' is defined in terms of the relationship between family pride and economic need:

> Lady Agnes was less optimistic than her daughter, and such optimism as she cultivated was thin tissue, with a sense of things as they are showing through it . . .
> 'It's all very well to say that in public life money isn't necessary, as it used to be,' her ladyship went on, broodingly. 'Those who say so don't know anything about it. It's always necessary.'
> Her daughter was visibly affected by the gloom of her manner, and felt impelled to invoke, as a corrective, a more cheerful idea. 'I dare say; but there's the fact – isn't there? that poor papa had so little.'
> 'Yes, and there's the fact that it killed him!'

In the drama of the relations between mother and son her high inherited idealism is seen being strangely distorted, under economic and psychological pressure, into an almost farcical cynicism. At the crisis of this family drama:

> The most painful thing in this painful hour was perhaps this glimpse of the strange feminine cynicism that lurked in her fine sense of injury. Where there was such a complexity of revolt it would have been difficult to pick out particular complaints; but Nick could see that to Lady Agnes's imagination

he was most a fool for not having kept his relations with the
actress, *whatever they were* [italics are mine] from Julia's knowledge.

Nick's story is intended by James as a study of a 'complex';
we see as relevant the means his mother adopts to try to enforce
her desperate demand that he should make a brilliant marriage
with the rich, beautiful and public-spirited Mrs. Dallow, and
seek a political career: 'Your father would have valued it for you
beyond everything. He's with you always; he takes with you, at
your side, every step that you take yourself.' We may relate this
to the picture of Nick, alone, after his decisive choice: 'He gazed
before him into the gloom produced by the unheeded burning-
out of the last candle. The vague outer light came in through the
tall studio window, and the painted images, ranged about, looked
confused in the dusk. If his mother had seen him she might have
thought he was staring at his father's ghost.' Lady Agnes herself
engages our sympathy: 'It almost frightened Nick to see how
she hated her life.' Her reaction to Nick's failure to comply with
her plans is pathetic: 'She struck him [Peter Sherringham] as a
woman who had received her death-blow. She looked ten years
older; she was white and haggard and tragic.' She is an example
of the growing ineffectiveness and desperation of the old governing class in a changing world; politics for her has been a family
affair (they are a 'governing family'); thus we see her '. . . engaged with them [her letters] at the big brass-mounted bureau
which had belonged to his father, where, behind an embankment
of works of political reference, she seemed to herself to make
public affairs feel the point of her elbow'. But, as this last quotation
shows, she is in the book largely for our amusement. She is one
of Arnold's Barbarians; we have the 'note of provinciality' also,
at the beginning of the book, when Peter Sherringham and
Gabriel Nash are discussing Balzac and the plays of Augier:
'"What an extraordinary discussion! What dreadful authors!"
Lady Agnes murmured to her son.' And towards the end Nick
says of her: 'She has the wildest ideas about it [art] – the wildest
theories. I can't imagine where she gets them; partly, I think,
from the general conviction that the "aesthetic" – a horrible
insidious foreign disease – is eating the healthy core out of English
life (dear old English life!).'
But in the world of *The Tragic Muse* the Barbarian and the

Philistine are at one: we see this brought out by the contrasting Mrs. Rooth: 'Mrs. Rooth was very fond of a moral and had never lost her taste for edification. She delighted in a beautiful character and was gratified to find so many represented in the contemporary French drama' – a species of art which, as his drama-criticism makes clear, James himself rates no higher than did young Bernard Shaw. Mrs. Rooth, of course, presents herself vaguely as also out of the top drawer ('one of the Neville-Nugents'). She is preoccupied with gentility, as Peter Sherringham, Miriam's admirer, notes but as to that 'Sherringham very soon gave up the futile task of piecing together her incongruous references to her early life and her family in England. He renounced even the doctrine that there was a residuum of truth in her claim of great relationships, for, existent or not, he cared equally little for her ramifications.' James, in fact, is dealing with English civilization at a crucial phase. He has as much interest as the classical English novelists in English snobbery, but, from the point of view from which he approaches it in *The Tragic Muse*, its surface variations are unimportant: what matters is that it is all permeated with Philistinism. More particularly, the presentation of Lady Agnes, and the world in which she has her being, is in line with similar treatments of the theme (the failure of sensibility and intelligence related to deeper failures of living) in such things as *Lady Barberina* or *An International Episode*; we might compare the Warburton theme in *The Portrait of a Lady*.

Mrs. Dallow also represents high society, and its conception of the active life ('She *was*, indeed, active politics'); but *her* rejection of Art is of a very different order from Lady Agnes's. Over and above her obvious place in the design as the symbol of the world of public affairs and public duties – she reads articles on the British Constitution – Julia Dallow stands for something deeper. True her rejection proceeds in the first place from instinctive antipathy to Miriam: 'She's dreadfully vulgar', and a further personal factor is hinted at, her revulsion from the dilettante futilities of her late husband. Nor is her high seriousness presented without irony; we appreciate the point, with Nick, of Nick's pardonable misunderstanding when, after a friend of theirs has said: 'Julia lives so in public. But it's all for you,' and continues with 'It's a wonderful constitution': 'Nick at first failed to seize her allusion – he thought it a retarded political reference, a sudden tribute to the great unwritten instrument by which they were all governed. He was on the point of saying: "The British? Wonderful!" when he perceived that the intention of his inter-locutress was to praise Mrs. Dallow's fine robustness.' Neverthe-less, that 'fine robustness' is very real in the book, and Mrs. Dallow, with her beauty – 'the pure style of her capable head, her hair like darkness, her eyes like early twilight, her mouth like a rare pink flower', and her intelligence – consider her conversation with Nick in VI, with its light shrewdness and in-sight (the whole scene reminds us of *Coningsby*) – stands for aristocratic England at its best, with its intelligent sense of responsibility and duty. In Julia's case this sense is bound up with, and helps to form the quality of, her love for Nick Dormer: 'She desired no experience for the familiar and yet partly myster-ious kinsman in whom she took an interest that she would not have desired for herself; and indeed, the cause of her interest in him was partly the vision of his helping her to the particular emotion that she did desire – the emotion of great affairs and of public action.' For Gabriel Nash she is merely the conventional English lady. But for the reader she is a great deal more; she represents in the scheme of the book something importantly human and valuable. The effective symbolism of the lake scene (in XV) where Nick makes his proposal of marriage because the situation seems to demand it rather than out of any deep convic-tion, brings this out clearly, but for us rather than for him: since she is for Nick, he reflects early in the book, his 'doom'.

It is a point in favour of Mr. Wilson's reading that James should resort, when it becomes necessary, to an itself rather evasive presentation of Nick's evasiveness:

> He might have said [to himself] that the effect she produced upon him was too much a compulsion; not the coercion of design, of importunity, nor the vulgar pressure of family ex-pectation, a suspected desire that he should like her enough to marry her, but something that was a mixture of diverse things, of a sense that she was imperious and generous – but more probably the former than the latter – and of a certain previous of doom, the influence of the idea that he should come to it, that he was presented.

And it is true and well known that Henry James is not a full-blooded writer, and that he rarely unites lovers. But we have no general feeling in this book that James's sense of value has gone wrong, or that there is something peculiar, something unrecognized by the author, about his presentation of Nick's retreat from marriage. The fear which underlies, and is the ultimate motive for, so many of the behaviour-patterns and valuations of conventional social living, is here plainly and objectively exposed; it is part of James's subject:

> 'There is one thing [Nick tells Mrs. Dallow] one can always do for one's country, which is not to be afraid.'
> 'Afraid of what?'
> Nick Dormer hesitated a moment, laughing: then he said:
> 'I'll tell you another time.'

However, the presentation of Nick is not among the stronger things in the book. For the same theme, better handled, we may point to Peter Sherringham, brother of Julia and admirer of Miriam: a brilliantly sketched study of the effect of being in love on a sensitive but egoistic and *au fond* conventional young upper-class Englishman. He is seen at first as the rising diplomat, very much aware of his training, but going through a period of flirtation with the Theatre and Art. Early on in the book he sees himself, in contrast with Nick, as having, in a sophisticated way, gone native in Paris. 'Nick Dormer's express enjoyment of Paris . . . struck his companion as a sign of insularity; the appreciation of such things having become with Sherringham an unconscious habit, a contended assimilation.' But even the initial impact of Miriam has an effect which shows how far Sherringham is not 'assimilated' to the spirit of Gabriel Nash:

> The girl hesitated, and for an instant she appeared to make a vain, convulsive effort. In this effort she frowned portentously; her low forehead overhung her eyes; the eyes themselves, in shadow, stared, splendid and cold, and her hands clenched themselves at her sides. She looked austere and terrible, and during this moment she was an incarnation the vividness of which drew from Sherringham a stifled cry. '*Elle est bien belle – ah – ça!*' murmured the old actress; and in the pause which still preceded this issue of sound from the girl's lips Peter turned to his kinsman and said in a low tone:
> 'You must paint her just like that.'
> 'Like that?'
> 'As the Tragic Muse.'

The Tragic Muse herself gives us the opportunity for distinguishing between what might be called the 'thesis' and the 'poetic' aspects of the book. As to the 'thesis', she was conceived by James to illustrate the hint about the actor's art which he got from Mrs. Kemble: 'The interest, I say, would be as a study of a certain particular nature d'actrice . . . The thing a confirmation of Mrs. Kemble's theory that the dramatic gift is a thing by itself – implying of necessity no general superiority of mind' (*Notebooks*, ed. Matthiesson and Murdock, p. 64). And much of the book's rich comedy does certainly derive from the contrast pointed between the transcendent gifts of Miriam – the future Rachel – and the cheerful vulgarity of her natural personality and accustomed social surroundings. The world of the Theatre people is shown as very much a part of the complacently Philistine world against which the romantic 'theatre-lover' tends to place it in dazzling contrast; not so different, either, as far as its taste and culture are concerned, from the world of 'Lord Bottomley and the young slim uninitiated gentleman who is engaged to the Honourable Jane, his lordship's second daughter' – about which James in this novel makes some of his most mordant comments. When Sherringham explains to the actor Basil Dashwood – whom, significantly, Miriam is eventually to marry – '. . . that this art was serious work and that society was humbug and imbecility; also that of old the great comedians wouldn't have known such people. Garrick has essentially his own circle.

"No, I suppose they didn't call, in the old narrow-minded days," said Basil Dashwood.' And a little later: 'Dashwood defended the taste of London, praised it as loyal, constant, faithful; to which Sherringham retorted with some vivacity that it was faithful to rubbish.' James (who was to have a long and sad struggle with the commercial stage) notes with regret that the actors are not highbrows. And it is with the same quizzical irony that he presents the naïve egoism of the actress, of her habits, dispositions and interests. For though, 'in the presence of famous pictures and statues', Miriam has 'some remarkable flashes of perception'. 'She felt these things, she liked them . . . always because she has an idea she could use them . . . "I could look just like that, if I tried."

"That's the dress I mean to wear when I do Portia."' So that it is not surprising that poor Sherringham wonders: '. . . if there were necessarily something vulgar in the histrionic conscience – something condemned to feel only the tricky personal question.'

This aspect of the Muse, then, is adequately done for James's purposes; he gives us (especially in sketches like that of the 'old actress', Mme Carré) some admirable reporting; and he seems to know more, and more from the inside, about the stage and theatrical people, than about painters and painting (*that* part of the book, brought in with relevance to Nick Dormer, is clearly inadequate). Our criticism is that it *is* largely 'reporting'; not only did he not have to be a genius to do it, he has not assimilated it sufficiently to the mode in which the finer things in *The Tragic Muse* are presented. The major interest of Miriam, in fact, is not on this plane at all – the plane of the speculative and excogitated, on which James, in this matter of the histrionic temperament at any rate, has many competitors. Her real value as a dramatic creation is, as the *poetic* embodiment of art – expansive, florid, and lively as she is; an art not cut off from direct first-hand living. The 'beauty' she represents (it is the key-word in most of the descriptions of her) is of a very different kind from that displayed for homage in 'the great religion of beauty'. Whatever hints James may have taken from her namesake in Hawthorne's *The Marble Faun*, she is most convincingly realized for us as a believable physical presence, and, for all the intentional contrast she offers to the proud, reserved, sensitive Mrs. Dallow, as a sympathetic figure. And, whatever her mental limitations, she is intelligent and shrewd: she puts her finger on the moral weakness in Peter Sherringham: 'He wants to enjoy every comfort and every appearance, and all without making a sacrifice.'

The case of Sherringham is central to the book. It is in the nature of that case that he is radically disturbed by Miriam: 'There were moments when Sherringham tried to think that Miriam's talent was not a force to be reckoned with.' But the attempt is not successful. He is not presented unsympathetically; but we are not allowed to ignore his profound conventionality, and the fear that underlies it: 'Reflection taught Peter further that the matter was altogether a delicate one, and suggested that it was odd he should be mixed up with it in fact when . . . he had wished only to keep out of it.' To 'keep out of it' in this case means a kind of refusal of life more serious than Sherringham's own way of putting it reveals, when he thinks of 'art' as '. . . the strange temptress with whom he himself had been wrestling and over whom he had finally ventured to believe that wisdom and training had won a victory'. It is significant, therefore, that Peter Sherringham, opting for his diplomatic career, should finally settle down with little Biddy, who goes in for 'art' in a very different spirit: 'He smoked a cigarette, because she begged him to, said that people always smoked in studios – it made her feel so much more like an artist.' ('*Anch'io son pittore,*' she announces proudly.) It is she too who puts the alternatives in a way in which James throughout dissuades us from putting them:

> 'Oh, his [Nick's] attitude is very noble, Peter; his state of mind is wonderfully interesting,' Biddy pleaded. 'Surely *you* must be in favour of art,' she said.
> Sherringham stared. 'He's going to chuck up his seat?'
> 'I think his mind is made up to it. He has talked me over – we have had some deep discussions. Yes, I'm on the side of art!' said Biddy, ardently.

Biddy is a wholly sympathetic character, which Sherringham – because he is more intelligent, and sees more – is not: the spirit in which he makes his *gran rifiuto* is, in James's eyes, a comment, and an adverse one, on the 'wisdom and training' upon which he sets such store.

The opposition of 'Art' and 'Society' in *The Tragic Muse*, is, then, not a simple matter. On the one hand, there is nothing idealized or sentimental about James's presentation of actual art and actual artists – this is a measure of the development of his powers since *Roderick Hudson* which, distinguished novel as it is, rests overmuch on the more or less conventional *donnée* of 'the celebrated artistic temperament'. On the other hand, the old aristocratic order, whatever its present-day short-comings (i.e. later nineteenth century) is revealed in depth and surrounded by a certain glamour of idealization. The historical imagination assists in the idealizing process; we have a parallel to Strether's famous reverie in Paris in Nick's vision of the past of England (the 'apprehended revelation of his country') as he strolls round an old abbey.

This last element may be criticized as too much a wistful indulgence typical of Henry James, the sensitive American visitor, and not sufficiently 'in character'; but it seems to me that it gives a perspective to Nick Dormer and his problems which help to make them more of a dramatic reality than they would otherwise be. In any case, even if the idealization in that part of the book may be somewhat too overt, the occasion for Nick's reverie is his visit to Mr. Carteret, a heroic Whig survivor of the heroic age of 1832; and Mr. Carteret is the subject of some of James's most amusing, and most critical, comedy. The handling of him is satirical: 'He had never proceeded in any ironic way from the particular to the general; certainly he has never made a reflection upon anything so unparliamentary as Life.' The tragi-comedy of his illness is in the same key: 'He laid his liberal hand on Nick's with a confidence which showed it was not yet disabled. He said very little . . . but from time to time he murmured with a faint smile: "Tonight's division, you know – you mustn't miss it." There was to be no division that night, as it happened, but even Mr. Carteret's aberrations were parliamentary.' This shows the influence of Dickens. But Mr. Carteret is more than an opportunity for providing amusement. There is real pathos in his dim consciousness that Nick's refusal to marry Mrs. Dallow, and to take his generous gift, strikes at the root of his whole 'philosophy'; there is pathos as well as humour in his struggle with Nick on the issue of what constitutes the noble life:

> Nick says, 'I think the noble life is doing one's work well. One can do it very ill and be very base and mean in what you call a high political career. I haven't been in the House so many months without finding that out. It contains some very small souls.'
> 'You should stand against them – you should expose them,' stammered Mr. Carteret.
> 'Stand against them – against one's own party?'
> The old man looked bewildered a moment at this; then he broke out: 'God forgive you, are you a Tory – are you a Tory?'

However, this part of the book is, of course, predominantly satire, and the satire is integral with the whole scheme; that scheme which relates the commonplace of Victorian Liberalism (with its Whig component) to the Philistinism, provinciality, and the moral and spiritual limitations of the society the novelist shows us – a society presented astonishingly effectively: astonishingly, I mean, when one thinks of what is usually said about James.

The weakness of *The Tragic Muse*, as I have suggested, is Nick Dormer. We may put the main adverse criticism of the book in this way: despite the masterly handling of the subject-matter (though not always, it must be granted, always on the same plane of success), we are left with a feeling of something in an unfavourable sense *constructed*, something arbitrary, about the novel as a whole. The treatment of Nick brings our dissatisfaction to a head. His case, to begin with, is too ostensibly and deliberately a 'case' – a special contrived situation. For there is nothing artistically inevitable about the equation of the sphere of public duty, and a conventionally successful career, with the 'life' the relation of which to the living art of Miriam is the subject of the book. There is something suspicious about the explicitness with which the 'divided nature' of Nick is brought into prominence: 'The difficulty is that I'm two men; it's the strangest thing that ever was . . . I'm two quite distinct human beings, who have scarcely a point in common; not even the memory, on the part of one, of the achievements or the adventures of the other. One man wins the seat – but it's the other fellow who sits in it.' But our objection here is not only to the over-special nature of the case; it is also to James's too manifest drawing together of the themes that he started with, so that the novel should be something more than the sum of its attractions; and especially in view of the writer's failure to make Nick throughout a convincing character, we cannot take the will for the deed.

However, in considering just what James has undertaken to do in *The Tragic Muse*, we may find a partial answer (though not, I think, a complete one) to these criticisms; and, incidentally, to the criticism of Mr. Edmund Wilson I began by quoting. Nothing is more notable about James's work as a whole than its range and variety; and this comment can be applied locally, to his work of the later eighties; for the major novels of that period are all very different, and require very different kinds of critical adjustment and discrimination. Compare, for instance, *The Tragic Muse* with *The Bostonians*. The centre of *The Bostonians* is a psychological study; for all the importance in the novel's total effect of the world of 'old abolitionists, transcendentalists, and spiritualists', the comedy of the Boston culture, this comedy is subordinated to the treatment of the relationship between Olive Chancellor and Verena ('one of those friendships between women which are so common in New England'). In *The Tragic Muse*, on the other hand, there is no deep psychological interest; the psychology of the characters is developed adequately for James's purposes, but these do not include a plumbing of the depths of the personality. Rather, we should appraise the novel in terms of James's success in justifying the interests we can see that he began with: see it as an experiment in a kind of novel (the *roman à thèse* which is also something else) and a kind of subject-matter (a realistic handling of English upper- and upper-middle-class society) which James never repeated.

That last sentence, with the word 'experiment' emphasized, suggests also the limits of the claim that can be made for it. It must perhaps be placed below *The Bostonians*, where James had a subject-matter that he could deal with more inwardly and more surely. But I suggest that it is considerably superior to *The Princess Casamassima*, the other novel of this period. For *The Princess Casamassima, pace* Mr. Lionel Trilling, is not one of James's best works (though there are fine things in it, the Princess herself, for instance, the *femme fatale* of the revolutionaries, is superbly done). Whatever note-taking James may earnestly have done in the London streets, the London, and the lower class, in that novel, come too much out of literature. If *The Tragic Muse* and *The Princess Casamassima* may both, with some point, be called *tours de force*, the former shows far less discrepancy between intention and achievement.

1954

XVI

KIPLING'S LATER STORIES

Kipling never wrote a line of prose or verse for the purpose of 'expressing his personality'. As *Something of Myself* makes plain, he maintained a reticence about his private thoughts and feelings which modern readers may think old-fashioned, and in his personal life he clung to privacy with all the determination of Tennyson. His theory of art, furthermore, was 'classical' and 'impersonal'. He believed in inspiration – the Daemon – but he thought of it as something coming from outside, not generated by the conflicts within: in his story *Wireless* he works out as a sort of sustained metaphor the likeness between wireless telegraphy (then a novelty) and the temporary invasion by Keats's genius of the soul of a consumptive chemist's assistant. He asked his critics to 'seek not to question other than / The books I leave behind'. Yet no author is more strongly personal than Kipling. When we think of his books, what comes to mind is not this or that character, Orde or the Lama or McIntosh Jellaludin, Mrs. Hauksbee, or Bagheera, or Mary Postgate – though no one else could have created them – but Kipling himself; not the biographical personality, but the typical composite of anecdote, reminiscence, and photograph with the vaguer but still powerful impressions drawn from his writing, which makes up what we call 'the man behind the work'. And it is this personality-pattern, holding the work together, which must ultimately be the subject for any general criticism of Kipling. But this does not mean that the critic is necessarily concerned with biographical inference. For one thing, this is so risky. We know very little of people, even when they are there to be studied; and though no doubt Kipling was a 'human case', like everyone else, it is surely unwise

to interpret his art by evidence much of which must be fragmentary and conjectural, and which is anyway mostly available
only in the artistic treatment Kipling gave to it. External reference
can be misleading, even where the basis of the fiction is certainly
autobiographical, since it may make us overlook interpretations
of the story in question which do not happen to fit in with the
imaginary biography we have in mind.

A case in point is the early story *Baa, Baa, Black Sheep*, which
has been so much quarried by biographical critics. Now certainly
the young Rudyard Kipling *had* sojourned in the House of
Desolation; he *was* Black Sheep. But what psychological critics
tend to overlook is that someone so warped and morally in-
capacitated by his childhood traumas as Kipling is said to have
been could never have written the story. For our very natural
pity and indignation at the treatment of Punch – who could feel
anything else? – must not allow us to ignore the element of
diagnosis which is so important in the tale. Punch came from India
an attractive little boy, but already with the potentiality of
arrogance towards lesser breeds, and his reaction when treated
as a pariah and thrust among them is to despise them more and
identify them, in self-defence, with his persecutors. Now it is
true that the author feels 'sympathy and understanding' for the
victim, but we must emphasize 'understanding'; he knows more
than the boy does about what has happened; the return of the
beloved mother seems to make everything 'all right' for the boy,
but we know, and Kipling knows, that it does not and cannot
make everything 'all right'. The story might be compared with
Sartre's *Enfance d'un chef*. Kipling has imaginatively created the
genesis of the state of mind which leads to fascism; he has done
it from within, but we feel the constant co-presence of a mind
more adult than Black Sheep's; sentimentality is not absent from
Kipling's work, but it does not appear in this story. Critics have
used the story to 'explain' the alleged cruelty of Kipling and his
tendency, springing from fear, to take the side of the bully. It
would be just as easy to use it to account for Kipling's horror of
religious bigotry, which appears everywhere in his work. We
recall the wretched Mulcahy's terror of death in *The Mutiny of the
Mavericks (Life's Handicap)*: 'He remembered certain things that
priests had said in his infancy, and his mother . . . starting from
her sleep with shrieks to pray for a husband's soul in torment.'
The narrator in the futuristic fantasy *With the Night Mail (Actions*

and Reactions) speaks compassionately of 'the men of the old days, each one of them taught (*that* is the horror of it!) that after death he would very possibly go for ever to unspeakable torment'. Religious tolerance is the lesson of Kabir in *The Prayer* (from *Kim*): 'His God is as his Fates assign, / His prayer is all the world's – and mine.' And young readers may have got from *Kim* their first understanding of the simple fact that people in other lands can believe just as sincerely in their very different religions as Christians do in theirs. It cannot be denied that Kipling's work illustrates his interest in cruelty, and this preoccupation may well have been due to his early sufferings; but what the literary results seem to show is, not that it made him cruel, but that it gave him a deeper insight into cruelty, and strengthened his conviction of the need for compassion.

A slighter instance of the dangers of the biographical approach is the use of the Balestier episode in Vermont to explain the anti-American phase of Kipling's writings. The most pungent of these stories is *An Error in the Fourth Dimension*. But this story was first published in 1894, before the Balestier episode; and the only safe inference is that this episode may have confirmed Kipling's already existing distrust of American lawlessness. Indeed, if the author in question had been someone other than Kipling, critics might have credited him with an intention not so much motivated by topical or personal considerations, but the typical *artist's* intention to show 'the other side' of a theme which interested him, the American hustle and irreverence for stagnant traditions which he makes so attractive in *Captains Courageous*. Again, in the later story *As Easy as ABC*[1] (1912), another futuristic fantasy about the Aerial Board of Control, it is easy to point out, as critics have done, that the Utopia of the story reflects Kipling's hatred of democracy because it encourages crowds and 'invades privacy'. What they frequently fail to notice is that the story is a *tour de force* of sustained irony, in which the narrator, a typical product of this Wellsian future in which *Transport is Civilisation*, unwittingly reveals the spiritual emptiness of a world which has banished struggle and suffering from life. The Archangel of the English, in the very late story *Uncovenanted Mercies*[2] (1932), says of his people: 'I am giving them each full advantages for self-expression and realization. These will include impeccable surroundings,

[1] *A Diversity of Creatures.*
[2] *Limits and Renewals.*

wealth, culture, health, felicity (unhappy people can't make other people happy, can they?) and – everything commensurate with the greatness of the destiny for which I – er – destine them.' But it is plain that neither the Archangel's immediate audience, nor Kipling himself, share this attitude.

Of course it is undeniable that public and private events left their mark on Kipling's work. It was not for nothing that he began his writing career as a journalist, and his political pre-occupations are everywhere obvious; the protusion of opinions can spoil a story which otherwise might have been a self-contained whole, as, for example, at the end of the South African story *The Comprehension of Private Copper*. What I am maintaining is rather that we should be careful not to apply too ready-made an image of the private or the public Kipling to the interpretation of his art: in particular, to the pattern of its evolution.

For one of the peculiarities of Kipling's art in his short stories is that, while showing obvious variety and range, it does not in any obvious sense show *development*. Of no author is it more true than for him 'in my end is my beginning'. This can readily be illustrated from what every reader of Kipling must have noticed, the characteristic unevenness of his work; unevenness, that is, not within a particular story, but in any of his collections of stories considered as a whole. It is not only that the stories are not all equally good; in a prolific author that might well be expected. The case is odder than that. Masterpieces as assured as anything he ever wrote can be found, at any period of his work, side by side with very inferior things; and yet on these inferior things the same minuteness of care and skill seems to have been expended. So in his work of the eighteen-eighties we find the poignant and noble tale of *The Man who would be King* inhabiting the same collection as *The Strange Ride of Morrowbie Jukes*; and at the very end of his career, in the collection called *Limits and Renewals*, which contains work as subtle and complex as he ever wrote, such as *Dayspring Mishandled*, we find so unpleasant and negligible a piece as *The Tie*. In any book of Kipling's stories ostensibly written for adults we must be prepared to find the ethos of *Stalky & Co.* cropping up in places where it is inappropriate. Beetle represents a self that he never outgrew.

But of course the statement that Kipling did not develop needs both qualification and explanation. Like most writers, he made some false starts before he found his real bent. And, as in most writers, a certain balance of loss and gain can be seen in comparing his later with his earlier work. The fresh vividness of the early work, registering the impact of India on a boy journalist of genius, he never perhaps quite recovered. On the other hand, some irritating immaturities, typified by the recurrent 'But that is another story' of *Plain Tales*, vanished from his style; his technical ingenuity increased; his skill took more complex and intellectualized forms; and he brought to its strange perfection that narrative manner of implication, abstention, and obliquity of which the first considerable example is *Mrs. Bathurst* (1904). He turned to new subject-matter, the Sussex countryside, the historic past of England, the Navy, and, in his last phase, the work of mental and spiritual healing of war-sufferers. But all this seems extension rather than growth; what insights Kipling had, he seems to have had from the beginning; we do not get from his later work the sense of a profound and radical change of outlook, the discovery of a new spiritual dimension, issuing from the author's changing response to his changing experience: the sort of change we can detect in the life-work of a Melville or a Dostoevsky. Quite apart from any question of relative value, Kipling does not seem to be that *kind* of artist at all. Even his best work shows this curious undeveloping poise: a formal self-sufficiency which suggests a fixity. We may contrast Joyce's *Dubliners*: in reading these stories we feel that the author could and must broaden his form and develop his insights by going on to something quite different. But in reading Kipling's stories in chronological succession, we come to feel that our knowledge of the sense of life transmitted by this writer is only being quantitatively increased; there is no perceptible modification of its quality. He seems to have worked out his distinctive technical formulas, themselves reflecting a narrow range of fixed sympathies and antipathies and set attitudes, and applied them to a variety of subject-matter which, while giving the stories their sensationally contrasting surfaces and colourings, leaves these formulas essentially unchanged.

This art, however, produced remarkable triumphs; there are compensations for the reader in Kipling's invariable realization of his particular intention, even if at times we mistrust the intention and dislike what is done. The unceasing craftsmanship,

the rigorous subduing of the matter in hand to an artistic discipline itself becomes a moral quality and an important, if always
implicit, part of the author's 'message'. Henry James, as is well
known, complained that the pursuit of this particular kind of
perfection necessitated a descent 'from the less simple in subject
to the more simple – from the Anglo-Indians to the natives, from
the natives to the Tommies, from the Tommies to the quadrupeds,
from the quadrupeds to the fish, from the fish to the engines and
screws'. This of course is not an accurate description of the
progress of Kipling's work; the bent which produced such *tours
de force* as *The Ship that Found Herself* and *The Maltese Cat* and
.007, or the various kinds of beast-fable ranging from *Just So
Stories* and *The Jungle Books*, where didactic allegory can be far or
near as the author chooses, to such relentless fables as *The Mother
Hive* or *A Walking Delegate* or *Below the Mill Dam*, where the
message is continuous and insistent – this bent was not just a
middle-period preoccupation of Kipling's, but was something he
reverted to at every stage of his literary career. Nor can James's
account be extended to Kipling's later work, which was yet to
come, and which cannot be said to be 'simple' in subject-matter.
Nevertheless, James's remark points at something fundamentally
true about the frequent results of Kipling's intent desire to have
the completest possible *control* of his form and his medium. This
desire can lead to impressive achievements in the realm of allegory, satiric fantasy, and fable – sometimes to the attainment of
the higher reaches of symbol and myth. But it can also lead to a
simplification and distortion of human character and human
behaviour which, in an author with so recurrent and emphatic a
didactic purpose as Kipling, can become irritatingly tendentious.
The danger of a strongly symbolic art, when it deals directly
with human beings, is that it makes the reader feel he is being
illicitly 'got at'; he is receiving, in the place of the really seen and
the strongly imagined, nothing but the author's theory of life.
Kipling's supreme achievements in prose fiction seem to be those
in which his genius as a fabulist and myth-maker is felt to be
shaping the story without detriment to the author's true and
sensitive perceptions of actual human beings, *They* and *Mrs.
Bathurst* and *The Wish House*, *Mary Postgate* and *The Gardsner*
exemplify this power of the short story to suggest the *distillation*
of a human life, the rendering of its essence as latent within a
momentary situation, or an anecdote, or an episode. Without the

artistic economy, in which every detail is significant, these stories would not have their power; but the power of this selectiveness depends upon our conviction that behind the selection there is a latent reserve of fuller knowledge. They have what Kipling calls in *The Bull that Thought (Debits and Credits)* 'a breadth of technique that comes of reasoned art, and, above all, the passion that arrives after experience'.

This 'reasoned art', the conscious craftsmanship of Kipling, is the most obvious and distinctive feature of everything he wrote, and it is the only aspect of his work about which he permitted himself to depart from his usual reticence. His emphasis in these remarks – strange as it must seem to those who still equate Kipling with the Jelly-bellied Flag-Flapper – is less on a 'message' or a 'self' to be expressed, than on a medium to be manipulated.

I made my own experiments in the weights, colours, perfumes, and attributes of words in relation to other words, either as read aloud so that they may hold the ear, or, scattered over the page, draw the eye. There is no line of my verse which has not been mouthed till the tongue has made all smooth, and memory, after many recitals, has mechanically slipped the grosser superfluities.[1]

And, in speaking of the *Puck* books, he says, 'I worked the material in three or four overlaid tints and textures, which might or might not reveal themselves according to the shifting light of sex, youth and experience.'[2] The drawbacks, as well as the pleasures for writer and reader, of this passion for manipulation are clear. There is the danger, to which Kipling too often succumbed, of overwriting. 'My gold,' says the narrator in *Their Lawful Occasions*,[3] with a tinge of regret, 'I have lacquered down to dull bronze, my purples overlaid with sepia of the sea, and for hell-hearted ruby and blinding diamond I have substituted pale amethyst and mere jargoon.' There is the excess of detail which is apt to occur in a writer so microscopically concerned with the texture of his writing; George Moore said of a description of evening in *Kim* that 'Mr. Kipling seems to have followed it about

---

[1] *Something of Myself*, Chapter Three.
[2] op. cit., Chapter Seven.
[3] *Traffics and Discoveries*.

R

like a detective employed in a divorce case'. Sometimes, of course, this detail can be very charming, as in the illuminated manuscripts of the Middle Ages:

> The Sub-Cantor looked over his shoulder at the pinned-down sheet where the first words of the Magnificat were built up in gold washed with red-lac for a background to the Virgin's hardly yet fired halo. She was shown, hands joined in wonder, at a lattice of infinitely intricate arabesque, round the edge of which sprays of orange-bloom seemed to lead the blue hot air that carried back over the minute parched landscape in the middle distance.
>
> 'You've made her all Jewess,' said the Sub-Cantor, studying the olive-flushed cheek and the eyes charged with fore-knowledge.[1]

But sometimes, as all readers of Kipling know, it can be a tiresome mannerism; and the defect inherent in this manner of writing, its extreme self-consciousness, may be suggested by these lines from the prefatory poem to *The Captive* (*Traffics and Discoveries*):

> And the words of his mouth were as slaves spreading carpets of glory
> Embroidered with names of the Djinns – a miraculous weaving –
> But the cool and perspicuous eye overbore unbelieving.

There can be a bad sense to the word 'manipulation', and even in Kipling's best work we may be reminded of the assertion, in *The Village that Voted the Earth was Flat*, that 'Advertisin' is the most delicate of all the sciences.'

But this long practice in word-painting reaped its true artistic reward in those stories where it is used with tact and restraint; the sudden, vivid descriptive touch can be unforgettable, Manallace drawing on his black gloves at the end of *Dayspring Mishandled*, Helen Turrell of *The Gardener* in the army graveyard:

> She climbed a few wooden-faced earthen steps and then met the entire crowded level of the thing in one held breath. She

[1] *The Eye of Allah, Debits and Credits.*

did not know that Hazenzeele Third counted twenty-one thousand dead already. All she saw was a merciless sea of black crosses, bearing little strips of stamped tin at all angles across their faces. She could distinguish no order or arrangement in their mass; nothing but a waist-high wilderness of weeds stricken dead, rushing at her. She went forward, moving to the left and the right hopelessly, wondering by what guidance she should ever come to her own. A great distance away there was a line of whiteness. It proved to be a block of some two or three hundred graves whose headstones had already been set, whose flowers were planted out, and whose new-sown grass showed green.

Less charged and intense, but even more typical of Kipling's mature style, is the opening of *Friendly Brook* in *A Diversity of Creatures*:

The valley was so choked with fog that one could scarcely see a cow's length across a field. Every blade, twig, bracken-frond and hoof-print carried water, and the air was filled with the noise of rushing ditches and field-drains, all delivering to the brook below. A week's November rain on water-logged land had gorged her to full flood, and she proclaimed it aloud.

Two men in sackcloth aprons were considering an un-trimmed hedge that ran down the hillside and disappeared into mist beside those roarings. They stood back and took stock of the neglected growth, tapped an elbow of hedge-oak here, a mossed beech-stub there, swayed a stooled ash back and forth, and looked at each other.

'I reckon she's about two rod thick,' said Jabez the younger, 'an' she hasn't felt iron since – when has she, Jesse?'

'Call it twenty-five year, Jabez, an' you won't be far out.'

'Umm!' Jabez rubbed his wet handbill on his wetter coat sleeve. 'She ain't a hedge. She's all manner o' trees. We'll just about have to —' He paused, as professional etiquette required.

'Just about have to side her up an' see what she'll bear. But hadn't we best —?' Jesse paused in his turn, both men being artists and equals.

'Get some kind o' line to go by,' Jabez ranged up and down till he found a thinner place, and with clean snicks of the hand-bill revealed the original face of the fence. Jesse took

over the dripping stuff as it fell forward, and, with a grasp
and a kick, made it to lie orderly on the bank till it should be
faggotted.

By noon a length of unclean jungle had turned itself into a
cattle-proof barrier, tufted here and there with little plumes of
the sacred holly which no woodman touches without orders.

It would be easy to find openings of stories, like the famous first
paragraph of *Love o' Women*, that proclaim Kipling's authorship
more flamboyantly than this, but none more essentially typical of
him. Here, unmistakably, is this personal style, which, without
ostentatious economy, establishes at once the brook itself, the
animistic 'hero' of the tale; the November weather; the two
hedgers, with their pride in their ancient craft, their knowledge-
ableness, their ceremonious etiquette of 'artists and equals'; the
real if modest triumph of human endeavour ('By noon a length
of unclean jungle had turned itself into a cattle-proof barrier'),
and the final touch, that hint of 'inside' knowledge which in its
blatant manifestations can be so tiresome in Kipling's stories,
but is here perfectly right in its tone of respectful approval
('. . . little plumes of the sacred holly which no woodman touches
without orders'). Kipling had implicitly criticized much in his
own early work when he complained, in *Wressley of the Foreign
Office*, that 'one of the many curses of our life in India is the want
of atmosphere in the painter's sense. There are no half-tints
worth noticing. Men stand out all crude and raw, with nothing
to tone them down, and nothing to scale them against'. This
chastened later style is the opposite of 'crude and raw'; it is full
of 'half-tints'; and much in these later stories which the reader
vaguely recognizes as 'background' and 'atmosphere' is there
precisely to 'tone down' and to 'scale against'.

One of the first stories in the distinctively 'late' manner is
They[1] (1904), and it is convenient to open discussion of the later
Kipling with a work so totally different from the conventional
account of him. Even that account allows Kipling an interest in
the eerie and the occult (in one mode *Wireless* or *The Finest Story
in the World*, in another *The Mark of the Beast* or *At the End of the
Passage*). But the first thing to be noticed about *They* is that the
part played by the ghostly children and the blind childless woman
whose love draws them to the beautiful house she has made for

---

[1] *Traffics and Discoveries.*

them, has nothing to do with a ghost-story strumming on the nerves. The mode of the tale is nearer to *Burnt Norton* than to *The Turn of the Screw*. The appeal of the fantasy is to poetic feeling and imagination. Not that we are to take the ghosts as simply the projection of the blind woman's longing or the narrator's bereavement (he, it is finally made known to us, has lost a child, whom he is to find again, once, at the end of the tale). They exist for other people in the tale, the butler, his wife, and the village mother. But their 'reality' is equivocal: 'When I paused in my work I listened, but the wood was so full of the noises of summer (though the birds had mated) that I could not at first distinguish these from the tread of small cautious feet stealing across the dead leaves.' One effect of this potently evocative use of the sound of the children's footsteps, whispering, and laughter is to assimilate the narrator's and our perception of them to the blind woman's; an effect echoed in the final fading-out of the story, after the blind woman has told the narrator he must never come again: 'She left me to sit a little longer by the screen, and I heard the sound of her feet die out along the gallery above.' The reason for the equivocal status of the earth-bound spirits is plain when the significance of the story as a parable is taken; the fancied glimpse of the world of the dead is there to confirm that it *is* another world, and the living must go back to the world of the living.

All this is part of the manifest meaning of the tale. But there is another theme in *They* interwoven with the theme of the children, and its presence has puzzled some readers, who may not have been conscious of its distinct existence, but who have noticed certain elements in *They* which do not seem relevant. What, for instance, is the point of the incident of the dishonest tenant-farmer (who is terrified by the ghosts) at the end? We may approach this more hidden theme by asking another question: why is there so much about the narrator's motor-car? This car is one of those somewhat comic early models which frequently appear in Kipling's work, usually (as in *They*) breaking down at some point in the story. It introduces a note of stridency into the dreamland of the beautiful house with its lawn and yew trees: 'It was sacrilege to wake that dreaming house-front with the clatter of machinery.' The narrator's references to it tend to have a *gaucherie* and a blatancy which contrast with his generally quiet and sympathetic tone: 'In two minutes I was blowing all the horns of Jericho in front of the House Beautiful, and Madden, from the pantry, rose to the crisis like a butler and a man.' This sentence by itself could be used to exemplify Kipling's bad style. But in the context this manner of referring to the car seems to be part of a social or sociological observation. The narrator is very conscious of not being one of what the fat village woman calls 'carriage folk'. This comes out in what he says to the blind woman, who *is* one: 'If you had done your duty as a pillar of the State and a landed proprietress you ought to have summoned me for trespass when I barged through your woods the other day.' And it is twice repeated in the story, with significant emphasis, that he comes 'from the other side of the country'. Of course this last touch refers also to the mystical theme. But this way of contrasting the old England and the new, the motor-car and modern people with the House Beautiful and the villagers, 'deep-rooted trees of that soil', runs right through the story. The imaginative bias of the writing is *against* the modern world; the least sympathetic character is the dishonest tenant-farmer, who is represented as a characteristically modern product. And the narrator feels it 'sacrilege' to 'wake that dreaming house-front with the clatter of machinery'. On the other hand, it is the car which takes the narrator to the House Beautiful – the second time he feels that 'my car took the road of her own volition'. And it is thanks to the car that the sick child is saved. '"Useful things, cars", says Madden the butler. "If I'd had one when mine took sick she wouldn't have died . . . Croup. No one knew what to do . . . I drove eight miles in a tax-cart for the doctor. She was choked when we came back. This car'd ha' saved her. She'd have been close on ten now."' One function of this incident of the sick child is to safeguard against idealization of the past.

We may wonder whether Kipling showed artistic tact in inter-weaving these two themes. Other stories in which the motor-car plays a prominent role can show him in a more defiantly philistine mood; and hostility to the 'county' undoubtedly occurs in stories like *The Village that Voted* and *Beauty Spots*, in such a way as to suggest that the author is working off some personal resentment. But in *They* the narrator, with his sensitive humanity and quiet grief, is an entirely sympathetic figure, and, with his poise between wistfulness and renunciation, the best possible spokesman for the present in relation to a past which it knows is irrecoverable. The two themes join delicately in the symbolic moment early in the tale, which foreshadows the end: 'Here, then, I stayed; a horse-man's green spear laid at my breast; held by the exceeding beauty of that jewel in that setting.'

This wrenching-apart of the thematic materials of *They* must give a false impression of the tale itself, where the fabric is continuous and delicate. But for close working and subtlety of means it is far surpassed by the later story *The Wish House*[1] (1924), which has claims to be regarded as the most remarkable story Kipling ever wrote. Certainly it is difficult to think of any other short story in the language which is richer in content, and yet gives no suggestion of overcrowding. When it is brought together with *They* we see at once a parallel, in the skill with which in both tales the element of the supernatural (or non-natural) is introduced into the tale without disturbing the reader's sense of the human centrality of the story; and another in the importance of both of the mysterious powers of a woman. But *The Wish House* represents a far rarer order of achievement. The setting and atmosphere of *They*, with its beautiful old house set in an idealized English countryside, gives a licence for a daydream indulgence of fancy; in *The Wish House* we are never for a moment allowed to forget the hard realism of the poor suburban villa, the two ageing women in the little room shaken by charabancs, one of them going blind, the other dying of cancer. The story cannot be summarized; everything is done by means of touches, implications, details. Through the ordinary, realistic talk of the old countrywomen (this is one of the tales in which the suggestion of dialect is not overdone, as it sometimes is in Kipling, and is essential to the effect) there emerges the wholly credible picture of their two interconnected lives; by way of the secondary story of Liz Fettley, in response to her confidence and her sympathetic questions, we learn from Grace Ashcroft the story of the Wish House, which for her represents the sacrifice of her health and life she believes herself to have made for the man she loves. The story of the Wish House, reduced to the bare bones of anecdote, is fantastic. A Sussex cook, Grace Ashcroft, goes to a little empty house in a back street of London to speak through a letter-box to 'the Token', whom she asks to let her 'take everythin' bad that's in store for my man, 'Arry Mockler, for love's sake'. This

[1] *Debits and Credits*. For a particularly interesting examination of this and other late Kipling stories, see Miss J. M. S. Tompkins' admirable study *The Art of Rudyard Kipling*, Methuen, 1959.

decision has to be taken over and over again, until it becomes part of the irrevocable pattern of her life. Everything that happens to Harry, who has left her and does not requite her love, she thereafter attributes to her pledge to make him, without knowing it, 'take his good from her'. At the end of the story she is facing death, but still pleadingly insistent that 'the pain *do* count to keep 'Arry – where I want him. Say it can't be wasted, like'. The tale closes with the arrival of the District Nurse; Mrs. Ashcroft becomes 'the self-contained domestic once more', and Mrs. Fettley, before she leaves,

> . . . leaned over, and kissed Mrs. Ashcroft on the waxy yellow forehead, and again on the faded grey eyes.
> 'It *do* count, don't it – de pain?' The lips that still kept trace of their original moulding hardly more than breathed the words.
> Mrs. Fettley kissed them and moved towards the door.

Even this outline may suggest something of the moving and compassionate quality of the tale. But judgement of its human significance must partly depend on how we are to regard Grace Ashcroft's sacrifice. Clearly the business of the Token is literally incredible, and Grace is a superstitious woman. The distinction of the story is that she is none the less convincingly established for us as a tragic figure. The Wish House comes to stand for those forces in human life which are not under the control of man, but which the stoic confronts and accepts. That we do not find Grace's behaviour incredible, or a neurotic vagary, is due to the completeness with which we are made to believe in her as an ordinary person – ordinary in so far as we admit that we ourselves are ordinary people. She is seen as real and immediate, with her early amorous waywardness (so well brought out in the account of her relationship with her husband), and her later proud resignation and pathos, all conveyed amid the crisp brevities of her speech. But she is also a figure of history; for through the tale, as in *They*, but quite differently and more subtly, there runs the sense of the changing English life, both local and national, which changes her individual life and the lives of her friends; the moves from country to town, and from town to country, the displacement of horse-drawn traffic by motor-buses and everything that that implies – all are brought in, not as mere background, but as a means to establishing her reality as a living reminiscence of older ways and older habits of thinking and feeling. In front of us is the little house in the modern village, a heavy tea laid out (Grace was a cook who never 'owed me belly much'), and geraniums on the window-sill; in the nearer distance is London, with that other horrible little house of the walled garden and the basement kitchen; farther back still the Sussex countryside of the women's youth. The richness of this treatment might lead us to suppose that the story required development at fuller length; but on reflection we see that something correspond-ing to the laconic stoicism of Grace Ashcroft is artistically appro-priate; without this economy there could not be that sense, at once sympathetic and ironic, of the distillation of a whole life, of the universal tragedy of possessive love, in one bizarre encounter with the powers of darkness.

There is much in *The Wish House* that would repay analysis; T. S. Eliot, while praising it, has called it 'hard and obscure', and in a fuller treatment of the story due consideration should certainly be given to the use of the symbolism of cancer which recurs, some would say obsessively, in Kipling's later work; we notice its association, though perhaps this is non-significant in *The Wish House*, with blindness, another recurring symbol. (We remember the terrible image of 'a blind face that cries and can't wipe its eyes' in *At the End of the Passage*.) No doubt these symbols meant something intensely personal to Kipling. But in our impulse to psychological investigation of the author we should not forget the actual force these symbols have in the stories, and the insight (as shown in *The Wish House*) which leads us, not back to the author, but to ourselves and the world. (And if Kipling *was* obsessed with cancer, is it not the characteristic obsession of modern man?)

These questions about the degree of insight and the general human significance of Kipling's more 'unusual' stories are posed in a sharper form by *Mrs. Bathurst*,[1] which has always been one of the *cruces* in the criticism of his work. Here the obsession of the sailor Vickery with the kind and pleasant and motherly Mrs. Bathurst is powerfully done – her 'blindish look' as she walks forward in the news-reel picture (the 'biograph') is unforgettable, as is the grotesque business of 'Click' Vickery's four false teeth, by which he is identified as a charred corpse at the baffling end of the story. But what exactly happened, and what is the significance

[1] *Traffics and Discoveries.*

of what happened, many readers have puzzled over. Some have thought that Kipling in this story has overdone his passion for 'cutting'. *Mrs. Bathurst* (1904) is one of the earliest of Kipling's experiments in indirect or suppressed narrative, and its experimental character might make that explanation plausible. But it may well be that the point of the story lies in this obscurity. Pyecroft, the observer of the story, does not claim to understand Vickery and his doings. He knows, and his friends can confirm, the power of love ('it takes 'em at all ages'), and its destructiveness. This is what the story is 'about'. *The Wish House* also testifies to this destructiveness in love. But there the effect is totally different, because we have heard Grace Ashcroft's own story, seen the pattern of her life as she sees it, and seen her 'close to' through the eyes of Liz Fettley. In *Mrs. Bathurst* we see only glimpses of a stranger through the eyes of a boon-companion who, despite his assurance to the contrary, has very little essential idea of 'what transpired'. The emotion generated in us, as in Pyecroft and his friends, is a sort of impersonal awe or terror. We feel no incongruity when the incongruous Vickery can say 'The rest is silence'. Any one of us, in his relationship with his mother, may have lived through the experience of a childish Hamlet; and the rest – indeed, most – of Vickery's story *can* be silence. That the woman whom Vickery is found dead with in the teak-forest is never identified in the story is psychologically right; the sense of a pattern of life (and death) from which certain things have been dropped or repressed is essential to its human significance. Kipling makes a shell-shocked soldier say in *Epitaphs of the War*:

> My name, my speech, my self I had forgot.
> My wife and children came – I knew them not.
> I died. My Mother followed. At her call.
> And on her bosom I remembered all.

Vickery, as we hear of him, was in something like that condition of shock.

Mrs. Bathurst, with its cryptic quality, might be dismissed as a mere oddity. When we turn to *Mary Postgate*, however, the challenge to our human and moral judgement cannot be evaded. Here nothing is hidden; we are looking at Mary Postgate from beginning to end of the story, and everything relevant to understanding and judging her is supplied. *Mary Postgate* has been more attacked than anything else Kipling wrote. No one denies that his full powers are engaged in this story, and some have regarded this as clinching their condemnation of him as a cruel writer who is here vicariously indulging a morbid passion of hatred and revenge. Now undeniably Kipling's writings during the First World War do show bitterness. There were poignant personal reasons for that. And he did not make the critical defence of *Mary Postgate* easier by appending to it a poem about how 'the English began to hate', nor by including in the same volume, *A Diversity of Creatures*, the queer fantasy called *Swept and Garnished*, a sort of parody of *They* in a Berlin setting, which does show some signs of a desire for reprisal. But I believe that *Mary Postgate*, horrible as it is, can be shown to have the intelligence and insight which those who hate it wish to deny. It is certainly a tale of horror. The middle-aged English spinster gloating over the dying German airman – it is not a tableau that the reader will want to revert to very often. No one will deny that, in the circumstances of the story, Mary Postgate's indulgence is understandable, if still terrible. What is at issue is the author's attitude towards it.

From the outset we must be conscious that Mary Postgate is 'placed'. We are shown her limitations, and her unimaginativeness:

> Mary was not young, and though her speech was as colourless as her eyes or her hair, she was never shocked [i.e., by her elderly woman employer's *risqué* stories]. She listened unflinchingly to every one; said at the end, 'How interesting!' or 'How shocking!' as their case might be, and never again referred to it, for she prided herself on a trained mind, which 'did not dwell on these things.'

Her inarticulate devotion to her employer's nephew, the 'unlovely orphan of eleven' who '. . . repaid her in his holidays by calling her "Gatepost", "Postey", or "Packthread", by thumping her between her narrow shoulders, or by chasing her bleating round the garden, her large mouth open, her large nose high in air, at a stiff-necked shamble very like a camel's'. Later on, we are told, 'he filled the house with clamour, argument and harangues as to his personal needs, likes and dislikes, and the limitations of "you women", reducing Mary to tears of physical fatigue, or, when he chose to be humorous, of helpless laughter'.

The presentation of young Wynn is consistent; as a young man he remains painfully callow. He joins the Flying Corps and is killed during a trial flight; the effect of his death on Mary is cataclysmic, but with her usual inarticulateness she cannot express it; her immediate reaction to the news is to say, 'It's a great pity he didn't die in action after he had killed somebody.' Later, she is burning his belongings in the incinerator – the interminable catalogue of Wynn's possessions is dwelt on with all Kipling's relentless detail – when she hears the dying German airman groan in the shrubbery. To herself she justifies her own cruel behaviour – she refuses to help the man, brings a revolver, hums to herself ('Mary never had a voice'), shouts, finally 'drinks in' the sounds of his dying agony – by remembering the child who has just been killed in the village, and whose body she has seen; a bomb has been dropped, perhaps by the airman who is dying in front of her. She speaks to him, as she has been thinking, in Wynn's idiom:

> 'Stop that!' said Mary, and stamped her foot. 'Stop that, you bloody pagan!'
> The words came quite smoothly and naturally. They were Wynn's own words, and Wynn was a gentleman who for no consideration on earth would have torn little Edna into those vividly coloured strips and strings. But this thing hunched under the oak tree had done that thing.

The crowning horror is in the last sentence of the story, where we see the plain dull spinster satisfied and fulfilled as a woman, 'taking a luxurious hot bath before tea, and . . . looking, as Miss Fowler said when she saw her lying all relaxed on the other sofa, "quite handsome!"'

It will be clear that the diagnosis of Mary Postgate's contradictory state of mind, due to her emotional upheaval, is fully given; we have only to reflect on the contrast between her words on hearing of Wynn's death, and her self-justification for hating the German airman. What those who condemn Kipling would say is that the author is quite aware of the moral incoherence of Mary, but exploits her as a vent for the release of emotions which a sahib himself cannot admit that he feels; women, as contradictory and inferior beings, can be allowed the indulgence which the author himself desires. But this amounts to attributing to Kipling – the Kipling of this story – the outlook of young Wynn. It ignores the careful art of the story in avoiding any sentimentalization of Mary or Wynn or the relationship between them. Above all, it ignores the essential identity – symbolic, of course, not literal – between the dying airman and Wynn. (He too, like Wynn, has fallen from his aeroplane.) The tale perhaps could not have been written by someone who had not experienced the agony of the bereaved civilian in war-time. But what it gives us is not a self-indulgence, but art: the imaginative understanding of what has happened to a Mary Postgate, and the moral intelligence to direct our horror to what *is* horrible, the stripping of a human soul, war and the cruelty of war.

It is natural to contrast the compassion of the later tale, *The Gardener*,[1] with the cruelty of *Mary Postgate*. But this contrast need not be used to emphasize a change of heart in Kipling. No doubt the dates are significant; *Mary Postgate* belongs to 1915, *The Gardener* to 1926. But the dramatic self-sufficiency of each tale is complete. *The Gardener* is a piece of grave irony; the ironic tone is sustained to the very end. What is remarkable is that this irony does not preclude – indeed, is the medium for – compassion. 'Everyone in the village knew' that Lieutenant Michael Turrell was not Helen Turrell's nephew, but her son. She has lived a lie, and we are made to feel that there was nobility in this lie, but only the truth can make free. Helen is not free; her silence cuts her off from the human response which she desires to make, after Michael is killed and she goes on a pilgrimage to the war-cemetery, to the woman whom she meets and who has confessed to a love like hers. The woman is repelled by Helen's apparent coldness and lack of sympathy. Release from the past is given by the man she takes for the gardener, when she is searching for Michael's grave:

A man knelt behind a line of headstones – evidently a gardener, for he was firming a young plant in the soft earth. She went towards him, her paper in her hand. He rose at her approach and without prelude or salutation asked: 'Who are you looking for?'

'Lieutenant Michael Turrell – my nephew,' said Helen slowly and word for word, as she had many thousands of times in her life.

The man lifted his eyes and looked at her with infinite

[1] *Debits and Credits*.

compassion before he turned from the fresh-sown grass towards the naked black crosses.

'Come with me,' he said, 'and I will show you where your
son lies.'

Even after this cathartic moment, the irony does not cease; the
story ends with Helen turning away, still 'supposing him to be
the gardener'. The reader will pick up the reference to the Gospel,
but Helen can be left to assume that the gardener was mistaken.
Thus the symbolic force, for the reader, of Helen's alleviation
can be conveyed without the explicit assurance that for her it
was a religious experience. This deliberate ambiguity is not there
because of Kipling's own equivocal attitude towards Christianity.
It is the imaginative delicacy of art: the art that we find in the
best of Kipling's later stories.

But it may be said that, though *The Gardener* is one of Kipling's
best stories, it is hardly typical of him. And, indeed, it may well
be that Kipling's best stories are not his most representative. We
do not find, in the stories I have discussed, the typical Kipling
'world-picture', the emphasis on the tribal and the arcane, the
passion for being an initiate, 'one of the brotherhood', in the
know, and above all, the overriding insistence on the Law.
Certainly this 'world-picture' never disappears from Kipling's
work, and it is one of the things that makes it hard to describe
his art as showing development. To bring out the essential line
of continuity in Kipling's work we may look finally at one of his
latest stories, *Dayspring Mishandled* (1928).[1] This tale is so sombre
and bitter in feeling, as well as so complex and elliptical in style,
that it is not at first easy to recognize the closeness of its relationship to one of Kipling's most characteristic and frequently exploited *genres*: the story of a hoax. The place of these stories in
Kipling's work, and his sense of the ludicrous in general, is not
always understood. Often the *ethos* of his comedies seems to
contradict what we all tend to regard as the most fundamental of
Kipling's beliefs – the necessity of obedience to the Law. It need
not be stressed how often this is reiterated, in different keys, all
over Kipling's work. It is the message of the *Jungle Books*. Purun
Bhagat, in his withdrawal to the contemplative life, is 'looking
for a law of his own'. St. Paul in another story tells the neurotic
sea-captain to serve Caesar: then, at least, he will be following

[1] *Limits and Renewals.*

some sort of law. Yet, in the farces, law and order is constantly being flouted with the author's evident approval. This comes out oddly in *Stalky & Co.* The message of the book is ostensibly the breaking-in of the young colts by the benevolent Chirons. But most of the action in fact consists of a series of rags and practical jokes in which the school authorities are constantly being disobeyed and outwitted. How is this contradiction reconciled in Kipling's world-picture?

The answer seems to be that Kipling's emotional interest in hoaxes is closely connected with his feeling about imaginative creation. All his practical jokers are artists, but artists in the manipulation of men and circumstances rather than the usual media of art. There is no mistaking the creative joy of the impresario Bat Masquerier in his organizing of the vast hoax of *The Village that Voted*. It may be, as indeed is indicated in the story, morally irresponsible. But by itself it represents a triumph of imagination, as much as the scheme of conquest in *The Man who would be King*. In imaginative creation man seems to be a free agent, no longer the powerless victim of circumstances and forces outside his control. So Kipling's delight in the farcical hoax is not really in contradiction with that sense of the impotence of the lonely individual which makes him insist so strongly on the necessity of subordination to the law or the tribe. The hoax, as work of art, supplies an emotional holiday, in allowing man the illusion of freedom.

What is remarkable about *Dayspring Mishandled* is that, uniquely in Kipling, it is both the story of a hoax and a tragedy. And the tragedy resides precisely in the eventual demonstration, in the story, that human freedom *is* an illusion and that man is powerless. *Dayspring Mishandled* is a tale of revenge; or rather, of a plan for revenge to which a man devotes his whole life without ever carrying it out. The scheme of revenge thus remains a pure imaginative creation, but one in the elaboration of which the essence of a man's life has been drained away. Manallace, a middle-aged writer of popular historical fiction, conceives a subtle scheme of revenge on an unpleasant highbrow man of letters, Castorley, who has wronged (in some way which is left rather obscure) the woman Manallace loved. Castorley has made himself an international authority on Chaucer, and it is at this reputation that Manallace resolves to strike. His scheme requires the forging and 'planting' of a medieval manuscript containing a hitherto unknown fragment of a tale by Chaucer. Castorley is to 'discover' it, become famous, get a knighthood, and then be shattered, by the irrefutable proof of the forgery which Manallace has cunningly worked into the 'discovery'. The account of the forgery and 'planting' is done with all Kipling's beloved technical expertise and know-how. The scheme succeeds up to a point; Castorley duly makes the 'discovery' and is elevated to the pinnacle of renown from which Manallace plans to topple him. But now Manallace incomprehensibly delays his revenge. He finds all sorts of excuses and ways of delaying (he has by now become the close collaborator in Castorley's learned labours). Meanwhile Castorley is ailing of a mysterious disease, obscurely connected – as disease often is in Kipling – with his sense of guilt about the wrong he has done. Manallace in the outcome never carries out his revenge. The ostensible reason is that he feels that Castorley's wife, aided and abetted by another sinister character, Castorley's doctor, has in some way found out his secret intention to destroy her husband, and is using him to further her own plan to get rid of Castorley. The tale ends with Manallace at Castorley's funeral, pulling on his black gloves; he is left with the *raison d'être* of his life gone, accepting the role of good friend and loyal collaborator of Castorley that he has so long pretended to be. Lady Castorley and the doctor are left in possession of the field.

Many readers have found *Dayspring Mishandled* difficult. In its elliptical mode of narrative, significant turns and developments are played down. The point at which Manallace's 'real life-work' began is indicated cryptically. It is never quite clear just what Castorley's original offence was – the offence that has poisoned two lives. And the business of Lady Castorley and the doctor, Gleeag, remains somewhat obscure. But these obscurities are appropriate in a tale which deals so much in the hidden springs of action. Manallace himself cannot have been clear about the motive which led him first to delay and then to abandon the consummation of his life's work. We must not overlook the element of compassion. But it would seem that the main reason was that he was an artist, a worker in the imagination. The plot against Castorley became an end in itself. He could not bear to see his art transposed into the world of action, because in that art, although the impulse to create it sprang from hatred and revenge, he could feel the creator's delight. *Dayspring Mishandled* can thus be seen to occupy a similar place in Kipling's work to that of *Bartleby the Scrivener* in Melville's. Both are bitter parables of the artist and his illusory 'freedom'. It seems appropriate that a discussion of some of Kipling's later tales should close with so poignant an example of his general sense of men's powerlessness.

1964

XVII

D. H. LAWRENCE AND
WOMEN IN LOVE

The object of criticism, it is often said, is to obtain a 'balanced view' of the author criticized. But where the author in question is D. H. Lawrence this is peculiarly difficult. Lawrence tends to stir up (to use one of his own phrases) a 'bristling rousedness' in his critics, and estimates of him both as a man and as a writer tend consequently to be exaggerated, one way or the other. He is not an easy author for the would-be judicious. The first problem the critic has to face is the daunting mixture of kinds and levels in Lawrence's writing. It is easy to make rough-and-ready distinctions: to say, for example, that *The Woman who Rode Away* comes from the artist, *Fantasia of the Unconscious* from the preacher, and the poems in *Look! we have come through* from the man, the 'difficult' husband and lover, the subject for biographical speculation and psychological inquiry amateur or professional. But even in the works mentioned, the relation between the different elements in Lawrence's genius is not altogether simple, and when we come to consider such equally characteristic works as *The Captain's Doll* or *St. Mawr* or *The Man who died* the complexity of the treatment required is obvious. No simple critical formula can be proposed. This is largely because Lawrence is like Byron or Tolstoy, in that it is impossible to separate, for long, his work and his life. The work represents very often the writer's living-through of his personal problems and conflicts, as well as his more general preoccupations; while the life comes to take on the shape of a symbolic story or legend.

That story will be read over again, and probably with more

objectivity as the years go by and the personalities and topicalities involved cease to irritate or to divert. Lawrence is a person that future students of English literature and English civilization will have to meet; and it may be said that his 'personality' is the central subject for criticism for the student of his life – not only the Lawrence of anecdote, the brilliant letter-writer, journalist, and travel-book writer, but the wider personality-pattern which informs his creative work. Only one or two faces of Lawrence's 'personality' can be examined here; no comprehensiveness will be attempted, but merely a clearing-away of some of the manifest obstacles to judgement and appreciation.

Many of the works of Lawrence that follow his 'Nottingham' period do present obstacles. Now it should be said at once that where he is most completely a *poet* these seem to disappear; where, for example, he is evoking the life of nature: not merely the 'nature' of nature-poets, but the ancient feeling of the cosmic mystery, the pre-human and inhuman power of the universe, which we may suppose archaic man to have felt, and which Lawrence, with that strong 'archaic' strain in his genius, can make articulate more wonderfully than any other modern writer in English. When this poetry appears in Lawrence – more often in his prose than in his verse – our doubts, objections, and questions are silenced. But Lawrence is a novelist and story-teller as well as a poet of the cosmos, and when he deals in human relationships – and he himself described his own subject-matter as 'the relation between men and women' – we are often disturbed and challenged, and sometimes repelled, by what we sense of the point of view of the author. This is not only because Lawrence preaches to the reader, and many of us dislike being preached to anyway, apart from disliking what he preaches. Even when Lawrence is more fully an artist and makes us feel what he wants us to feel, instead of insisting that we ought to feel it, bafflement and irritation often occur. It is at such times that our attention is drawn away from the work to the man behind the work, and we cannot but deviate into thoughts about those well-known sexual obsessions and social unease which critics and biographers have so much dwelt on. So we lose contact with the world of the author's imagination and find ourselves on the plane of ideas and opinions. It is easy then to discover that Lawrence as a moralist is thoroughly incoherent. Any attempt to institutionalize his moral, social, or political teaching would produce chaos – assuming we could

imagine what the attempt would be like. Lawrence is too
obviously generalizing improperly, and at times erroneously,
from his own case. This is especially clear in the matter of sex.
There is obviously self-deception, hence insincerity, in a work
like *The Plumed Serpent* (1926), with its insistence that a woman
must not seek complete physical satisfaction from the act of sex,
but must find contentment instead in a reverent 'submission' to
male 'authority'.

But this disagreeable side of Lawrence, though it exists, is
relevant to the literary student only in so far as it reflects a failure
in Lawrence's art. It is true that this failure is frequent and
characteristic – perhaps especially in those post-war years when
the suffering and defeated mood of the author is more evident,
and coincides with, if it is not indeed partly due to, a decline in
his creative powers. But we must be careful to distinguish between those works of his which are disturbing in the wrong way
– those which deflect us on to the plane of opinions and arguments – and those which are healthily disturbing, which compel
us to a valuable reappraisal, and perhaps readjustment, of our
familiar assumptions and attitudes. Roughly speaking we may
say that in his successful works Lawrence makes us *see* the complexity of many of the concrete human situations to which moral
judgements are undoubtedly relevant, but which do not lend
themselves to description and analysis in straightforward moral
terms. Thus (whatever we may think of the success of the novel
as a whole) his presentation in *Aaron's Rod* (1922) of the deadlock
in Aaron's marriage, the impasse into which Aaron's life has got,
is so powerful that we are no more inclined than we would be in
real life to pronounce readily on the rights and wrongs of Aaron's
decision to leave his wife and children. It is not that we are
persuaded to excuse Aaron, though as the novel goes on we soon
realize that the author is on Aaron's side. It is rather that, owing
to Lawrence's art, we are able to see this sort of situation 'in
depth' – in a way that we rarely can, either in our own lives or in
the lives of others. When it comes to explaining *why* Aaron took
the step that he did, Lawrence is perhaps not able to translate his
own convictions about the matter into art – not able to dramatize
them; the amateur psychologist may indeed feel that this is because Aaron's decision is not consciously enough related, in the
book, to his difficulties revealed there in forming a relationship
with *any* woman and his curious quasi-homosexual relationship

with the writer Rawdon Lilly. But what Lawrence can and does do is to show *how* it happened. We *see* that the Aaron we meet in his pages would, and did, act in this way. Lawrence's imagination has been sufficient to provide the data, the 'facts' of the situation; though when it comes to interpreting them, his imagination – perhaps because of some personal psychological 'block' – seems to function less powerfully.

Even where Lawrence has clearly fallen into special pleading, we can find this fullness in the presentment of the *données* of the situation which gives us room to make up our own minds. And it should be added that Lawrence's didacticism is characteristically apt to turn into self-questioning; just as those works of his (like *Lady Chatterley's Lover*) where a kind of near-allegorical simplicity is clearly intended, turn into something more complex because Lawrence, in 'becoming' the gamekeeper, cannot but bring into the gamekeeper his own uncertainties and self-mistrust. (A simpler example is the short story *The Daughters of the Vicar*, in the character of the miner Durant, who represents instinctive 'life' in the fable, but who turns out to have intense inner difficulties.) It is notable that Lawrence's didactic prose is at its best when it reveals, in its oscillatory, fluctuating movement, this recurrent self-questioning.

Lawrence's over-insistence on 'telling' us things – and some-times telling us things we cannot accept – should not, then, be allowed to obscure from us the very real extent to which he often succeeds in conveying the feel of actual life and actual human problems. A man who spent so much of his life as Lawrence did in preaching to women, may fail (as Lawrence so often does) to pay due regard to the rules which govern valid argument, illus-tration, and proof; but this does not mean that he is lacking in the essential intelligence required of a novelist to realize the full human reality of the *people* who argue, puzzle, and suffer. Further-more, the inner stresses and strains which cause incoherence in the abstract thinker may in the novelist and story-teller provide the creative driving-force.

Perhaps it is something in Lawrence's manner of writing, rather than his matter, which has proved a stumbling-block for many readers. If we take up *The Tales of D. H. Lawrence* – the volume which contains a great part of his most unquestionably successful work as an artist – we will soon be struck by an obvious difference in quality between Lawrence's style and most of the educated English fiction we are accustomed to. Probably a superficial impression of lack of 'style' had counted for much in the opinion, once very common, that Lawrence is an uneducated writer. This opinion, stated baldly, is absurd. Nevertheless, the quality in Lawrence's style which prompts it is certainly there. When Lawrence lapses from his highest level he is apt to move towards Marie Corelli or Rider Haggard, not towards Galsworthy. In his good as in his inferior works he has something in common with the great 'lowbrow' best-sellers: the vitality which they have and the 'middlebrow' novelists have not, though the best-sellers are coarse where Lawrence is sensitive and spiritual. He can use a vocabulary perilously like theirs in which to register his sharpest intuitions into modern civilized life, and allow himself confident generalizations about racial, philosophical, and sexual matters which have a tone and ring uneasily reminiscent of the intellectual underworld of 'British Israel', Count Keyserling, or Max Nordau. This is a pity, because it nourishes the various animosities which ordinary vulgar snobbery, prudery, philistinism, or Bloomsbury superciliousness already have towards Lawrence on other grounds.

But it is now becoming common to praise the directness and vitality of Lawrence's style in general. What seems still an open question, even among his admirers, is whether he succeeded in expressing his full powers in self-sufficient works of art. It is well known that Lawrence rejected the traditional canons of structure and method in the novel. He wanted Arnold Bennett (the 'old imitator') to be told that the principles Bennett invoked held good only for novels that were 'copies' of other novels, and he spoke in exasperation about the 'ossiferous skin-and-grief' form which others wanted to impose on him. Some of what Lawrence said on this subject can be dismissed as mere special pleading. A judicious admirer of Lawrence will not cite *Aaron's Rod* or *Kangaroo* as triumphs of originality of form. They are meandering, repetitious, padded-out. Lawrence, especially in his later years, wrote too much and wrote it too quickly. Nor can the artistic objection to a great part of his work be regarded only as a misguided application of the Flaubertian principles which he rejected. Lawrence allows himself liberties, in what purport to be works of fiction – works of imagination – which are incompatible with the practice of any art, not merely the art of Flaubert. He openly abandons the pretence of dramatic objectivity and admits that this or that character is a mere mouthpiece. He addresses the reader directly, to explain, emphasize, or preach. He permits details from his personal life, not fully coherent with the presented fiction, to get into the book. It is unnecessary to elaborate these faults. Much can be urged in mitigation: the circumstances of Lawrence's life as a professional writer, the treatment meted out to the novels on which he *did* work hard, the growing urgency of his feeling (hence the overwrought, violent, didactic tone so frequent in those later books) about the decadence of modern civilized life. But faults are faults. If Lawrence is to be defended as an original artist of the novel, it will not be on the strength of *Aaron's Rod* or *Kangaroo*. Each has the makings of a good novel: but these are lost in a wilderness of preaching, autobiography, and journalism.

Nor will *The Plumed Serpent* or *Lady Chatterley's Lover* serve to substantiate the artistic claim for Lawrence. These he certainly worked hard on, especially the latter. They are different from one another, and their didactic messages differ. But they have this in common, that the writer is concerned with a single-minded intentness to 'put over' those didactic messages. Certainly his own maxim (in *Studies in Classic American Literature*, 1923) 'Never trust the artist. Trust the tale' applies to those two books. The tale can get the better of the artist. The fantasy-revival of the old Mexican paganism in the one, and the insistent sexual outspoken-ness in the other, do not make up the whole interest of *The Plumed Serpent* and *Lady Chatterley*. The fables themselves, in important points, do not serve the unequivocal purpose they were meant to serve. *The Plumed Serpent* in places can impress and move the reader who is most convinced that Lawrence's aim in this book was tragically mistaken and perverse – as well as being somewhat absurd. *Lady Chatterley's Lover* can inspire a sympathy with Clifford which was probably not intended, but can be genuinely grounded in what the story tells us. But neither book can be 'lived in': that is, neither book created an imagined domain in which the reader simply finds himself, and finds *for* himself the moral bearings of the world which the artist has imagined; a world which we are not just told about, but which seems to exist in itself and be discovered by us. In these books, as in other stories of Lawrence, the poles of truth and falsity, good and evil, sickness and health are imposed by the direct moral intervention of the author. The books cohere as wholes and make sense (morally speaking) only if looked at from a point of view already predisposed to accept the author's ideas. Too much of what seems to come out of genuine experience has passed through the moralist's filter. The high proportion in these books of merely sketched, diagrammatic characters is significant.

Now it is easy to show – from explicit remarks of Lawrence's in the novels, as well as in his criticism and in letters and so on – that in this didacticism Lawrence was going against his own proclaimed principles. What is harder to make out is just what *positively* those principles come to: just what is the formal character of the works that do come more or less completely out of 'pure passionate experience'. Some may think that *Sons and Lovers* is the text to choose in order to discover this. It is rightly one of the best known and most popular of Lawrence's books. But much that is essential to the study of Lawrence would be missed if we took that novel as fully representative. It is certainly the easiest to understand, being the only one of his first-rate books which is like an ordinary novel. Though much of it takes on a fuller significance when we know the rest of Lawrence's life and work, it is self-sufficient and undoubtedly the novel that a reader ignorant of him should begin with. Futhermore, the life-choices that the hero, Paul, makes in *Sons and Lovers* show their consequences in Lawrence's later work. Some have thought that in Paul's failure to see through his mother's pathetically false values, and in the cruelty, due to his mother's thwarting of his development, and shown in his attitude to his father and later in his treatment of Miriam, we discover Lawrence himself taking the wrong turning. But however this may be, Paul's choices are self-explanatory within the book itself. If in some respects it seems to be a confessional work, the power of the literary artist is shown in the objectivity with which the confession is treated. Yet *Sons and Lovers* is the work of a potential rather than an actual genius. Its great superiority over Lawrence's previous novels – *The White Peacock* (1911) and *The Trespasser* (1912) – lies in its freedom from literariness. They are over-written: the directness and naturalness of *Sons and Lovers* mark the great *literary* evolution which is the result of Lawrence's decision (encouraged by 'Miriam') to deal directly with urgent personal matter. But the reason of its very merits it cannot be a triumph of imagination. There is little in the book to make us feel that the author's future strength would

lie in the imagining of characters and themes outside his immediate
personal situation. In this respect it shows no clear anticipation of
the best parts of *The Rainbow*.

It is *The Rainbow*, together with *Women in Love* (1920) and the
best of the tales, on which Dr. F. R. Leavis, in his study of
Lawrence, has chosen to lay the main stress.[1] And whether or
not we can go all or most of the way with Dr. Leavis in what he
says about Lawrence in general, I am sure his selection here is
right. And out of this selection *Women in Love* seems a suitable
particular choice to illustrate Lawrence's mature art. Lawrence
seems to have thought it, together with *The Rainbow*, his greatest
work – though in later years his preoccupation with the Chatterley
book may have caused him to alter his judgement. Dr. Leavis,
having given good reasons for treating it (despite the carry-over
of names of characters) as a separate work from *The Rainbow*,
ranks it above the earlier novel. Whether this is so or not, it
seems clear that it is best considered as a separate work (though
one initial problem that confronts the reader of *Women in Love*,
the uncertainty about the social status of the two girls Ursula and
Gudrun who we meet in the first chapter, is cleared up if we come
to the later novel from the earlier). Perhaps it is a pity that
Lawrence did not change the names of the characters who are
carried over when he separated out the two works from the
originally envisaged single novel of *The Sisters*. The Ursula of
Women in Love is not like the Ursula of *The Rainbow*. To simplify
for the moment, Ursula of *The Rainbow*, though quite convincingly
dramatized and a girl, lives mainly out of the experience of the
young Lawrence himself. The Ursula of *Women in Love* has much
more in her of Lawrence's wife Frieda. Any effort by the reader
to fuse the two Ursulas in his reading of *Women in Love* would
lead to difficulties. It is true that the later part of *The Rainbow* –
what bears on the failure of the affair between Ursula and
Skrebensky – contains germinally some of the substance of
Women in Love. But the connexion is thematic, rather than narrative. *Women in Love* is thus best treated separately.

There are two reasons for choosing it, rather than its predecessor, for discussion. First, the cyclical, repetitive method of *The
Rainbow* is not hard to grasp, once it is seen for what it is. The
book contains patches of local obscurity (as often with Lawrence,

[1] F. R. Leavis, *D. H. Lawrence, Novelist*, Peregrine Books, Harmonds-
worth, 1955.

T

the love-scenes are obscure), but it has not on the whole been found so radically puzzling as *Women in Love*. But above all *Women in Love* is the more 'modern' of the two, the one in which Lawrence is more concerned with what we recognize as contemporary life. There is something of a pastoral, idealizing, idyllic quality about *The Rainbow* – at any rate, in the earlier part, before the advent of 'modern' life in the story of the childhood and youth of the girl Ursula. That earlier part has a certain epic spaciousness which is unlike anything else in Lawrence. *The Rainbow* compares with *Women in Love*, in this respect, as *War and Peace* does with *Anna Karenina*. Its idyllic quality is beautiful. But that quality is only possible because of the background to the story, the older England which has gone for ever; it is the work of the Lawrence whom Dr. Leavis can see as the successor to the George Eliot of *The Mill on the Floss*. *Women in Love*, then, is chosen here as the more complex, difficult, and 'modern' of the two novels of Lawrence's creative prime – not necessarily as the better.

This novel can be, and has been, used (as in Dr. Leavis's treatment of it) to show how prose fiction takes over, in Lawrence's hands, the thematic and symbolic method of poetry. Such things as Gerald's treatment of his mare (in Chapter IX) or the episode of the cats (in Chapter XIII) will strike the reader even at a first reading as essentially poetic in this sense. But, effective as they are, they do not go far beyond the devices of previous fiction, in that they are the economical and vivid summing-up of a significance that has already been made explicit. In chapters like that called 'Rabbit' (XVIII), and most of all in the wonderful chapter called 'Moony' (XIX), where Birkin, watched by Ursula without his knowledge, throws stones into the water to shatter the moon's reflection, we seem to reach deeper levels. Their significance is not that they sum up what has gone before, but that they extend and deepen our awareness of what is happening in the novel. In chapters like these Lawrence justifies the claims that have been made for him as a formal innovator who extends the range of the art of fiction.

Dr. Leavis's method of analysing this novel has been to select representative themes and characters to illustrate its content and significance. But this analysis, though illuminating, does not bring out the total structure of the book. An account of the structure does indeed support and reinforce, to some extent, the critic's claims for Lawrence's artistry. But is also seems to me to reveal weaknesses which the critic's more selective analysis passes over.

What is *Women in Love* about? It is natural (though not, I think, best) to set about answering this question by beginning at the beginning of the novel, with the conversation between the two sisters, Ursula and Gudrun Brangwen. This opening scene impressively illustrates Lawrence's power of suggesting undercurrents of feeling and atmosphere: in this case the suppressed sexual tension and, more dimly in the background, the social unease of the girls – yet all is done dramatically, through the conversation, picking up and fading out in an apparently casual, natural way. Their conversation is about marriage; and there presently follows a description of a wedding at which the two are present, and during which we are introduced to most of the principal characters of the novel. All this is simply but adroitly done, and as the book gets going we are ready to assume that it is to be about marriage, and the varying attitudes of the two girls (who are already contrasted) to men in marriage. We are thus tempted to regard the girls as central characters. And indeed Gudrun's attitude to Gerald Crich in this chapter, the nature of her attraction to him, does point forward to what their relationship is to become. But it soon becomes clear that the organizing principle of the novel is not to be found in the difference between the two girls nor in the theme of marriage. True, we are given to understand at the end that Ursula, the more sympathetic of the two girls, does marry Birkin. But this marriage has no climatic effect. If, then, we begin our analysis of *Women in Love* from what seems the natural starting-point, we soon get into difficulties, such as have made less analytically minded readers in the past give up the book in exasperation.

It seems to me, then, that the structure – and hence the total meaning – of the book is better understood not by beginning at the natural starting-point suggested by the book's title and the first chapter, but by beginning at what might be called the logical starting-point, which is Birkin. This is not to assume that as an actual fact of composition Lawrence himself began here – though it seems significant that in an early draft of *Women in Love* the book did begin with Birkin's meeting with Gerald on holiday on the Continent. All that is claimed is that the effective structure of the book is more clearly revealed by taking Birkin to be the principal centre of interest. It may well turn out – indeed in my view it does – that Birkin does not in the end have quite the kind of central and standard-supplying role in the book which Lawrence may have intended. But he is, after all, virtually a self-portrait of Lawrence, and as such he carries whatever weight of doctrine about the relations of men and women is to be found in the novel. And it will be seen that all the other principal characters and themes of the book are in a sense causally dependent on the conception of Birkin.

Though modelled on the author, Birkin is definitely a character *in* the book and not overshadowing it. He is exasperating and touching, protean, sometimes unpleasant, sometimes likeable, in a credible way. If his peculiarities are Lawrence's own, they are presented by Lawrence quite objectively. It is not even clear that when Birkin and Ursula are in conflict the reader's sympathy is automatically presupposed to be with Birkin. This objectivity is comparatively rare in Lawrence. The passage in Chapter XIX, in which the two sisters discuss Birkin, suggests how this effect is obtained:

> 'Of course,' she [Gudrun] said easily, 'there is a quality of life in Birkin which is quite remarkable. There is an extra-ordinary rich spring of life in him, really amazing, the way he can give himself to things. But there are so many things in life that he simply doesn't know. Either he is not aware of their existence at all, or he dismisses them as merely negligible – things which are vital to the other person. In a way he is not clever enough, he is too intense in spots.'
>
> 'Yes,' cried Ursula, 'too much of a preacher. He is really a priest.'
>
> 'Exactly! He can't hear what anybody else has to say – he simply cannot hear. His own voice is too loud.'
>
> 'Yes. He cries you down.'
>
> 'He cries you down,' repeated Gudrun. 'And by mere force of violence. And of course it is hopeless. Nobody is convinced by violence. It makes talking to him impossible – and living with him I should think would be more than impossible.'
>
> 'You don't think one could live with him?' asked Ursula.
>
> 'I should think it would be too wearing, too exhausting. One would be shouted down every time, and rushed into his

way without any choice. He would want to control you entirely. He cannot allow that there is any other mind but his own. And then the real clumsiness of his mind is its lack of self-criticism. No, I think it would be perfectly intolerable.'

Ursula 'assents vaguely' to this, but she 'only half agrees', and presently she feels 'a revulsion from Gudrun'.

> She finished life off so thoroughly, she made things so ugly and so final. As a matter of fact, even if it were as Gudrun said, about Birkin, other things were true as well. But Gudrun would draw two lines under him and cross him out like an account that is settled. There he was, summed up, paid for, settled, done with. And it was such a lie. This finality of Gudrun's, this dispatching of people and things in a sentence, was such a lie.

It is a measure of the success in the presentation of Birkin that we are made both to feel the applicability of what Gudrun says and the understandableness of Ursula's reaction to it. We see him often as Ursula does in Chapter XI, where we hear of '. . . this duality of feeling which he created in her . . . his wonderful life-rapidity, the rare quality of an utterly desirable man: and there was at the same time this ridiculous, mean effacement into a Salvator Mundi and a Sunday-school teacher, a prig of the stiffest type'. In this treatment of his self-dramatization Lawrence shows himself one of the great realists of literature. Not that he is always convincing in his treatment of material facts, settings, and milieux: anyone who has read much of Lawrence will know that that is not so. But when he is at his best he can give expression in the most effective way – in the dramatic treatment of character – to the refutation of that 'finality' which Ursula here imputes to Gudrun: the moralist's wish for the ultimate and definitive 'placing' of live human creatures in their life and growth, in relation to some static and preconceived notion of purpose and value. And correspondingly the novelist's positive achievement is the communication of a sense of life as it is lived, not merely in the day-by-day or moment-by-moment fluctuations of perception and emotion, but in the shifts of judgement and attitude which are inevitable in any live human relationship. The result is that we are involved in the experiences described in a fuller way than as mere spectators, because we are made to feel that it is

continuous with ours. Sometimes, indeed, the involvement is
too great, as in the quarrels between Mr. and Mrs Morel in *Sons
and Lovers*, or Birkin's obscure battles with Ursula in this novel;
the 'frame' of the book is broken and we are drawn into the
quarrel as if it were real life, forced to take sides, to want to
intervene. This is a serious fault in the art, but it shows the
strength of Lawrence's conceptions: a strength which in his best
work is surprisingly compatible with the 'distancing' that good
art requires. But this compatibility would not be possible without
the dual role of the character Birkin. Lawrence is personally
involved in him but – in the best passages anyway – without this
interfering with our sense of Birkin as a dramatic character, open
to objections which are forcibly put, either by himself or by the
tenacious Ursula.

Birkin, then, is a spokesman for Lawrence's changing moods.
He is also, just credibly, a school-inspector; this enables Lawrence
both to give some trace of plausibility to the restless wandering
which seems to characterize his form of life, and to put him in
touch with Ursula in her fictional capacity as a schoolmistress.
But he is above all the opportunity for Lawrence to imagine an
experiment in life. Birkin is a man of religious temperament who
cannot believe in the God of Christianity, or in any formal
religion. He feels a revulsion from the mechanized wilderness of
the modern world, the loss of supernatural sanctions, the disappearance of clear significance and purpose in living from every
class of society. This revulsion is accompanied by a deep repugnance for the whole social structure of England. Birkin has no clear
positive idea of just what he wants changed, and what he wants
to put in its place. This no doubt deprives his jeremiads of any
definite political significance; but it does not invalidate them as
expressions of his state of soul. He evinces the same passionate
dislike of the *bourgeoisie* among whom he lives (with Bohemian
intervals) as the clever cultivated Gudrun does for the working-
class life in which she has grown up and from which she has
broken away. The book ends, as Lawrence's stories so often do
(*The Fox, The Daughters of the Vicar*, and others), with the 'fugue',
the flight abroad of the Lawrence-character with the woman he
loves, into a social void. But although Birkin can find no general
practical cure for the social disease that disgusts him, he seeks for
a personal way of salvation for himself. He wants to try to live
by a religion of love. This 'love' is not to be interpreted in a

romantic or Christian sense. It is to be a relationship between 'fulfilled' individuals, who remain individuals (Birkin shrinks in horror from the idea of any kind of 'merging', loss of individuality in the union of love) but who each achieve through the other some contact with a hitherto unknown, non-human, and trans-human power. One lover is to be the 'door' of the other to this unknown power, the life-source to which Christianity (as Birkin-Lawrence understands it), and still more modern humanitarianism and democracy, have no access.

The Birkin theme is thus mainly concerned with his choice of Ursula as the woman with whom he is to try this 'way of freedom' in love, and to whom he preaches – against her understandable resistance – a curious doctrine of sexual *Apartheid* that goes with it. His failure with another woman, Hermione, which we learn about early in the novel, and the consequent embarrassing, embittered, and prolonged epilogue to their love-affair, represent the wrong kind of relationship between a man and a woman. Birkin has to escape from this. He has also to escape from an inner temptation which he feels very strongly towards a cult of purely sensual, 'mindless' experience evoked in the novel by a West African statuette which is introduced, with effective dramatic symbolism, in the chapter called 'Totem'. Here, of course, we have an instance of Lawrence's famous primitivism. But we note that in the book it is a temptation which Birkin sees as such. That sensual mindlessness, which he calls the 'African way', is a sort of barbaric equivalent to the sentimental Western idea of love which he feels to be decadent: but it too he supposes to be a product of decadence. But Birkin also thinks he must educate Ursula out of the sentimental and romantic love-ideal which she wants to impose on their relationship. He senses behind it that devouring and essentially egocentric maternal possessiveness which readers of Lawrence will not be surprised to learn that he regards as the enemy of human life and growth. It is this would-be 'education' of Ursula which makes up the main positive part of the Birkin theme.

This purpose of Birkin's can be taken as the logical starting-point of the novel. We have it foreshadowed in Chapter V, in a conversation between Birkin and his friend Gerald Crich, in which Birkin asks Gerald the characteristically Laurentian ques-tion: 'What do you think is the aim and object of your life?' It is a characteristic question, because it demands, and permits, only a certain kind of answer, the kind that is suggested when Birkin says presently: 'I find that one needs some one *really* pure single activity.' It is also characteristic because it seems to be as much a question asked of himself as of Gerald. Gerald finds some difficulty in answering, and finally admits that he has no answer to it, or to the equivalent question: 'Wherein does life centre for you?' 'It doesn't centre at all. It is artificially held *together* by the social mechanism,' is what he eventually has to say. Birkin agrees, but presses his view that 'there remains only this perfect union with a woman – sort of ultimate marriage – and there isn't anything else'. Gerald's rejection of this idea of 'ultimate marriage', a rejection which expresses his essential nature, and the psychological consequences of that rejection, underlie the extended story of his relations with his chosen woman right down to its disastrous close, his extinction in an inhuman world of snow and ice.

The Gerald theme is thus both complementary and contrasting to the Birkin theme. It is so much easier to work out analytically, after reading the book, that to some readers it seems to be the main 'story' in *Women in Love*. But this is not its place in the intended structure of the work. The two men, Gerald and Birkin, show a kind of contrast which is familiar to all readers of Lawrence. No subject does he write about more, whether well or badly, in his fiction. It is a contrast easier to illustrate than describe: the contrast between what is meant to be represented, in their different ways, by the gamekeeper in *Lady Chatterley*, by Count Dionys in *The Ladybird*, or by Alexander Hepburn in *The Captain's Doll*, and on the other hand by Sir Clifford Chatterley, by Rico in *St. Mawr*, or by the Bricknells in *Aaron's Rod*. One says 'meant to be represented', because sometimes confusions and contradictions vitiate Lawrence's handling of it. But in its outlines the nature of the contrast is clear: that between the man who has the right kind of human naturalness, showing itself in a play of emotional spontaneity and mobility and a capacity for tenderness – a man whose form of life grows from that 'life-centre' without which Lawrence thought modern living was mere automatism; and the man who lets 'will-power', 'personality', and 'ideals', in the strongly derogatory sense Lawrence gives to such words, interfere with his proper relation to other men and women and the universe, and who thus lacks the emotional depth and the capacity for sincere relationships and tenderness which for

Lawrence were the evidence of a connexion with some power above and beyond the individual. In his various novels and tales Lawrence sees people's superficially different or unconnected characteristics – such as executive or intellectual domineering, sentimentality, aestheticism, flirtatiousness, smart flippancy – as all symptoms of living at too shallow a level, excessive 'consciousness' (as Lawrence likes to call it) drawing its perverse power from thwarted and misdirected emotional forces. He is apt to weigh the scales against such people by representing them as sexual failures, but it is clear that this is only the sign or symbol of a more general failure. And Lawrence in his later years came with an increasing bitterness to see people of Gerald's *Weltanschauung* as the real rulers of the modern world. Now we may argue that Lawrence's sense of proportion, and at times his sense of reality, desert him in some of his treatments of this theme. Rico and Sir Clifford Chatterley, for example, are too slight as characters to bear the symbolic weight which their part in the chosen fable imposes on them. Worse than that, many of them, like Rico (though unlike Sir Clifford), are badly drawn, unconvincing, and presented with such obvious animosity as to invalidate their functioning as art. But one of the notable things about *Women in Love* is that the treatment of the General theme is wholly convincing; Gerald as a character does really enact the symbolic role which he is assigned. He is done from within as almost no other characters of this kind are done in Lawrence: Lawrence *is* Gerald in important ways, and this identification is reflected in the strong and deep relation that there is in the book between Birkin and Gerald, who are close friends, ambivalent, intermittent, and obscure as the presentment of their friendship is in chapters like 'Man to Man' and 'Gladiatorial'. Lawrence is not weighing the scales this time; as a result he realizes much more fully the potentialities of the Gerald theme.

So thoroughly, indeed, is the Gerald theme worked out that Dr. Leavis is able to base on it the greater part of his account of *Women in Love*. Once the intention behind the creation of Gerald is grasped his drama is felt to unfold itself convincingly. Gerald's strength is a mechanical strength, a strength of 'will-power' and 'ideals'. He has not the inner reserves to meet the mounting crisis of his life, and the strain in him is felt like the tighter and tighter winding-up of a mechanical toy which at last flies loose and bounds away to its final destruction. It is worth noting that

Gerald's realistic status in the novel, as an efficient colliery-owner, does not (whatever Lawrence may have intended) derive its validity from any faithfulness to social history. The judgement on Gerald would still be valid even if there were in fact no general correlation between the qualities needed for success in industry and the particular *malaise* of which he is the victim. The point of making him an industrial tycoon is symbolic: he is a man who makes the machine his god, and it is a god that fails.

Yet Gerald himself is not a machine, but a human being, and by no means an unsympathetic one. Lawrence gives a pretty full account of his previous life and his background – his father, his mother with her significant 'queerness', due to the ruining of her life by her husband's 'idealism', the childhood in which he accidentally killed his brother. When he grows up his knowledge of his father's inefficient paternalism as 'industrial magnate' spurs him on to improve on and supersede his father. He makes himself efficient and ruthless, and though the colliers hate him they respect him as they did not respect his father, because even if he despises them and they know it, they are slaves themselves to the 'values' which he seems so successfully to embody. But his strength is not true strength. He has limitations. The machine fails him already in the 'Water-Party' chapter, where he 'assumed responsibility for the amusements on the water' – lest this 'responsibility' for what happens, the drowning of his sister, should seem too tenuous, the point is driven home by the failure of his attempt at rescue. And ironically this cruel expression of his limitations comes just at the moment when he has been able to achieve one of the rare moments of 'apartness' and peace with the woman he loves. It is not Lawrence's purpose to show that strength and tenderness are incompatible. On the contrary, it is Gerald's inner weakness which is the corollary of his incapacity for true love. The slow disintegration and death of his father brings sickeningly home to him the void in his life which 'will-power' is powerless to fill. He turns in his need to the woman, Gudrun. But it is part of the dialectic of their relationship – their similar incapacity for true love – that this need should call out in Gudrun the mocking, destructive, malicious side of her nature. This has throughout been shown as a possible development in Gudrun, and it is one of the ways in which the two sisters are shown as different types of woman. The dramatic consequences of the conflict between the lovers are worked out in the long chapter called 'Snowed Up'. The final death of Gerald in the snow is only the symbolic expression of the inexorable consequence of his life-defeating idealism. Lawrence often uses the contrast of warmth and cold in a symbolic way: human warmth is a spiritual reviving-power in stories like *The Horse-Dealer's Daughter* or *The Virgin and the Gipsy*. Here the intense cold is the symbol of spiritual death.

Everything in *Women in Love* that bears on this theme is finely organized. And it is noteworthy that, although the drama of Gerald and Gudrun mostly happens on an esoteric plane, most of it is made to happen also on a plane where the ordinary criteria for successful fiction can be employed. In spite of some *avant-garde* critics, a general credibility of characters and setting is necessary for successful fiction. 'People don't do such things' remains a valid adverse criticism of a novel. Now, once the total structure of *Women in Love* has been understood – and it is this on the whole that has been found difficult – the characters do affect us as belonging to a life we know, and behaving in keeping with it (given a certain amount of poetic licence in the presentation of the social setting).

This keeping in touch with ordinary reality is a remarkable achievement. It broadens the scope of the novel. It enables Lawrence to introduce, quite naturally, characters like Gerald's father and mother – indeed the whole of the Crich family – who are very relevant to the Gerald theme, and yet are given the kind of dramatic presence, natural dialogue, and ordinary credibility which the novel-reader expects. Some of them may be 'odd', but they are odd as people in real life are odd. Lawrence takes similar opportunities in depicting Birkin's relation to Hermione. Much of this is on an esoteric level, half-conscious swirls of emotion, since Hermione is a sort of feminine counterpart of Gerald, in her blend of domineering will-power and inner weakness, just as her need for Birkin, which he knows he cannot meet, is a counterpart of Gerald's need for Gudrun. Yet Hermione is vividly depicted as a picturesque serio-comic character, and her house-party makes the appropriate occasion for Lawrence to bring in some satire both on the 'Establishment' of the day and the sophisticated radical intelligentsia he had encountered in such quarters (he takes the chance to pay off an old score against Bertrand Russell). Even the chapters describing artistic Bohemian life, though their relevance is less obvious, have a function in making the Bohemian side of Birkin's and Gerald's life more real, and in one place at least – the night Gerald spends with Halliday's mistress – their bearing on the Gerald theme is important, as illustrating the superficiality of Gerald's attitude to sex. And there is no need to emphasize the functional importance of minor characters like the artist Loerke, who plays his part in the climax of Gerald's tragedy. Thus *Women in Love* has a structure which arises naturally from Lawrence's firm grasp of his dual theme. The filling-up and population of the book seems thereby also to be accomplished with inevitability and naturalness.

Women in Love, then, does seem in part to justify the unusualness of its formal conception: a novel whose 'plot', if it is to be so called, does not answer to the usual account of 'character in action'. There is development, but it is at a deeper level than that of 'personality'. If the whole book had a convincingness equal to what we find in the treatment of the Gerald theme, it could be judged an assured artistic success. But it suffers from a grave central weakness. The book's strong pattern derives from the contrast between the destinies of the two couples, and the subsidiary, though important, masculine relationship between Birkin and Gerald. (We may compare the strong pattern given to *Anna Karenina* by Tolstoy's use of the three marriages of Anna, Dolly, and Kitty, the 'unhappy', the 'ordinary', and the 'happy' marriages respectively.) But what is the significance of this pattern in expressing the intended total meaning of *Women in Love*? Dr. Leavis would have us believe that the Birkin–Ursula relationship sets up a standard – or at least moves towards a standard – from which the Gerald–Gudrun experience is a deviation. But do we feel this in reading the novel? Surely what we feel in reading the novel is that Birkin too is a sick and tortured man, who does not (except at a few ideal moments which give rise to some of the worst writing in the book) achieve with Ursula the kind of fulfilment which he has made his *raison d'être*. Perhaps if Lawrence had conveyed the positive quality of those moments – as distinct from the mere feeling of repose and relief after fighting and tension, which as always he conveys wonderfully – our sense of Birkin's 'normative' standing in the novel would have been induced. But as it is, those ideal moments – as in Chapter XXIII, 'Excurse' – are among the weaknesses of the book. Lawrence expresses the ineffable no better here by his obscure, repetitious, periphrastic style than he does in the notoriously direct passages of *Lady Chatterley's Lover*. And if it is urged that, given the nature of the experience in question, those portentous wordinesses are all he could do, this is enough to prove the enterprise mistaken.

But this is not the most radical question. To understand Birkin fully we must understand the state of mind of the Lawrence who wrote of him. It is true that *Women in Love*, as part of *The Sisters*, was presumable conceived before the horror of the war years had closed down on Lawrence: conceived during the happy interval between the break with 'Miriam' and the coming of the war. But it is hard not to see in Birkin the Lawrence of 1916, amid the penury and misery of his life in Cornwall, and in his mind always the horror of the war and the nightmare of suspicion and persecution. How else can we explain Birkin's hatred of human life? 'Mankind is a dead tree, covered with fine brilliant galls of people,' he says, and there is much in the same strain. But this is a defect in a work of imagination. Birkin's hatred is not clearly accounted for in particular terms. It remains in the book just a donnée, an idiosyncrasy, which is so strongly rendered that it seriously limits Birkin's value as a representative of the normal man. No doubt it is unfair to attack *Women in Love* on the ground that Birkin himself is obviously not a normal man. Some imaginative licence must be granted in the presentation of this experiment in love: for the character who thinks of making it to be at all convincing, he would have to be rather unusual. But it is clear that Lawrence intended Birkin to be searching for, and perhaps even eventually reaching, conclusions about the relations of men and women in marriage which *could* be held to be valid for normal men.

This suggests a more serious criticism. For we cannot ignore Birkin's own sense of his failure. After all, the last chapter, in which Birkin gazes down at the dead Gerald, is a final taking-up of the issues first proposed between them in the chapter called 'In the Train'. Birkin has come to realize that his ideal of 'ultimate marriage' was not sufficient. It needed completion by the male relationship with Gerald. But this too has failed. What makes Gerald's death tragic – and there is an unmistakable note of tragedy in Birkin's thoughts as he turns away – is not the death itself (Gerald is not a figure of tragic stature) but its effect on Birkin. And the whole effect of the book – though Birkin even at the end will not directly admit this to Ursula – is to show that the kind of love he wanted is illusory. And to say this is not to bring extrinsic standards to bear on a work of imagination. It is what the work itself seems to say: pointing a moral of its own, which is not the author's.

1961